The Broken Compass

The Broken Compass

Parental Involvement with Children's Education

Keith Robinson
Angel L. Harris

Harvard University Press

Cambridge, Massachusetts

London, England

2014

Library of Congress Cataloging-in-Publication Data

Robinson, Keith.
The broken compass : parental involvement with children's education /
Keith Robinson and Angel L. Harris.
pages cm
Includes bibliographical references and index.
ISBN 978-0-674-72510-2 (alk. paper)
1. Education—Parent participation—United States.   2. Home and school—
United States.   I. Title.
LC225.3.R64 2014
371.19'2—dc23   2013012420

To Robert F. (Bob) Schoeni, an excellent mentor who has meant so much to both of our careers

Contents

The Broken Compass

— 1 —

The Role of Parental Involvement in Children's Schooling

In the end, there is no program or policy that can substitute for a mother or father who will attend those parent/teacher conferences, or help with homework after dinner, or turn off the TV, put away the video games, and read to their child. I speak to you not just as a President, but as a father when I say that responsibility for our children's education must begin at home.

— President Barack Obama, address to a joint session of Congress, February 24, 2009

It is safe to say that most adults in this country believe that parent involvement is critical to improving educational outcomes for all children. Parents' contributions of time and effort are thought to be greatly beneficial in helping schools meet various state and community educational goals. This sentiment is well captured by Epstein (1996, 213), who claims, "We have moved from the question, Are families important for student success in school? To *If* families are important for children's development and school success, *how* can schools help all families conduct the activities that will benefit their children?" The idyllic conception of an effective school is one in which the responsibility of educating children is shared equally between parents and teachers—where teachers provide formal instruction and implement school curriculum, and parents reinforce these efforts by creating a cultural milieu outside of school that facilitates the learning process.

The benefits of parental involvement are thought to be important throughout youths' K–12 schooling careers. Involvement during early education is encouraged as a means of promoting positive attitudes and behaviors toward learning and mathematics development, and of improving student literacy (Englund et al. 2004; Jordan et al. 2009). For older children, parent involvement is thought to be important for reducing school delinquency,

1

improving discipline, and increasing college enrollment rates (e.g., Domina 2005; McNeal 1999). Overall, parents who are active participants in their child's education are thought to promote children's social, emotional, and academic growth (Green et al. 2007). Accordingly, it seems reasonable for educators to place increased responsibility on parents as a solution for enhancing school effectiveness and countering the academic failure of disadvantaged groups. In a system consumed with promoting value-added practices, parents are viewed as a policy lever integral for helping administrators outrun the juggernaut of high-stakes accountability.

The importance placed on parental involvement by educators is guided by their belief that poor achievement results from lack of involvement or valuing of schooling on the part of parents. For example, Souto-Manning and Swick (2006) report that a lack of parental involvement is the primary reason teachers cite for the achievement of students who perform below federal and state standards. Bol and Berry (2005) find that teachers (grades 6–12) invoke family support as more important than curriculum and instruction or school characteristics for youths' academic orientation. Their findings show that many teachers depict poor families as not valuing academic achievement or making education a priority (2005, 38). DeCastro-Ambrosetti and Cho (2005) show evidence that pre- and in-service teachers have negative attitudes toward parents of ethnic minority groups, question the value they place on education, and attribute low achievement to factors at home and the extent to which parents value education.

One cannot overstate the great deal of importance placed on parental involvement within the education arena. One indicator is the centrality of parental involvement in the discourse on school reform and education in general, particularly among policy makers. Several states—including Alabama, Arkansas, Florida, Georgia, Kansas, Minnesota, New Hampshire, New Jersey, New York, Ohio, Pennsylvania, Tennessee, and West Virginia— have declared one month a year, typically October, as parental involvement month. In fact, in 2011, the New Jersey State Parent Information and Resource Center (NJPIRC) offered fifteen stipends to public schools to host a family involvement activity and free Parent Involvement Pledge Cards to mark the importance of parent involvement in the educational process. The proclamations signed by governors that introduce Parental Involvement Month typically include a clause that states, "Research indicates that there is a positive relationship between high student achievement and the high expectations and educational involvement of parents. When schools, parents, and communities work together in partnership, our children succeed" and/or "the role of parents in creating a successful pre-school through college education system for [state's] children cannot be overstated."

Regardless of the discourse on parental involvement among academics, there is clear evidence that policy makers believe that parental involvement is a major factor in positive academic outcomes. For example, as then governor of Tennessee, Phil Bredesen stated, "Parents are a child's first teacher and we must encourage strong interaction between families, communities and schools.... Family involvement in a child's education can only lead to success and higher achievement" (Newsroom and Media Center, 2009). In his weekly address to Delawareans, Governor Jack Markell stated that "One point that's made over and over is how critical parental involvement is to student success ... what happens at home has a huge impact on what they are able to do at their desks.... This Monday ... educators and employers, PTA members and policy makers will be getting together to proclaim October 'Parental Involvement Month' in Delaware" (Markell, 2010). In a 2010 speech regarding the awarding of the Governor's Education Initiative Award for Parental Involvement to two school districts, Nebraska's governor Dave Heineman stated that "since 2007, the Nebraska Association of School Boards and my administration have been working together to focus on parental involvement. Parents play a critical role in education ... I applaud each of these school districts for the emphasis they place on getting parents involved in education. Parents and teachers working together is an essential element in student learning and academic achievement" (Heineman, 2010).

Statements that parental involvement "can only lead to success," has a "huge impact," and plays "a critical role" are often supported by the views held by high-ranking officials within the education sector. For example, the Department of Education of West Virginia states that "research shows that when families take an active interest in their children's schoolwork, students display more positive attitudes, behave better and learn more. Parent involvement is critical for children from diverse cultural backgrounds, who tend to do better when families and school staff join forces to bridge the gap between home and school cultures" (West Virginia DOE, 2010). In fact, some administrators attribute greater importance to parental involvement than socioeconomic factors. State Superintendent of Schools Steve Paine states that "caring, involved parents, not income or social status, is the most accurate predictor of student achievement in school.... Parents can make a difference in their children's achievement" (West Virginia DOE, 2010). State Board President Priscilla Haden states "If we want West Virginia students to be successful, and we do, parents must be encouraged to support their children's learning. . . . By working together, we can assure our children will be prepared for global success in college, in the workplace and in life" (West Virginia DOE, 2010). Even politicians at the national level have expressed similar confidence that parental involvement leads to high achievement, as evidenced by President Obama's quote at the beginning of this chapter.

This book represents our attempt to evaluate the enormous policy effort that has been administered toward this issue. Are the resources expended in efforts to increase parental involvement justified? Put another way, does existing evidence support the notion that parental involvement is the answer to underachievement? Our analytical endeavors in this book bring us closer to answering this question, yet we recognize the answer is partially based in one's own judgment and perspective. We are less concerned with the question of whether parents *should* be more involved and more concerned with whether greater parental involvement will solve many of the problems currently facing our schools. Ultimately, we are motivated by a high interest in identifying factors that can improve the state of education in this country. This book provides us an opportunity to examine a factor deemed critical to children's academic success and advance the discourse on parental involvement several steps further. We believe that an extensive study on the role of parental involvement in children's academic lives and the racial achievement gap is long overdue. Given the dawn of the high-stakes accountability era, we hope that this work ultimately helps to maximize whatever benefits are associated with parental involvement.

In this study we define "parental involvement" as practices that entail parent communication with their children about education, beliefs or behaviors parents hold or engage in with the exclusive aim of increasing academic outcomes, and parental engagement with schools and teachers. Some of these elements are included in other popular conceptions of parental involvement. For example, Epstein (2010) summarizes the ranges of family involvement within a classification system that includes school-home communications, parent involvement within the school and the community, home learning activities, and parents serving as decision makers. However, we are interested in factors parents employ that can be *directly* linked to achievement. This focus led us to exclude some activities that have been viewed as forms of involvement in previous research (Domina 2005), such as taking the child to museums and involving them in extra-curricular endeavors such as ballet or piano lessons. We consider these activities as intended to generally cultivate or to enrich the child rather than to specifically affect academic outcomes. There are forms of parental involvement that might be beneficial to youths' social and emotional development, psychological well-being, or general enrichment that we do not consider. Those outcomes can be regarded as stemming from good parenting. This is not a study about "parenting" in general or about whether parenting is beneficial for academic achievement.

Given our definition of parental involvement, it is more accurate to characterize our study as focusing on aspects of parental involvement parents employ only because academic outcomes exist. Therefore, in this study, a finding that parental involvement *(for a given academic outcome)* is not beneficial for achievement does not mean parental involvement is not important for other dimensions of child development or that parents should become less involved in their children's lives. Such a finding would simply mean that parental involvement measure x is not associated with increases in achievement. Another interpretation is that parental involvement measure x as currently implemented by parents—on average—is ineffective. This could be useful because these types of results highlight aspects of parental involvement educators and parents should focus on adjusting.

In this chapter, we describe the existing educational problems in this country, giving particular focus to differences in academic performance both by social class and by race within America's schools. We then discuss the policy and research response to these problems as they relate to parental involvement. We conclude this chapter with an overview for the rest of the book.

Despite the limitations of testing, we focus much of our discussion in this chapter on achievement as measured by test scores. Although school is also very much about students' grades, it is standardized test scores that concern policy makers most. Despite being *one* assessment of students' academic proficiency, standardized tests have become *the* defining motif of school reform initiatives. For this reason, standardized testing has been characterized as the tail wagging the dog (McNeil 2000; Meier 2000; Sacks 1999). In fact, in many cases good grades are not enough to graduate from high school or to gain admission to top-flight colleges, graduate programs, and professional schools. Twenty-six states (encompassing two-thirds of the nearly seventeen million youth in high school) require high school exit exams (Center on Education Policy 2009), and standardized tests serve as the primary mechanism of stratification for colleges (Scholastic Assessment Test/American College Testing), graduate programs (Graduate Record Exam), and professional schools (Medical College Admission Test/Law School Admission Test). Since policy makers seem to focus entirely on test scores, any discussion of achievement (and achievement gaps) must document the trends in standardized test scores.

The Problem of Raising Achievement in America's Schools

Determining whether greater parental involvement leads to higher academic achievement is an urgent policy issue, particularly given some of the worrisome trends in U.S. education. Data from national and international assessments indicate that America's students are performing at relatively low levels. A 2006 report from the Program for International Student Assessment (Baldi et al. 2007) compared the scientific literacy of fifteen-year-olds in the thirty member countries of the Organization for Economic Cooperation and Development (OECD) and twenty-seven non-OECD countries and found that the U.S. scientific literacy score was 489, which was below the average score of 500 for the thirty OECD countries. The average U.S. score in math was 474, lower than the OECD average score of 498, and lower than thirty-one jurisdictions (23 OECD and 8 non-OECD). Additionally, among public high schools in 2005–6, only three-fourths of incoming freshman graduated on time, and the graduation rate was below 70% in eleven states and Washington, DC—which account for over one-third of all students in public high schools within the U.S. (Planty et al. 2009).

In 2009 the National Assessment of Educational Progress (NAEP) assessed the proficiency in reading and math of U.S. students in grades 4 and 8. Among fourth graders, only 33% scored "Proficient" or greater in reading, and 39% scored "Proficient" or greater in math. Among students in the eighth grade, roughly one-third attained "Proficient" scores in both reading (32%) and math (34%). Writing was assessed in 2007 for students in grades 8 and 12. Less than one-third of these students tested at the "Proficient" or greater level in writing. The proficiency levels were even more alarming for U.S. history in 2006, in which less than 20% of students in grades 4, 8, and 12 tested at levels considered to be "Proficient" or greater.

These percentages are clear indicators that this country has much ground to cover in ensuring a quality education for its youth.

Further Cause for Concern: Achievement Gaps

Another major problem facing American schools is the struggle to close achievement gaps. There are drastic differences in achievement by social class and by race. These differences have persisted for decades and remain a vexing problem for parents, schools, and policy makers. Its implications can be felt at all levels of schooling and in the U.S. labor force. In their book, *50 Ways to Close the Achievement Gap*, Downey and colleagues referred to it as "the most complex and compelling educational dilemma facing schools" (Downey et al. 2009, 1).

Achievement Differences by Social Class

One of the major ways in which achievement varies across youth is by social class. On average, youth from more affluent backgrounds have higher levels of achievement than those from less resourced backgrounds. We highlight this pattern in Figure 1.1, which shows achievement levels for youth in reading, math, and grades by youths' social class backgrounds (see Appendix C for a detailed description of the achievement measures). We measure social class by both parents' educational attainment and family income.[1] The data are from the National Educational Longitudinal Study (NELS), a nationally representative study of nearly twenty-five thousand U.S. students who were in the eighth grade during the first wave of data collection in 1988 and were followed through 2000 (see Appendix A for further information on all data sets used in this study). It serves as one of the primary data sets used in this study to examine the role of parental involvement in achievement because it contains a rich collection of measures of parental involvement during a key transition period (middle school) and measures of academic achievement in grade 12, which approximate the academic skills youth have toward the end of compulsory schooling.[2]

Figure 1.1 displays the average achievement in reading, math, and grades for three categories of parental education—parents who (1) hold less than a high school diploma, (2) are high school graduates, and (3) have earned a four-year degree or greater—and three categories of famiy income—those with incomes (1) below the national median, (2) from the median to twice the median, and (3) twice the median or greater. In addition to the achievement levels, which are displayed as circles, triangles, and squares for the high, middle, and low categories of social class, respectively, Figure 1.1 also shows the standard deviations (tails) for each group. The tails are useful because they illustrate the middle 66.8% of the achievement disrtibution for each social class category.[3] To indicate where the average achievement levels for each group are situated within the achievement distribution, we show the achievement distribution (a bell-shaped curve) and highlight the scores that represent the 25th and 75th percentile for each outcome. We also dispay the standardized gaps in achievement by parental education and family income relative to the top social class categories of these factors. Thus, Figure 1.1 shows the average achievement by social class, the location of each group's average achievement within the achievement distribution, the amount of overlap in the achievement distribution for each category of social class, and the achievement gaps in both actual and standardized units (see Table B.1 in Appendix B for the sample sizes for all analyses of achievement outcomes throughout this book).

In general, the patterns are virtually identical for all three measures of achievment and both proxies of social class. Specifically, regardless of how social class is measured, youth from the high social class category (4-year degree or greater and twice the median family income or greater) have higher levels of achievement than their counterparts from the lower categories of social class. Conversly, youth from the low social class categories (parents have not completed high school or live in homes in which the family income is below the national median) have the lowest levels of achievement. For all three achievement outcomes, youth from the high social class categories have levels of achievement that place them near the 75th percentile of the achievement distribution. Youth in the middle categories of social class (parents' highest level of education is high school graduate or family incomes from 1 to 2 times the national median) have average levels of achievement near the center of the achievement distribution.

We repeat this analysis using data based on the Child Development Supplement (CDS) to the Panel Study for Income Dynamics (PSID)—the second primary source of data we use in this study—which we display in Figure 1.2. The CDS contains a rich collection of parental involvement measures for a nationally representative sample of 3,563 children collected in 1997 when youth were between the ages of 0–12, which can be linked to achievement in 2002 when they were between the ages of 5 and 18. As

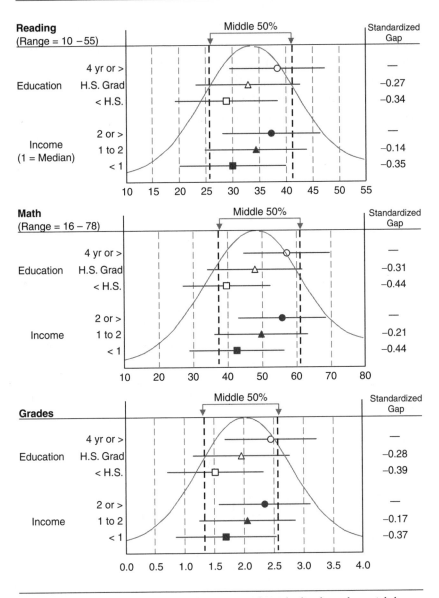

FIGURE 1.1. Achievement, standard deviations, and standardized gaps by social class: NELS. *Note:* The graph displays the unadjusted estimated achievement (shapes) and standard deviation (tails) for each group. Unweighted number of observations for reading, math, and grades is 8,352, 8,350, and 9,028, respectively.

such, the CDS allows us to assess the parental involvement–student achievement link throughout the K–12 schooling cycle. In general, the patterns in Figure 1.2 are identical to those observed in Figure 1.1.

It is important to note that although the gaps in achievement are substantial, the overlap in the achievement distributions for the social class categories displayed in Figures 1.1 and 1.2 suggest that while social class is strongly related to achievement, it does not entirely determine youths' achievement. Nevertheless, it seems that there are advantages to having a high social class background that are associated with academic success. It

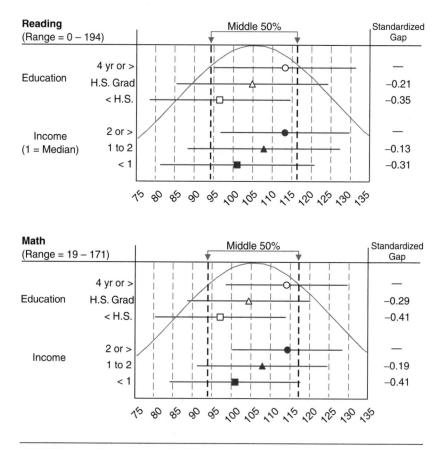

FIGURE 1.2. Achievement, standard deviations, and standardized gaps by social class: CDS. *Note:* The graph displays the unadjusted estimated achievement (shapes) and standard deviation (tails) for each group. Unweighted number of observations for reading and math are 1,304 and 1,299, respectively.

is possible that parental involvement is the mechanism by which youth with advantaged backgrounds attain their high achievement levels relative to their less advantaged counterparts.

Achievement Differences by Race

Another major problem facing American schools is the struggle to close what is called the minority achievement gap—lower average test scores and grades (and even high school completion and college attendance rates) among black and Hispanic/Latino students. It has appeared in the four major geographic regions in the United States, and within different cultures, ethnicities, and socioeconomic strata. The minority achievement gap is large, persistent, and pervasive. Consider the following:

- From 1999 to 2005, Asian Americans (henceforward Asians) had the highest mean Advanced Placement (AP) exam score, whereas blacks had the lowest.
- On the 2009 NAEP reading test administered to students in grades 4 and 8, more than twice the proportion of Asian/Pacific Islanders and whites (over 40%)scored at or above "Proficient" than did black and Hispanic students (less than 20%) at both grade levels. The same relative racial differences apply to math.
- In 2008, white students outscored black students on the SAT—which was scored on a scale from 200 to 800—by an average of 98 points in reading and 111 points in math. They also outscored Hispanics by an average of 74 points in both reading and math.
- In 2009, NAEP data show that the achievement gap between white and Hispanic fourth graders in reading and math was not measurably different than it was in 1992 and 1990. The same applies for the black-white and Hispanic-white gaps in both reading and math among eighth graders.
- The college enrollment gap was greater in 2006 than it was in 1972; 69% of white high school graduates in 2006 enrolled in college the next academic year, substantially more than their black (56%) and Hispanic (58%) counterparts (Planty et al. 2008, 140).

These points capture just some of the many facts indicative of the vast racial differences that exist in the American school system.

Data from the NAEP show that by age 17 the average Hispanic and black student is four years behind the average white student; Hispanic and black twelfth graders score lower than white eighth graders in reading, math, U.S. history, and geography (Thernstrom and Thernstrom 2003). Barely half of Hispanic and black students graduate from high school, compared to nearly 80% for whites and over 80% for Asians (Alliance for Excellent Education 2008). Though Asians are a minority in number in the United States (approximately 4.4% of the total population), on many educational outcomes they are more similar to whites than they are to blacks and Hispanics and thus are not included in our usage of the term "minority achievement" throughout this book.

Without question, racial differences in achievement—particularly as assessed through testing—have garnered the most attention nationally within education. We highlight the racial achievement gap in Figure 1.3, which shows the achievement levels in reading, math, and grades for twelfth graders from various racial groups. Given the heterogeneity within the Asian population, throughout the book we sort Asians into two groups: Asians A—groups often characterized as "model minority" (Chua 2011; Kao 1995; Osajima 2005)—and Asians B—socioeconomically disadvantaged Asian groups (see Appendix B for further details). Similarly, Hispanics are disaggregated into two groups: non-Mexican Hispanics and Mexican Americans (henceforward non-Mexicans and Mexicans, respectively).[4] These group classifications are far from perfect. However, in order to capture some of the heterogeneity within each group we believe it is more appropriate to disaggregate in this manner than to treat each as one group. These data are representative of students in the early 1990s. Figure 1.3 shows the presence of a gap in twelfth grade reading, math, and grades. Minority students had lower performance compared to whites and both Asian groups.

What makes the racial achievement gap such a headline feature is that unlike racial gaps in rates of college enrollment or high school graduation, the racial achievement gap in testing spans twelve years of schooling (i.e., grades K–12) and has persisted for decades. The former point is highlighted in Figure 1.4, which shows the achievement levels for various racial groups contained in the second wave of data collected for the Child Development Supplement (CDS) to the Panel Study for Income Dynamics in 2002. The figure suggests the presence of a minority achievement gap in reading and math from grades 1–12. The top panel indicates that the first five years of school are marked by substantial differences between minority

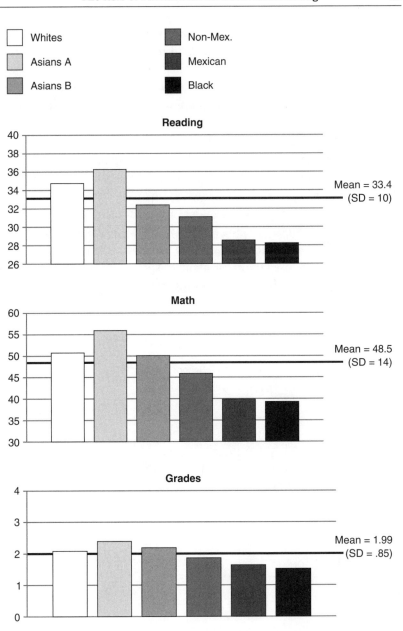

FIGURE 1.3. Achievement by race: NELS. *Note:* The bold line represents the mean achievement level for the entire sample.

and nonminority groups; this gap becomes even larger after elementary school. For instance, Asian students held roughly an 11-point advantage over Hispanic students in math in elementary school. This advantage is approximately 17 points among adolescents. Similar to Figure 1.3, Figure 1.4 illustrates that minority students are well below the population mean for achievement in both reading and math—a level of underperformance that spans the entire period of K-12 schooling.

In terms of change over time, the achievement gap in testing has fluctuated over the past several decades. There was a convergence in the gap from the early 1970s to approximately 1990; since then, the convergence has been slow. This stagnation has given many in the educational community a cause for concern since bringing minority test scores closer to parity with those of nonminorities has proven to be an intractable problem. Hedges and Nowell (1999) raised the alarm about the persistence of the black-white gap in testing a decade ago, illustrating that the prospect of test-score

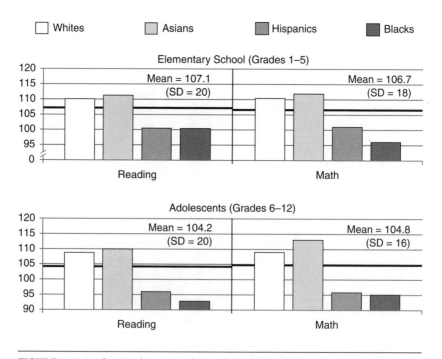

FIGURE 1.4. Academic achievement for youth by race: CDS-II. *Note:* The bold line represents the mean achievement level for the entire sample. Since the CDS does not disaggregate the racial groups, we report results for the traditional racial categories.

equality between these groups is not in the foreseeable future. Using nationally representative data for each decade from the 1960s to the 1990s, the authors concluded that given the rate of decline during that time, convergence in the black-white gap would take approximately six decades in reading and over a century in math. As if the projections were not disconcerting enough, analysis of achievement trends in the 1990s indicated that the modest convergence in reading and math gaps made in the 1970s and 1980s has either ceased (Smith 2000) or reversed (Grissmer, Flanagan, and Williamson 1998).

This trend is demonstrated clearly in Figure 1.5, which shows SAT scores for whites, Asians, Hispanics, and blacks from 1996 through 2012. The data are for seniors who took the SAT any time during their high school years through March of their senior year. If a student took the test more than once, the most recent score is used. The graph shows that minority achievement gaps remained remarkably stable between 1996 and 2012 for both reading and math. Analysis based on the NAEP also shows that

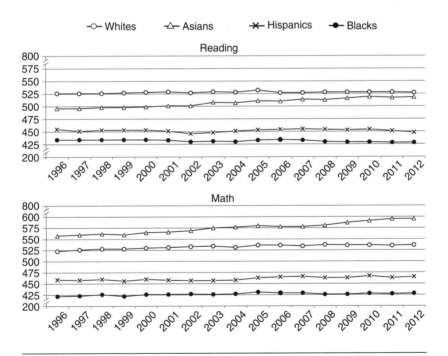

FIGURE 1.5. SAT scores since the mid-1990s. *Source:* College Entrance Examination Board, National Report on College-Bound Seniors, years 1995–96 through 2011–2012.

minority achievement gaps were relatively stable over the past two decades. One of the findings that highlighted the severity of the black-white testing gap was that racial inequality exists even among high achievers. Hedges and Nowell (1998, 167) note that "blacks are hugely underrepresented in the upper tails of the achievement distributions, and this underrepresentation does not seem to be decreasing."

The same pattern exists with regard to students' grades. In Figure 1.6, we show the grade-point averages (GPA) for high school seniors in 2001 and 2011 by race. The bold line represents the overall average in achievement for all students (3.30 in 2001 and 3.34 in 2011), and the bars represent the difference in achievement for each racial group relative to the average overall GPA for all students. The actual average GPA for each group is displayed above (or below in the case of Hispanics and blacks) the bars. The figure shows that although GPA has risen slightly over time for most students, the subgroup differences have remained the same.

When you consider that academic performance is an important determinant of educational attainment and that students with higher grades or test scores are more likely to complete high school, enroll in and complete college, and attend better quality colleges (Behrman et al. 1998; Hanushek

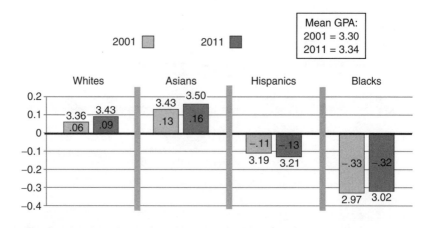

FIGURE 1.6. High school grade-point averages (GPAs) and points above/below the mean GPA for all students, 2001 and 2011. *Note:* The numbers outside the bars represent students' GPAs and the numbers within the bars correspond to the points above or below the mean GPA for all students. *Source: SAT Trends: Background on the SAT Takers in the Class of 2011.* http://professionals.collegeboard.com/data-reports-research/sat/cb-seniors -2011/tables.

and Pace 1995; Rivkin 1995), the minority achievement gap may warrant even greater attention from policy makers interested in reducing racial inequality in general. For instance, academic achievement (i.e., test scores) actually explains some of the racial disparities in earnings later in life, even among those with similar levels of educational attainment. In fact, racial wage gaps are smaller between people with similar test scores than among those with different scores (Farkas and Vicknair 1996; Murnane, Willett, and Levy 1995; Neal and Johnson 1996; O'Neill 1990).

The importance of racial differences in educational attainment and achievement extend beyond their implications for individual incomes. Increases in educational outcomes are associated with improved physical and mental health (Cutler and Lleras-Muney 2008), reduced crime (Lochner and Moretti 2004), and even improved civic participation (Dee 2004; Milligan, Moretti, and Oreopoulos 2004). Some reports indicate that the effects of education become stronger over the life course, particularly with regard to health (Lynch 2003; Ross and Wu 1996), and that racial differences in health are partially explained by racial differences in educational attainment (Hayward et al. 2000; Warner and Hayward 2006). Therefore, reducing the racial achievement gap seems to be a vital first step in addressing racial inequality within the United States and in realizing the democratic values that U.S. laws and social policies strive to achieve.

Parental Involvement as a Solution for Low Achievement

Given the importance of the minority achievement gap, it is critical for scholars to focus on potential causes and solutions for the gap. Numerous theories have emerged over the past half-century that might explain racial differences in academic skills. Some explanations have centered on genetic differences (Herrnstein and Murray 1994; Jensen 1969), racial bias in standardized testing (Kozol 2000; Meier 2000; Sacks 1999), differences in socioeconomic characteristics such as family structure (Moynihan 1965), exposure to poverty (Brooks-Gunn, Klebanov, and Duncan 1996; Duncan, Brooks-Gunn, and Klebanov 1994), and residential segregation (Massey and Denton 1993; Wilson 1987, 1996). Social reproduction theorists argue that schools maintain existing patterns of inequality because they are structured to reproduce the current social order. Bowles and Gintis (1976) and Bourdieu and Passeron (1977) argue that schools reflect and reproduce social class inequality; schools socialize children to occupy the segments in society from which they originate. It has even been suggested that Hispanics and blacks promote an oppositional culture resistant to academic goals (Ogbu 1978). These theories represent just a subset of those used to explain low achievement and achievement gaps, yet the diverse set of factors they employ to explain the problem is evidence of the problem's complexity.

Encouraging parents to become more involved in their children's academic lives has been an important component of school reform efforts to enhance the achievement of America's school children for the past twenty years (Comer 1992; Epstein 1985). For example, in the late 1990s, states were being mandated by Congress to find ways to improve educational outcomes for students in poor and underachieving schools. The Improving America's Schools Act of 1994 (IASA) proposed to reduce the minority education gap by "affording parents meaningful opportunities to participate in the education of their children at home and at school." At the time, most public schools were using parental involvement as an educational strategy to improve students' academic outcomes. A 1998 report issued by the National Center for Education Statistics (NCES) found that 82 to 89% of all public elementary schools provided parents with information aimed at promoting learning at home, and roughly 90% held various activities intended to encourage parental involvement, including parent-teacher conferences and academic exhibitions (U.S. Department of Education 1998).

The next major federal policy to address schooling in the United States—the No Child Left Behind Act of 2001 (NCLB)—also addresses the issue of parental involvement in children's schooling. The central purpose of NCLB is to close achievement gaps in reading and math proficiency tests among students from different racial/socioeconomic backgrounds by 2013–14. One of the important goals of the NCLB is to increase parental involvement in children's schooling affairs (see Section 1118). Thus, despite the copious factors contributing to achievement gaps, parental involvement in children's schooling has been an important goal of major federal education policies of the last two decades—IASA and the NCLB. These initiatives are partially driven by the belief that families are critical for establishing and maintaining good academic performance and improving the achievement of poor performing students (Berger 1983; Epstein 1983; Marjoribanks 1979; National Education Association 1985; Seeley 1984).

The Need for Further Research on Parental Involvement

Despite the central role parental involvement occupies within the mindset of educators and policy makers, scholars have questioned whether these policies have taken full advantage of empirical research on parenting (e.g., see Epstein 2005; Karen 2005). Though numerous researchers have focused on variation in parental involvement in children's education (Domina 2005; Jeynes 2003; Stein and Thorkildsen 1999; Zellman and Waterman 1998), scholars still disagree about how parents should be involved and which aspects of parental involvement are associated with improvements in children's academic outcomes.

One major reason for this lack of consensus among scholars is that parents' involvement has been measured differently across studies. For example, Hoge, Smit, and Crist's (1997) conception of involvement entails four components: parental expectations, parental interest, involvement in school, and family and community. Mau (1997), however, claims the most important involvement measure is parental supervision of homework. Hango (2007) emphasizes the relational aspect of parents' time with children, claiming that involvement is important primarily because of the social capital it provides children in being able to mediate the harmful effects of financial deprivation. Such conceptual differences have led to inconsistent findings, creating a fair amount of confusion over the impact of involvement. The way that parental involvement is measured impacts the estimated effects of that participation on children's schooling (Domina 2005; Epstein 2001; Reay 1998; Sui-Chu and Willms 1996).

Additionally, many studies have used small samples making it difficult to generalize parents' degree of involvement and its impact on children's achievement to larger populations of families (Dearing et al. 2006; Gillies 2008). Complicating the importance of involvement even further is the fact that some have examined the parental involvement-student achievement link for elementary school children (Dearing and Taylor 2007; Schulting, Malone, and Dodge 2005), whereas others have focused on adolescents (McNeal 1999). Though parents tend to change their levels of involvement over time, there are very few (if any) studies that follow families over K-12 schooling. Finally, one of the most surprising aspects regarding parental involvement is that even though it has been widely suggested as a way to close achievement gaps between minority and nonminority students, the literature is unclear about which aspects of involvement actually improve achievement for minority students. Jeynes (2003) noted that "no meta-analysis that examines the effect of parental involvement on minority student educational outcomes has ever been published in an academic journal" (202).

When we first began research on this topic we were struck by three factors that heightened our urgency for completing this book. First, the numerous studies conducted on this subject have produced an unclear picture of the link between parents' involvement and academic outcomes. This lack of clarity is a result of the mixed findings from a variety of studies—some show that parental involvement is beneficial, whereas others show that it is associated with modest changes in students' achievement or even inconsequential. Second, the existing literature lacks coverage on whether racial/ethnic groups differ in the particular parental involvement activities they typically employ and on which of these activities matter for different racial (and class) groups. Thus educators can provide little empirically based guidance to parents regarding which activities promote academic success that are specific to each racial group.

Finally, for more than thirty years the federal government has heavily endorsed parental involvement as a strategy for improving the state of education in this country. Many school districts share the belief that parents are critical to the academic success of all schoolchildren. This belief has been steadfast for several decades among policy officials, members of Congress, and school personnel despite much uncertainty within the existing research literature about the effectiveness of parental involvement on children's academic outcomes. Thus the lack of clarity surrounding the parental involvement-student achievement link necessitates careful attention that considers social class and race beyond black and white and focuses on identifying strategies that lead to increases in academic outcomes for a wider range of youth.

Purpose and Guiding Framework for This Book

The purpose of this book is to provide an in-depth examination of the association between parental involvement and academic outcomes. This book represents our attempt at providing parents, teachers, policy makers, and the social scientific community with an extensive examination of how parental involvement in children's schooling both at home and at school varies both by social class and by race. We also examine how various parental involvement strategies are associated with academic outcomes separately by social class and by race and the extent to which parental involvement can be expected to lead to gap convergence. When examining social class, we consider both parents' education and income. When considering race, we go beyond the typical black-white comparison and include Asians and Hispanics whenever the data permit.

It is important to note that we are not conducting a study on parenting in terms of styles based on Baumrind's (1971) classic configuration of parenting approaches.[5] More specifically, we focus on activities that require parents to directly communicate the importance of schooling to their child. Although some forms of involvement, such as placing a premium on having a large number of books in the home or taking one's child on trips to the museum, can be regarded as measures of how parents are oriented toward the education of their child, our focus is on types of involvement that convey the importance parents attribute to schooling more directly (e.g., provide advice on post–high school plans or help with homework). These forms of involvement require minimal financial resources and are thus accessible to all parents.

We provide the outline for the chapters that follow in a conceptual framework in Figure 1.7. Arrows represent the relationships between the concepts written within the boxes. The figure depicts the relationship between

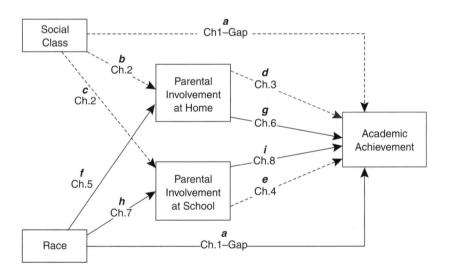

FIGURE 1.7. Chapter outlines and guiding conceptual framework.

parental involvement and achievement by social class (dashed lines) and race (solid lines) and the order in which these links will be examined. Thus, whereas the top portion of the figure corresponds to social class, the bottom portion corresponds to race. The paths denoted by *a* signify that differences in academic achievement exist by social class (dashed) and race (solid), which we described in this chapter.

In Chapter 2 we examine whether parental involvement varies by social class when the involvement consists of measures parents can implement at home and those that can be implemented at schools (denoted by paths *b* and *c*, respectively). In Chapters 3 and 4 we turn our attention to paths *d* and *e*, respectively, which propose that parents' involvement at home (path *d*) and at school (path *e*) is consequential for youths' academic achievement. These links are examined separately by selected categories of social class. We consider parental involvement at home and at school separately primarily because existing evidence suggests that involvement in these two domains may be distinct and have their own distinct effects on children (Pomerantz, Moorman, and Litwick 2007).

We turn our attention to race beginning in Chapter 5, which examines whether parental involvement at home varies by race (path *f*), and in Chapter 6, which examines the link between parental involvement at home and achievement by race (path *g*). The next two chapters are analogous to Chapters 5 and 6 using forms of involvement that require parents to come into contact with schools. Specifically, in Chapter 7 we determine whether racial differences exist in how parents interact with teachers and in their patterns of involvement with schools (path *h*). We then examine whether these forms of involvement are consequential for students' achievement (path *i*). We also assess the implications of parental involvement for achievement gaps by social class (Chapter 4) and race (Chapter 8).

We shift gears in Chapter 9 and turn our attention to parents' preferred strategy for dealing with their child's poor academic performance. Despite numerous studies on parental involvement in children's academic schooling, there is a dearth of knowledge on how parents respond specifically to inadequate academic performance. Therefore, in Chapter 9 we assess the degree of racial variation in (1) parents' philosophies for responding to inadequate academic achievement and (2) the implications these parenting philosophies have for children's achievement. Our results show that white and black parents have markedly different philosophies on how to respond to inadequate performance, and these differences appear to impact chil-

dren's achievement in dramatically different ways. In Chapter 10 we introduce a new conception of parental involvement that does not rely on the
more traditional forms of parental involvement (e.g., help with homework,
meet with teachers). We report the results of focus groups that help lay the
foundation for our understanding of how parental involvement actually
operates in children's schooling. Finally, we discuss the theoretical and
practical implications of the findings from this book in Chapter 11. Our
findings suggest that the one-size-fits-all mantra of parental involvement
and the reliance on parental involvement as a major strategy for amelio-
rating class- and race-based achievement gaps should be reconsidered by
educators and policy makers.

Chapter Summary

The belief that parental involvement is critical in establishing and maintaining good academic performance is widespread and regarded as common sense. Increasing parental involvement has been an important goal
for policy makers at the local, state, and federal levels of government. The
popularity of the parental involvement narrative might be partially fueled
by the sense of urgency among educators to address the persistence of low
achievement among youth from lower social class backgrounds and some
minority groups. However, the empirical literature is unclear regarding
the extent to which parental involvement is beneficial to achievement and
which forms of involvement are effective.

Although we have heard the calls for parents to play a greater role in
education (and certainly understand the logic behind this request), we are
puzzled by the strong belief that parental involvement will lead to improved
achievement for all children and to convergence in achievement gaps. We
have sufficient reason to be skeptical that this will lead to substantial
improvement in students' achievement, a convergence in the seemingly
intractable racial achievement gap, or positive changes in youths' overall
academic orientation. Our skepticism is based on (1) inconsistent evidence
on whether parents positively impact children's academic success, (2) relatively few studies documenting the impact parental involvement has on
academic outcomes for different racial and ethnic groups, (3) concerns about
the generalizability of findings from studies using small samples of families, and (4) lack of a comprehensive picture of the importance of parents
across the K–12 span. As it currently stands, two competent researchers

could begin studies on this topic and have widely divergent results—from one finding that parental involvement is beneficial for the schooling process to the other finding that parental involvement is mostly insignificant. It is likely neither researcher would consider all of the major racial groups within the United States or study parental involvement throughout K–12, which are limitations dictated by the scale of this issue and the narrow focus often required for publishing empirical findings.

We know some parents are capable of enhancing their children's likelihood of being academically successful—however defined. These parents may have educational experiences that increase their effectiveness as aides to children's learning. For example, they may have the cultural capital that allows them to create cohesion between the school and home learning arenas or a socioeconomic standing that allows them to contribute greater educational resources to their child. Thus the possibility that parents could be a determining factor in academic success does warrant the call for them to be more involved in their child's schooling. However, this potential only pertains to *some* parents. This is not to say that only more educated, connected, and wealthier parents are capable of helping their child succeed. Furthermore, some children might best excel when parental involvement is minimal. In our view, the focus should be on systematizing any of the benefits associated with parental involvement for all parents, with the understanding that different activities might matter for some groups and not others.

There are many activities parents can engage in to help their child academically, but there is no single mode of parental involvement. Studies focusing on involvement generally consider seven aspects of involvement: parent as (1) communicator, (2) supporter of activities, (3) learner, (4) advocate, (5) decision maker, (6) volunteer, and (7) home activities teacher (Hickman 1996). Although most studies on involvement are informative about the effectiveness of parental involvement in children's education, they often consider a limited set of practices that fall under one or two of these categories. To be clear, such studies have merit and advance our understanding about this process. At the same time, we believe that a more comprehensive assessment is necessary. Thus we assess over sixty forms of involvement in this study in order to provide an extensive assessment of what "works" for each social class and racial group.

The truth is that we should expect the benefits of parent involvement only for some children. Our conclusions suggest that when asked if parent involvement is critical for academic success, the answer depends on the form of involvement and the social class or racial group in question. There is no reason to assume that all forms of involvement will lead to better achievement or that the effects of particular involvement activities will be the same across groups, particularly given that members of different social class or racial groups can have substantially different life experiences within the United States. This factor is what makes the literature unclear on the importance of parents and the growing national emphasis on increasing their involvement wholesale perplexing. Parents continue to hear that they should be more involved, but in what ways? Should we be prescribing the same forms of involvement to all parents? To answer these questions, one would have to know what works for which groups. This information is currently the missing link in parental involvement research that we seek to address in this book.

We hope that this book answers three questions that are central to this study: (1) Do social class and racial differences exist among parents in the level of involvement they have in their children's academic lives? (2) Which forms of parental involvement—both at home and with schools—are associated with increases in achievement for children in each class/racial group? (3) What portion of the achievement gap can parental involvement account for? Our findings weigh in on important issues relevant for policy and address whether the notion that affluent parents care more about their children's education than their less affluent counterparts is justifiable. This belief has been long-standing among some educators (Deutsch 1967), and evidence suggests school personnel interpret parental involvement as a reflection of the value parents place on their children's educational success (Bol and Berry 2005; Lareau 1987). Our findings weigh in on the same for white and Asian parents relative to Hispanic and black parents and provide some insight into which parental practices work and for whom, and whether parental involvement explains a larger share of the achievement gap than socioeconomic factors. We also highlight the forms of involvement that are associated with increases in academic outcomes and those that parents and educators should work toward making effective or, in some cases, less detrimental for achievement.

— 2 —

Parental Involvement and Social Class

One of the major changes to the educational system since the early twentieth century is the policy mandate for parents to serve as home assistants to schools in educating children. Formerly, parents' primary role in the home with regard to schooling was to ensure that children were properly fed, adequately dressed, and ready to learn when they attend school. Since the 1950s, educational policy has made parental involvement at home an integral part of the wider educational system. De Carvalho (2001) notes that "by prescribing family education or aligning home education to the prevailing school curriculum, it penetrates the private realm and formalizes family educative practices" (11). Schools now place the obligation of actively supporting academic learning onto parents, communicating to parents that it is their responsibility to help with curricular goals. If parents do not perform to the school's satisfaction, it becomes the task of schools and teachers to guide disadvantaged or negligent parents (De Carvalho 2001).

Although parents can participate in their children's schooling in numerous ways, researchers typically characterize involvement into home-based and school-based subtypes. Such categorizations are useful because they capture distinct, yet important, activities expected of parents in most U.S. school systems (Green et al. 2007). Prior operational definitions of involvement at home include parents' communication with their children on school issues (Keith et al. 1986) and home involvement such as helping with homework (Shumow and Miller 2001; Singh et al. 1995; Sui-Chu and Willms 1996). Some scholars have also considered parental expectations for children's achievement as a form of involvement (e.g., Keith et al. 1998; Singh et al. 1995). Unlike behavioral forms of involvement, such as reading to the child or imposing rules about grades, parental expectations represent a different construct because they are beliefs. Previous studies have found that expectations have the strongest impact on achievement relative to other involvement types, such as parent-child communication (Fan 2001; Fan and Chen 2001). Therefore, it is important to include parents' expectations in studies on parental involvement.

School-based involvement reflects activities on the part of parents that require them to come into contact with schools. Such practices include, but are not limited to, attending parent-teacher conferences, attending school events, and being present at general school meetings. Common operational definitions of school-based involvement in previous studies include participation in school activities (Izzo et al. 1999; Miedel and Reynolds 1999; Shaver and Walls 1998) and the number of hours parents volunteer in their children's schools (Okpala and Okpala 2001). The most typical route to school-based involvement among U.S. parents is through attendance at general school meetings and parent-teacher conferences (U.S. Department of Education 2004).

In this chapter, we examine the link between social class and parental involvement. When considering the implications of social class for parental involvement, the distinction between home-based and school-based involvement is important. The forms of involvement that parents can employ at home can often occur with minimal (if any) material resources and are therefore more accessible to parents regardless of their social class standing. In contrast, forms of parental involvement at school often require parents to have access to reliable transportation and flexible work schedules to facilitate parent-school interaction. Therefore, throughout this study we treat involvement at home as conceptually and empirically distinct from involvement at school.

For the purposes of reorienting readers, we highlight the links that guide the analysis in this chapter in Figure 2.1. The figure depicts the hypotheses that both home-based and school-based parental involvement will vary by social class. In the following section, we provide a brief review of the research literature that leads us to these propositions. We then move to an empirical assessment of these hypotheses using an extensive set of measures of parental involvement from the NELS and CDS, two datasets that rely on nationally representative samples. We conclude this chapter with a summary of the results and a brief discussion on the implications of the findings for the literature on parental involvement and social class.

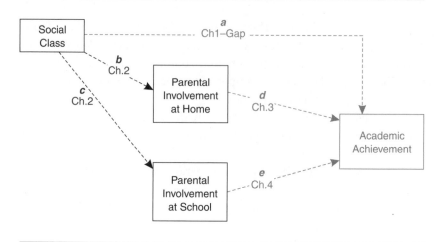

FIGURE 2.1. Chapter outline.

Previous Research on Parental Involvement and Social Class

Studies suggest that parents from lower social class backgrounds are less involved in their children's education both at home and at school than those from middle- and upper-class backgrounds. With regard to parental involvement at home, Baker and Soden (1998) compared opportunities for literacy learning among families from different income levels and found that children from low-income homes had fewer opportunities for informal literacy learning than children from middle-income families. Low-income parents were far less likely to take their child to the library (43%) than middle-income parents (90%) and less likely to engage in joint reading exercises with their children. The findings by Baker and Soden (1998) on the link between social class and opportunities for literacy practice have been replicated by studies that rely on both ethnographic (Delgado-Gaitan 1990; Goldenberg, Reese, and Gallimore 1992; Teale 1986) and quantitative methods (Bee et al. 1982; Brooks-Gunn, Klebanov, and Liaw 1995; Smith, Brooks-Gunn, and Klebanov 1997). Some studies suggest that these patterns might stem from social class differences in how parents perceive their role within the educational domain. Parents from lower social class backgrounds may be more likely to view children's achievement as residing within the school's arena and not wish to disturb the educational process (Barnard 2004; Gillies 2008). The separation between home and school arenas can prevent parents from responding to teachers' requests to help their children with at-home learning (Lareau 2000).

As with home-based forms of parental involvement, it is reasonable to expect that parents from disadvantaged backgrounds exhibit lower school-based involvement for a number of reasons related to their economic circumstances (Bradley et al. 2001; Bradley and Whiteside-Mansell 1997). According to Epstein and Dauber (1991), social class disadvantage isolates parents from school efforts intended to increase their participation. They note that school programs and teacher practices designed to connect parents with school are prone to favor more educated and more socioeconomically advantaged parents. Therefore, it is not surprising that parents with higher socioeconomic status and educational attainment are more likely to attend general school meetings and parent-teacher conferences (Pomerantz, Moorman, and Litwack 2007), which are the most typical routes to school-based involvement among parents in the United States (U.S. Department of Education 2004).

Why Does Social Class Matter?

Reasons why and how social class matters can be captured by three concepts: economic capital, cultural capital, and social capital. One's level of economic or material capital is related to the amount of access one has to economic resources such as money or assets that can be converted into cash (Bourdieu 2008). Research suggests that the disadvantages associated with economic capital constrain parents' ability to supplement and intervene in their children's education (Lareau 1987; Miller and Davis 1997). Lareau (2003) finds that middle-class families have disproportionately more reliable private transportation and flexible work schedules, facilitating their ability to interact with authority figures in their children's lives. By contrast, parents with financial hardships are often the primary targets of parental involvement initiatives because they are less visible in schools. Their ability to be involved is typically constrained by lack of job flexibility, lower likelihood of paid child care, and economic isolation from school efforts designed to stoke participation (Epstein and Dauber 1991; Haskins and Sawhill 2003; Lareau 1987). Further, as Federman et al. (1996) showed, many have experienced a home eviction, crowded housing, and a utility disconnection. These deprivations generate considerable amounts of instability that likely inhibit the extent to which parents can produce stimulating home environments.

Yet disadvantages associated with social class go beyond economic resources. Cultural capital is a useful concept for understanding the non-material relationship between social class and parental involvement. Introduced by Bourdieu and Passeron (1977) and elaborated by Bourdieu (1984), cultural capital refers to the constellation of knowledge, preferences, tastes, codes of appropriate conduct, and consumption practices that stem from one's upbringing in a particular social class stratum. The use of culture in the term "cultural capital" should not be viewed as indicative of parents' intent and ambitions for their children's education. Lareau (1987) finds that educational values of working-class and middle-class parents do not differ; regardless of social class, parents want their children to succeed in school and believe that they support and help their children academically. Nevertheless, one's human capital (i.e., level of education) and economic capital structures one's experiences, aesthetic disposition, and interpretations of the social world. Typically, those familiar with the styles, tastes, and dispositions of the higher-class culture are said to possess high amounts of cultural capital. In contrast, individuals from lower social class backgrounds are said to have forms of cultural capital considered less valuable than middle- and upper-class individuals. In general, all forms of capital are highly correlated; possessing one form of capital—say economic—increases the ease with which one can obtain and accumulate other forms of capital—say social or cultural.

The concept of cultural capital became a popular explanation for persistent patterns of unequal academic outcomes within the education research community. Bourdieu and Passeron's (1977) central premise was that inequality is perpetuated through the valorization of particular forms of cultural expressions. Schools value and operate within the culture and ideology of the upper classes; those who effectively enact these arbitrary cultural tools are said to have the "cultural capital" critical to achieving academically. In regard to parental involvement, parents with the cultural capital needed to navigate the school culture feel competent communicating with school personnel, which results in a high sense of entitlement in their interactions with educators (Lareau 2002). Therefore, they are in a better position to take advantage of the schools' requests. In contrast, working-class individuals are more deferential and outwardly accepting, and they have the added burden of acquiring the middle- and upper-class-specific cultural knowledge that schools and teachers promote (Kim 2009; Lareau 1987, 2000).

Previous studies have linked cultural capital to parent involvement in school. For example, Lareau and Horvat (1999) find that the possession and activation of cultural capital in school settings varies by social class, leading to variations between groups in the extent to which they are socially included (e.g., behaviors are recognized and legitimated) and excluded (e.g., marginalized and rebuffed) from the academic institutional setting. Furthermore, Lareau (2003) finds that middle-class parents have more opportunities than their working-class counterparts to build cultural capital through greater exposure to "middle-class institutions," which is closely linked to their greater involvement in the institutional dimension of their children's lives.

As greater cultural alignment between middle and upper class parents and educators leads them to have a more inclusive relationship with school personnel, they also have more interactions with teachers than their working-class counterparts. It is through these interactions that parents learn important information about school policies and teacher expectations (e.g., Epstein 1987; Lareau 1987). The product of these interactions has been referred to as social capital—actual or potential resources derived from social networks or relationships (Bourdieu 2008)—which parents accumulate as their bonds with teachers and other school personnel become stronger and more developed (Lareau and Horvat 1999).

In sum, the differences in both economic and cultural capital between lower- and upper-class parents are consequential for their school involvement. Lareau (2003) notes that whereas working-class and poor parents perceive educators as their social superiors, middle-class parents have greater confidence in criticizing educational professionals and to intervene in school matters. Although Lareau (2002) observed that middle-class parents sometimes appeared anxious during parent-teacher conferences, their anxiety was slight; they still spoke more frequently and asked educators more questions than their working-class and poor counterparts. Therefore, given the literature on the implications of social class and cultural capital within education, one should expect that analyzing a wide range of parental involvement measures will yield substantial variation by social class. Specifically, parents from higher social class backgrounds should have greater levels of involvement than those from lower social class backgrounds by virtue of their access to various forms of capital.

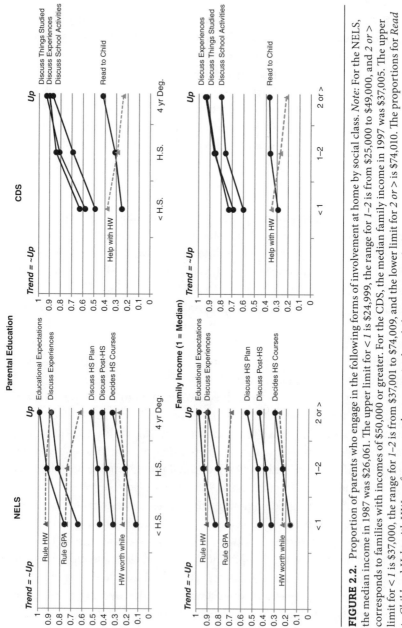

FIGURE 2.2. Proportion of parents who engage in the following forms of involvement at home by social class. *Note:* For the NELS, the median income in 1987 was $26,061. The upper limit for < *1* is $24,999, the range for *1–2* is from $25,000 to $49,000, and *2 or >* corresponds to families with incomes of $50,000 or greater. For the CDS, the median family income in 1997 was $37,005. The upper limit for < *1* is $37,000, the range for *1–2* is from $37,001 to $74,009, and the lower limit for *2 or >* is $74,010. The proportions for *Read to Child* and *Help with HW* are for parents who engage in these behaviors every day.

Does Parental Involvement Vary by Social Class?

We determine whether parental involvement varies by social class using both the NELS and CDS, two nationally representative data sets. We consider social class along two dimensions—parents' education and family income—with the samples stratified into three categories for each dimension. For parents' education, the comparison is made between (1) parents with less than a high school diploma, (2) those with a high school diploma, and (3) those with a four-year degree or greater. For family income, parents are divided by those with incomes (1) below the national median, (2) from the median to twice the median, and (3) twice the median or greater. Our analysis is straightforward; we assess the proportion of parents that engage in various measures of parental involvement for each category. Although these categories might not perfectly correspond to whether parents are from low-, middle-, or upper-middle-class backgrounds, this sorting strategy enables us to provide some key insight into the link between social class and parental involvement. That is, if an association exists between these concepts, then one should expect that the proportion of parents who engage in the measures of parental involvement is higher for each successive category of social class.

Figure 2.2 contains the results for the first set of analyses, which shows the proportion of parents who engage in various measures of parental involvement at home (see Appendix C for a detailed description of the measures used throughout this study). Whereas the forms of parental involvement that are not positively associated with social class are listed along the left-hand side of their respective quadrant (and illustrated by dashed lines), measures for which high levels of engagement increase with social class are listed on the right-hand side of their respective quadrants. The top panel shows the findings for social class along the lines of parents' education, and the findings in the bottom panel are for social class by family income.

The top panel of Figure 2.2 shows that in general, parental involvement at home increases with parents' level of education; an upward trend in parental involvement exists on 9 of the 13 (more than two-thirds) measures of parental involvement. The first quadrant shows that three of the eight measures of parental involvement at home based on the NELS are not positively associated with social class: having rules about homework and grades, and believing that homework is worthwhile. However, an upward trend in involvement exists for the other five measures of involvement:

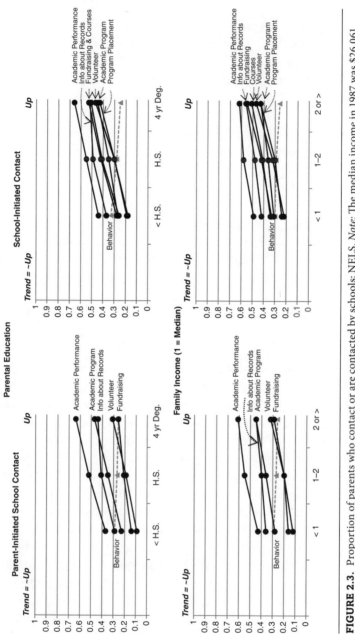

FIGURE 2.3. Proportion of parents who contact or are contacted by schools: NELS. *Note:* The median income in 1987 was $26,061. The upper limit for *< 1* is $24,999, the range for *1–2* is from $25,000 to $49,000, and *2 or >* corresponds to families with income levels twice the median or greater ($50,000).

parents' educational expectations for their child (i.e., how much education they would like for their child to attain); whether parents have a role in the courses youth take in high school; and parent-child discussions about school experiences, high school plans, and post–high school plans. The second quadrant shows that analysis based on the CDS similarly suggests a positive relationship between social class and parental involvement at home. Whereas helping with homework seems to decline as social class increases, the proportion of parents who discuss topics of study, school experiences, and school activities, and who read to their child increase with each successive level of education. The findings in the bottom panel of Figure 2.2 show the patterns are nearly identical when social class is measured by family income.

There are four primary points of interests in the results displayed in Figure 2.2. First, nearly 70% of the measures for parental involvement at home show a positive association with social class. Second, both dimensions of social class yield nearly identical results. Third, both data sets yield the same general upward trend for measures of parent-child discussion. Finally, parents from high social class groups appear to prefer forms of parental involvement that can be considered as nonauthoritarian for how youth should approach schooling; all nine measures of parental involvement that show a positive association with social class are forms of involvement that do not infringe on youths' autonomy. For example, six of the nine measures capture parent-child discussions related to schooling, another two capture parents attempts to serve as a resource to their child (read to child and help decide high school courses), and finally their educational expectations for their child. In contrast, three of the four measures of parental involvement that do not show a positive association with social class are more invasive forms of involvement; rules about both homework and grades, and helping with homework. We elaborate further on this pattern in the chapter summary.

We shift the focus to forms of parental involvement at schools in Figure 2.3. Specifically, the measures of parental involvement capture various reasons that bring parents into contact with schools, and whether the contact was initiated by the parent (left-hand panel) or by the school (right-hand panel). Similar to the findings for parental involvement at home displayed in Figure 2.2, the results displayed in Figure 2.3 are nearly identical for social class measured by parents' education (top panel) and family income (bottom panel). Twelve of the fourteen measures (or 86%) of parent-school

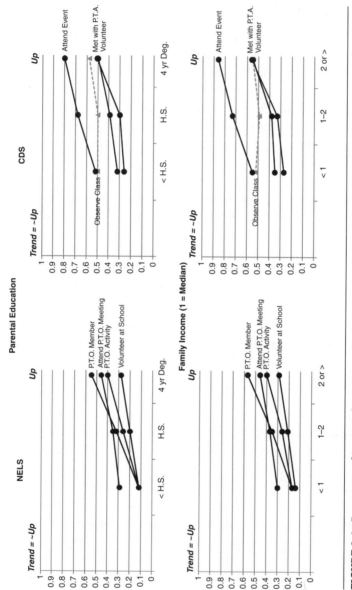

FIGURE 2.4. Proportion of parents who engage in the following forms of participation at school. *Note:* For the NELS, the median income in 1987 was $26,061. The upper limit for < *1* is $24,999, the range for *1–2* is $25,000 to $49,000, and *2 or >* corresponds to families with incomes of $50,000 or greater. For the CDS, the median family income in 1997 was $37,005. The upper limit for < *1* is $37,000, the range for *1–2* is from $37,001 to $74,009, and *2 or >* refers to families with incomes of $74,010 or greater.

contact are positively associated with social class; only contact with school about a child's behavior—both parent- and school-initiated—is not positively associated with social class. The findings in Figure 2.3 are consistent with the hypothesis that parents with higher social class backgrounds are more comfortable communicating with their child's school than those with lower social class backgrounds. The findings also suggest that schools are more likely to contact parents from higher social class backgrounds than those from lower social class backgrounds. Thus, Figure 2.3 lends support to Bourdieu and Passeron's (1977) notion of the role of cultural capital in schooling; namely, schools' expectations regarding parent involvement seem to be more in line with middle-class parents' beliefs, capacities, and involvement styles than those of working-class parents.

In Figure 2.4, we show results for analyses that examine the link between social class and measures most often associated with parental involvement at school. These measures capture parental participation at school in the form of parent-teacher organizations, attendance at school events, class observations, and volunteer efforts. Both the top and bottom panels show that higher social class is associated with more parental participation at school, regardless of whether social class is assessed by parents' education or family income. Similar to the trend in Figure 2.3, an upward trend in Figure 2.4 exists for 87% (7 out of 8) of the measures of parental participation at school. The only measure that does not show an upward trend is class observation, which is the only passive form of parental participation assessed.

The final set of analysis is displayed in Figure 2.5. The measures of parental involvement in Figure 2.5 are intended to capture parents' level of assertiveness with teachers. The left-hand side of the figure contains measures that assess whether parents engage in forms of involvement that require them to take initiative with school personnel by obtaining information on their child's teacher, meeting with the teacher, or requesting a particular teacher prior to the start of the school year. The measures on the right-hand side of the figure are intended to capture whether parents engage school personnel in either casual conversation or more formal interactions regarding their child. Specifically, these measures capture whether parents have had a conference with their child's teacher and school principal, or simply engaged them in informal conversations, met with the school counselor, and given some form of presentation to their child's classroom (e.g., read to children).

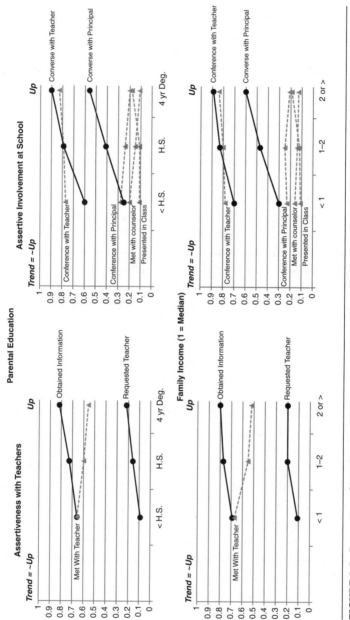

FIGURE 2.5. Proportion of parents who display assertiveness with teachers and school: CDS. *Note:* The median family income in 1997 was $37,005. The upper limit for the *< 1* is $37,000, the range for *1–2* is from $37,001 to $74,009, and *2 or >* refers to families with income levels twice the median or greater, which corresponds to $74,010 or greater.

The findings show that the proportion of parents who meet with the teacher appears to decline as social class increases. However, the proportion of parents who obtain information about their child's teacher and who request a particular teacher prior to the school year increases as social class becomes greater. In contrast to the former measure, which seems innocuous, the latter two measures can be characterized as an attempt by parents either to monitor or to influence the child's learning environment; they require parents either to engage in some form of research, perhaps by utilizing social networks, or to have the self-assurance and temerity to make changes to classroom rosters. Given that individuals from higher social class backgrounds have both more social capital (Lareau and Horvat 1999) and greater confidence in criticizing educational professionals and intervening in school matters (Lareau 2003), it is not surprising that these measures show a positive connection with social class.

The findings in the right-hand panel show that only two of the six measures of assertiveness at school are positively related with social class: informal conversations with teachers and with principals. The other measures— conference with teachers, or principals, meeting with counselor, and class presentations—do not seem to be related to social class. The two measures that show a positive connection with social class are those that are more optional in nature than the four measures that do not show an upward trend. Engaging in informal conversations with school personnel may be a function of cultural capital as it requires that parents have a certain level of comfort in interacting with authority figures. As discussed earlier, the culture and communication style in schools is often more in line with the norms and expectations of parents with middle- or upper-middle-class backgrounds.

Chapter Summary

The purpose of this chapter is to establish whether parental involvement varies by social class. Previous research has established that social class is positively related with parental involvement both at home and at school. Scholars have used a number of conceptualizations to describe the nature of parents' involvement in their children's education. This chapter extends the literature by accounting for two dimensions of social class—parents' education and family income—and relying on a wide range of measures from two nationally representative sources of data that capture parental involvement both at home and at school.

The findings from this chapter for the relationship between social class and parental involvement are consistent with those from previous studies. The results unequivocally show that parents with higher social class backgrounds are more involved in their children's schooling than those with lower social class backgrounds. This finding is the case regardless of whether the form of involvement takes place at home or at school, and regardless of whether social class is assessed along the lines of parents' level of education or family income. It appears that low levels of social class can inhibit parents' involvement in their children's education, even net of similarities in the educational values of working-class and middle-class parents (Lareau 1987).

We summarize these results in Table 2.1. The four general subheadings by which the measures of parental involvement were sorted (home, school contact, participation at school, and assertiveness at school) are listed in the first column. The findings reported in this chapter are consistent with the notion that parenting patterns are class driven. In total, 72% (32/44) of the measures of parental involvement examined in this chapter are employed more by parents with higher levels of social class than by those with lower levels of social class (listed in the second column of the table). In contrast, there are only 12 forms of involvement that did not have a positive association with social class (listed in the third column of the table). The combination of measures that show an upward trend versus those that do not is revealing. In general, it seems that a greater share of parents with higher social class backgrounds show a preference for more active or optional forms of involvement than parents from lower social class backgrounds. The opposite appears to be the case when it comes to forms of involvement that can be characterized as either more passive (e.g., rules about homework and grades) or appear to be mandatory (e.g., conferences with teachers, principals, or meeting with counselors); these measures either do not show a discernible upward trend or are adopted by a greater share of parents from lower social class backgrounds.

The work of Lareau (1987, 2003) yields a framework useful for summarizing the findings reported in this chapter. Lareau (2003) finds that social class creates distinctive parenting styles. Specifically, she finds that parents differ by class in how they define their own role in their children's lives and in how they perceive the nature of childhood. She notes that middle-class parenting conforms to a cultural logic of child rearing she terms "concerted cultivation." In addition to enrolling their children in numerous

TABLE 2.1. Summary of findings for parental involvement by social class

Involvement type	Upward trend	No upward trend
Home	Educational expectations[a] Discuss school experiences[a] Discuss high school plans[a] Discuss post-high school plans[a] Decides high school courses[a] Discuss things studied[b] Discuss school experiences[b] Discuss school activities[b] Read to child[b]	Rule about homework[a] Rule about grades (GPA)[a] Homework is worthwhile[a] Help with homework[b]
School contact	Contact school about academic performance[a] Contact school about academic program[a] Contact school about information regarding records[a] Contact school about volunteering[a] Contact school about fundraising[a] Contacted about academic performance[a] Contacted about information regarding records[a] Contacted about fundraising[a] Contacted about volunteering[a] Contacted about academic program[a] Contacted about program placement[a] Contacted about courses[a]	Contact school about behavior[a] Contacted about behavior[a]
Participation at school	Parent-teacher organization (PTO) member[a] Attend PTO meeting[a] Participate in PTO activity[a] Volunteer at school[a] Attend event at school[b] Met with parent-teacher association[b] Volunteer at school[b]	Observe class[b]
Assertiveness at school	Obtained information about the teacher[b] Requested teacher[b] Converse with teacher[b] Converse with principal[b]	Met with teacher[b] Conference with teacher[b] Conference with principal[b] Met with counselor[b] Presented in class[b]

a. Denotes that the data are from the NELS.
b. Denotes that the data are from the CDS.

organized activities, middle-class parents stress language use and discipline through persuasion and reasoning, which facilitates greater language, cognitive, and social development in their children. In contrast, she notes that working-class and poor parents employ child-rearing strategies that she terms the "accomplishment of natural growth." Parents who adopt this parenting ethos do not focus on developing their children's special talents. Instead, they believe that their children will grow and thrive if they provide love, food, and safety. Furthermore, their disciplining style consists of more directives and, in some cases, physical discipline. Lareau's description of the role of social class for patterns in parenting is relevant for understanding both the greater level of involvement by parents from higher social class backgrounds and their preferences for which forms of involvement they employ more (and those they employ less) than less advantaged parents.

The class-driven parenting preferences have implications for children's interactions with school personnel. Lareau (2003) notes that concerted cultivation gives rise to a robust sense of entitlement that is particularly important in institutional settings, and which results in middle-class children learning to question adults, address adults as relative equals, be open to sharing information and asking for attention. However, the facilitation of natural growth leads to a clear delineation between the world of children and adults that inhibits the development of skills necessary for interacting with authority figures both in and out of the home. It seems that class-driven parenting preferences structure how actively youth manage their interactions in institutional settings. Because schools tend to reward students who bring class-privileged aesthetic dispositions to the classroom (Bourdieu and Passeron 1977), it is reasonable to expect that class-driven parenting preferences have implications for academic outcomes.

Although Bourdieu's (1984) concept of cultural capital is useful for understanding why higher levels of cultural capital usually accompany high levels of social class, it is important not to overstate the extent to which cultural capital mediates the effects of social class. Lareau (1987) argues that not all cultural resources are equally valuable within the education domain. She notes that aspects of class and class cultures typically associated with Bourdieu's (1984) conception of cultural capital—such as religion, taste in music, art, food, and furniture—seem to structure the behavioral norms of parents and teachers and the family-school relationship *less than* resources tied directly to social class—such as education, occupational prestige, and income. That is, although displays of school-relevant cultural capital seem to translate into class advantage, these mechanisms are ultimately tied to families' structural location with regard to social class.

Schools expect specific types of behavior from all parents, yet class-related factors shape parents' approach to involvement that are not always in line with the affluent dispositions and preferences that are valued in schools. Whereas working-class parents tend to turn over the responsibility for education to teachers, middle-class parents view education as a shared enterprise; they scrutinize, monitor, and supplement their children's schooling experience (Lareau 1987). If the goal in education is simply to increase parental involvement, then local, state, and national education initiatives intended to reach out to parents should focus primarily on disadvantaged parents. However, if the goal is to increase parental involvement because it is consequential for student outcomes, then further research is needed. In the next chapter, we examine whether parental involvement is beneficial for academic outcomes, assessing whether educators and policy makers should view parental involvement as an effective strategy for attaining or maintaining academic success in the first place.

— 3 —

Implications of Parental Involvement
at Home by Social Class

In Chapters 1 and 2, we observe that social class is associated with both higher levels of academic achievement *and* parental involvement in children's education. Naturally, one might conclude that students' achievement is greatly determined by their parents' level of involvement. With social class as the common denominator in rates of both achievement and parental involvement, the narrative that affluent youth perform better academically because their parents are highly involved seems logical. At the same time, the reciprocal narrative can emerge that the low achievement of youth from more disadvantaged class backgrounds stems from a lack of parental involvement. Many educators consider family support as more important for youths' academic outcomes than curriculum and instruction or school characteristics (Bol and Berry 2005). However, the extent to which both of these narratives are true remains somewhat unclear.

Although social class is a prominent factor for both parental involvement and achievement, one needs to be cautious about assigning predictive effects to parental involvement based on the social class–achievement link. Our guiding framework (see Figure 3.1) is helpful for illustrating this point. Socioeconomic background determines limits on family resources and may predispose certain attitudes and approaches, which seem to have implications for both achievement (path *a*) and parental involvement (paths *b* and *c*). However, the effects of social class on parental predispositions and children's achievement are completely separate from the role that parental involvement has for achievement; paths *d* and *e* are independent of paths *a, b,* and *c*. In short, the link between parental involvement and achievement might be spurious.

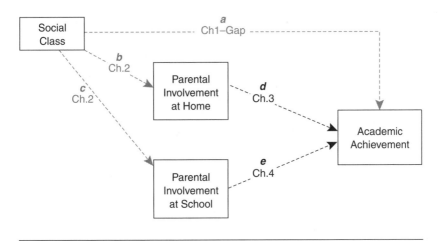

FIGURE 3.1. Chapter outline.

The notion that a link exists between social class and both parental involvement and achievement, but not between parental involvement and achievement, is easier to understand if one considers the difference between social class and parental involvement. Social class operates simply by virtue of the amount of economic, cultural, and social capital one has, or the social class group to which one belongs. The effects of social class might be latent; whether intentional or not, certain benefits come from having access to more resources. However, parental involvement requires activation—parental choices and activities driven by intentions for their children's lives and schooling (Hoover-Dempsey and Sandler 1997; Lareau 2000). Thus, the parental involvement–achievement link is not automatic. Furthermore, neither social class nor involvement determines the value parents place on education, their desires to be involved in their children's academic progress, or their wishes in having their children attain academic success (Delgado-Gaitan 1990; Eccles and Harold 1993; Lareau 1987). Indeed, many parents are able to secure positive educational outcomes for their children despite facing financial hardships and difficult life circumstances (Weiss et al. 2003). Basically, there are substantially more variables that can intervene in the involvement-achievement link than in the social class–achievement link—which might be more robust. That is, although high levels of social class might be a sufficient condition for academic success, academic success might require more than high levels of involvement.

In this chapter, we examine whether parental involvement at home is associated with achievement (path *d* in Figure 3.1). Specifically, we assess whether the measures of parental involvement at home employed in the previous chapter are related to increases in achievement. This link is assessed separately for each social class group both by parents' education and by family income. This allows us to determine whether the extent to which parental involvement is beneficial for achievement depends on one's social class. In the following section, we briefly summarize how the association between parental involvement and achievement has been understood within the research community. We then move to a description of the analyses and findings, and conclude this chapter with a summary of the results and a brief discussion on the implications of the findings for parents and educators.

Cultural and Social Capital and the Parental Involvement–Achievement Link

In addition to employing cultural capital to explain the connection between social class and levels of parental involvement, researchers have also employed the concept of cultural capital to explain how parents *transfer* educational advantages to their children. In this regard, cultural capital for parents exists in three forms: (1) connections to education-related objects (e.g., books, computers, and academic credentials), (2) connections to education-related institutions (e.g., schools, universities), and (3) personal attitudes and knowledge gained from experience (Lee and Bowen 2006). As discussed in Chapter 2, cultural capital within the educational context is determined by how closely aligned families' behavioral norms and overall knowledge and beliefs about schooling are with the values and practices of the educational system in which the family interacts (Lee and Bowen 2006). The more cultural capital parents possess, the more successful they will be in procuring additional cultural and social capital for their children. Parents with more cultural capital have been shown to be more adept at navigating and building useful connections in the educational systems in ways that translate to their children's academic success. In contrast, parents with less cultural capital tend to experience constraints that result in unequal access to institutional resources, which compromise their children's achievement (Lareau 2000).

In addition, the quality of relational engagement between parents and children *within* the household can have implications for the involvement-achievement link. For example, Coleman (1988) viewed social capital within the family as the product of relationships between parents and children, depending on both the physical presence of and attention from parents. Parents who invest greater time and effort in activities that support their children, such as shared activities or helping with homework, tend to generate more social capital within the family (Coleman 1988; Furstenberg and Hughes 1995) that children can use as a resource to generate higher achievement. However, studies have indicated that relative to socioeconomically disadvantaged parents, the conversations middle- and upper-class parents have with their children contain more contingent responsiveness that elicit children's speech, which results in their children having larger cumulative vocabularies prior to school entry than the children of their less advantaged counterparts (Bradley and Corwyn 2002; Hart and Risley 1995). Thus, children in families with greater cultural and social capital might benefit more from their parents' involvement than those from families with less cultural and social capital.

Achievement Returns to Parental Involvement by Social Class

Thus far we have demonstrated that parents do indeed vary in their involvement by social class and have suggested that they may also vary in the effectiveness of that involvement. Some evidence indicates that the benefits of parental involvement accrue differentially by socioeconomic status. The positive association between education and economic status means that parents will vary in their knowledge sets, and accordingly, the opportunities children have to learn and to practice academic tasks at home may differ (Kelly 2004; Lareau 2000; McCartney et al. 2007). In previous articulations of family capital, parent education is a resource that can be utilized to improve children's academic performance (Schneider, Martinez, and Owens 2006; Teachman, Paasch, and Carver 1997). Some scholars argue that the relative lack of social and human capital among parents from lower social class groups compromises the extent to which they can provide the type of academic involvement that would translate into academic benefits (Lott 2001).

In contrast, some evidence suggests that the benefits of parents being involved may be more beneficial to low-income children compared to higher-income children. Because poor children have fewer resources overall, the addition of one resource—say, strong parental involvement—may be especially important for their success (Cooper and Crosnoe 2007). For instance, Stanton-Salazar (2001) finds that poor children receive greater academic returns from supportive relationships with teachers and school mentors. Domina (2005) shows that lower social class parents have a more favorable influence on their children than parents with higher social class backgrounds when they help their children with homework and volunteer outside the classroom. Similarly, Cooper and Crosnoe (2007) find that children from lower-class backgrounds receive larger benefits from their academic orientation (a scored measure indicating how much children like school, think grades are important, and so forth) than nondisadvantaged children. Taken together, these studies suggest that poor children could benefit more from academic resources, such as parental involvement, than other children.

Another factor that influences whether the relationship between parental involvement and achievement is similar across different levels of social class is the great diversity among parents within class groupings (Furstenberg et al. 1999). For example, among less affluent parents, some have higher educational attainment than others. Therefore, previous research is mixed with regard to how the link between parental involvement and academic outcomes differs for parents from different socioeconomic backgrounds.

Parental Involvement at Home and Achievement

Our analysis on the association between parental involvement at home and academic achievement is based on data from both the NELS and the CDS. We display the results in a series of estimate graphs that show the gain or the loss in achievement attributable to each measure of parental involvement examined in Chapter 2 (see Appendix B for analytic details and sample sizes). Several points of clarification are warranted regarding these graphs. First, the names of the measures of parental involvement are listed on the left-hand side of the graph. Second, estimates on the negative side of the graph (to the left of the "0") suggest that the measure of parental involvement is associated with a decrease in achievement. Conversely, estimates on the positive side of the graph suggest that parental involvement is associated with increases in achievement. Third, estimates for which a significant relationship exists (either positive or negative) are highlighted, whereas those that are not significant—no systematic relationship exists between parental involvement and achievement—are displayed in gray.

Fourth, we display six estimates for each indicator of parental involvement. The first three estimates are displayed as an open circle, triangle, and square and correspond to the achievement points gained or lost for youth whose parents hold less than a high school education, at least a high school education, and a four-year college degree, respectively. The next three estimates for each indicator of parental involvement reflect the change in points that can be attributed to youth who live in households in which parents earn less than the median income, the median income to twice the median income, and twice the median income or greater, respectively. For the sake of consistency and parsimony, we sometimes refer to these categories as low, moderate, and high levels of parental education or income respectively. Fifth, all estimates show the gain or the loss in achievement attributable to the indicator for parental involvement after accounting for parents' marital status, youths' sex, and prior academic skills. Sixth, the standard errors are represented by the tails on both sides of the estimates.[1] Finally, given our goal to highlight the forms of involvement that are beneficial to students' achievement, we focus our discussion on those estimates that are positive.

The first set of findings on the association between parental involvement at home and academic achievement are displayed in Figure 3.2, which shows the results for reading (left-hand panel), math (center panel), and grades (right-hand panel). The top two panels for reading show that talking about school experiences and about high school plans is not associated with achievement for any group. In other words, the children of parents who engage in these two activities do not perform any differently in reading than the children of parents who do not engage in these activities.[2] The third panel for reading shows that talking about post–high school plans is associated with gains in achievement only for youth whose parents are moderate in terms of education (i.e., hold a high school diploma) and in terms of income (i.e., earn between the median and twice the median income). The bottom four panels show that having a rule about homework, parents' assistance in deciding youths' courses, and their help with homework are not related to increases in reading achievement for any group. Having a rule about grades is associated with increased achievement only for youth whose parents have low levels of education. Thus, only three of the forty-two estimates for reading (7 measures of parental involvement for 6 groups) suggest that parental involvement is beneficial for youths' achievement.

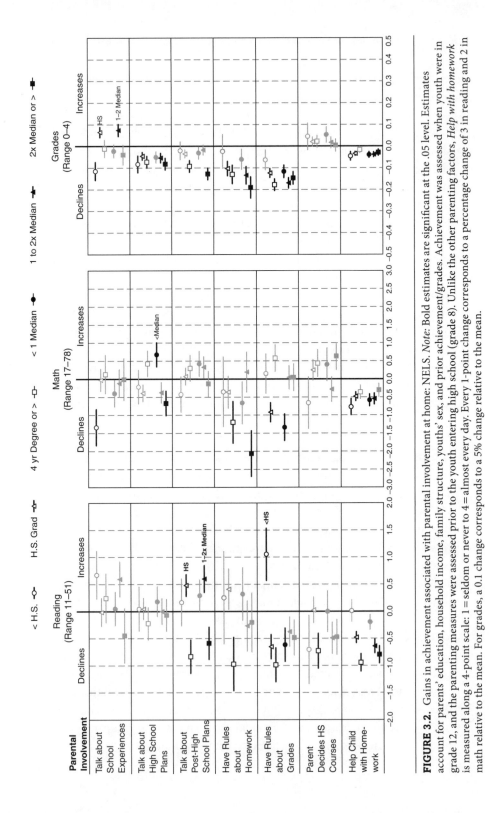

FIGURE 3.2. Gains in achievement associated with parental involvement at home: NELS. *Note:* Bold estimates are significant at the .05 level. Estimates account for parents' education, household income, family structure, youths' sex, and prior achievement/grades. Achievement was assessed when youth were in grade 12, and the parenting measures were assessed prior to the youth entering high school (grade 8). Unlike the other parenting factors, *Help with homework* is measured along a 4-point scale: 1 = seldom or never to 4 = almost every day. Every 1-point change corresponds to a percentage change of 3 in reading and 2 in math relative to the mean. For grades, a 0.1 change corresponds to a 5% change relative to the mean.

This pattern is similar when achievement is considered in terms of math and grades. Specifically, only talking about high school plans is positively connected to math achievement, but this connection exists only for youth from low-earning households. With regard to grades, talking about school experiences is the only measure of parental involvement that has a systematic positive association with achievement, but this appears to be the case only for youth from moderate social class backgrounds.

Although the findings displayed in Figure 3.2 suggest that parental involvement plays a minimal role for improving achievement, the top panel of Figure 3.3 conveys a different reality. Parents' estimates about the usefulness of homework appears to raise reading achievement for youth with moderate social class backgrounds, math achievement for youth with highly educated parents and parents with moderate earnings, and grades for youth with highly educated parents. Furthermore, the educational expectations parents hold for their children seem to be important for positive achievement for most youth, regardless of social class. If paired with the findings from Figure 3.2, these results suggest that parents' views about education are more predictive of higher achievement than more behavioral forms of involvement.

The findings in Figure 3.2 and the top panel of Figure 3.3 show the association between each measure of parental involvement and achievement. However, we recognize that although this strategy allows us to show the individual estimated effect of each involvement activity, it is unreasonable to expect that any single measure will have a substantial impact on the learning process. Rather, what might be important (and more aligned with the endeavor of parenting) is the collection of activities parents employ. In order to estimate the effectiveness of a more holistic approach to parental involvement in which parents engage in some activities rather than others, we present findings for scales created from the individual activities in the bottom panel of Figure 3.3.[3]

The bottom panel of Figure 3.3 contains the findings for two scales constructed from the parental involvement measures assessed in Figure 3.2 and the top panel of Figure 3.3. The *parent-child discussions* scale includes only the three measures for parent-child discussions: about school experiences, high school plans, and post–high school plans. The *full scale* combines all parental involvement activities, with the exception of the frequency with which parents *help youth with homework,* which is coded differently than the other measures. Because the scales were constructed by

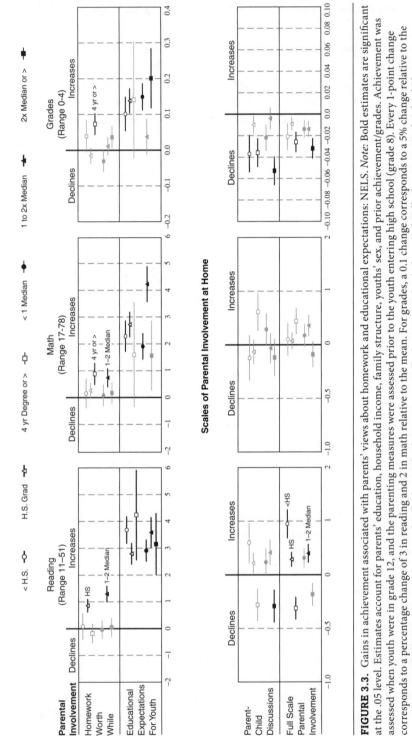

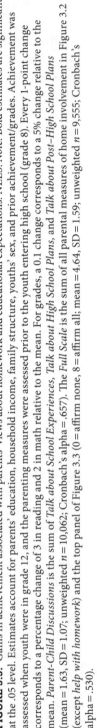

Scales of Parental Involvement at Home

FIGURE 3.3. Gains in achievement associated with parents' views about homework and educational expectations: NELS. *Note:* Bold estimates are significant at the .05 level. Estimates account for parents' education, household income, family structure, youths' sex, and prior achievement/grades. Achievement was assessed when youth were in grade 12, and the parenting measures were assessed prior to the youth entering high school (grade 8). Every 1-point change corresponds to a percentage change of 3 in reading and 2 in math relative to the mean. For grades, a 0.1 change corresponds to a 5% change relative to the mean. *Parent-Child Discussions* is the sum of *Talk about School Experiences, Talk about High School Plans,* and *Talk about Post–High School Plans* (mean = 1.63, SD = 1.07; unweighted n = 10,062; Cronbach's alpha = .657). The *Full Scale* is the sum of all parental measures of home involvement in Figure 3.2 (except *help with homework*) and the top panel of Figure 3.3 (0 = affirm none, 8 = affirm all; mean = 4.64, SD = 1.59; unweighted n = 9,555; Cronbach's alpha = .530).

simply adding the measures within the scale, their estimates can be interpreted as the change in achievement associated with each additional activity (within the scale) that parents employ or affirm. Despite treating the measures in combination, the results are similar to the nonscaled findings. The only measure for which a significant positive association with achievement exists is the *full scale* for reading achievement. The *parent-child discussions* scale is not associated with increases in achievement. We discuss this further in the chapter summary.

The findings based on the NELS capture parental involvement during middle school. In Figure 3.4, we present findings based on the CDS, which captures parental involvement from before youth enter school through middle school. This allows for analysis of the involvement-achievement link prior to adolescence (grades 1–5) and during adolescence (grades 6–12). Additionally, we use measures of parental involvement from the CDS-I to predict achievement during CDS-II. Therefore, for younger youth, we assess the implications that parental involvement prior to grade 1 have for achievement during elementary school (grades 1–5). For older youth, we examine how parental involvement during elementary and middle school is associated with achievement during middle and high school.

The first set of findings we present from the CDS is for parental involvement at home and is displayed in Figure 3.4. The top panel contains the findings for the younger subsample. It appears that reading to children is associated with increased reading achievement for youth from all social class subsamples except those from families with the highest income levels, for which the association is not significant. However, with regard to math achievement, being read to appears to be beneficial only for youth from the low and moderate social class categories based on parents' education. These findings are quite different when the analysis is conducted for adolescents, which are reported in the bottom panel. Having been read to as a child seems beneficial only for adolescent math achievement among youth from the highest income subsample. Interestingly, helping with homework is not associated with increases in reading or math achievement, regardless of whether the assessment is made for younger or older youth.

In Figure 3.5, we show the association between parent-child discussions about schooling and achievement. The findings suggest that parents' discussions about schooling with youth are more beneficial for children's achievement during adolescence. In general, the benefits of parent-child

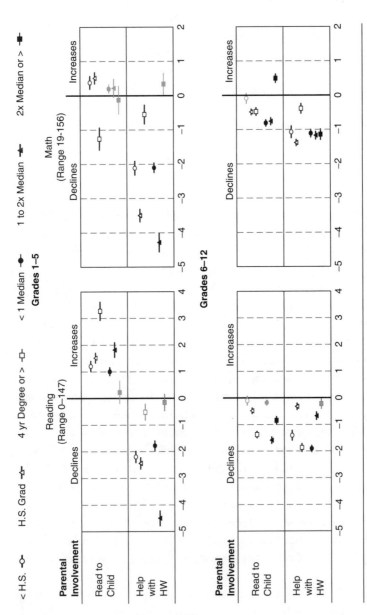

FIGURE 3.4. Gains in achievement associated with parental involvement at home: CDS. *Note:* Bold estimates are significant at the .05 level. Estimates account for parents' education, household income, family structure, youths' sex, grade in school, and prior achievement. Achievement was assessed from CDS-II, and the parenting measures were obtained from CDS-I. Every 1-point change corresponds to roughly a 1% change in reading and math relative to their respective means.

discussions prior to adolescence seem to apply only to youth from the lowest social class group; five of the eight positive estimates are for youth whose parents have not completed high school, and another two positive estimates are for youth from the lower income group. For adolescents, the benefits of parent-child discussions are more widespread, particularly for math achievement. Interestingly, the estimates for youth from the high social class group by parents' education show that parent-child discussions are associated with declines in reading achievement. Overall, the findings suggest that the benefits of parental involvement vary by both youths' stage of development and social class background. We elaborate on this in the chapter summary.

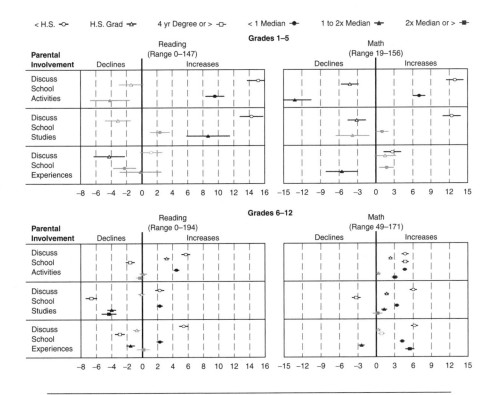

FIGURE 3.5. Gains in achievement associated with parental-child discussions at home: CDS. *Note:* Bold estimates are significant at the .05 level. Estimates account for parents' education, household income, family structure, youths' sex, grade in school, and prior achievement. Achievement was assessed from CDS-II, and the parenting measures were obtained from CDS-I. Every 1-point change corresponds to roughly a 1% change in reading and math relative to their respective means. Insufficient sample size for the top category for social class within the younger subsample did not allow for analyses of the *4-year degree or greater* and the *twice the median income or greater* subsamples.

Chapter Summary

In this chapter, we examine whether parental involvement at home is associated with achievement. In order to determine whether the extent to which parental involvement is beneficial for achievement depends on one's social class, the analysis was conducted separately for each social class group by both parents' education and family income. The relationship between involvement and achievement was assessed for each form of involvement by comparing the achievement of children whose parents typically engage in the involvement measure to those whose parents do not typically engage in the measure. Several findings are worthy of note.

First, parents' views about education are more predictive of higher achievement than more behavioral forms of involvement. With regard to the latter, there does not appear to be overwhelming support for the notion that parental involvement is associated with increases in achievement. For forms of parental involvement in the NELS that capture what parents *do* rather than what parents *think,* there are a total of forty-two estimates (7 measures of parental involvement for 6 groups) for each achievement outcome. The number of estimates that suggest a positive relationship between parental involvement and achievement is rather low: three for reading (talking about post–high school plans for youth whose parents are moderate in terms of parents' education and family income, and rule about grades for youth whose parents have low levels of education), one for math (talking about high school plans for youth from low earning households), and two for grades (talking about school experiences for youth from both moderate social class groups).

The findings are different for the measures that capture what parents *think.* Parents' views about the usefulness of homework is associated with higher reading achievement for youth with moderate social class backgrounds, higher math achievement for youth with highly educated parents and parents with moderate earnings, and grades for youth with highly educated parents. Parents' educational expectations are associated with increases in reading, math, and grades for most youth, regardless of social class.

Second, the findings based on the CDS show that the benefits of parental involvement vary by both youths' stage of development and social class background. Among younger youth, reading to children is associated with increased reading achievement for all social class subsamples, with the exception of youth from families with the highest income levels. However, among adolescents, reading to children seems beneficial only for math among youth from the highest income subsample. Additionally, parents' discussions about schooling with youth are more beneficial for children's achievement during adolescence. In general, the benefits of parent-child discussions prior to adolescence apply only to youth from the lowest social class group. In contrast, the benefits of parent-child discussions are more widespread for adolescents.

We organize the findings by social class in Figure 3.6. The figure shows the number of estimates that are positive, not significant, and negative by

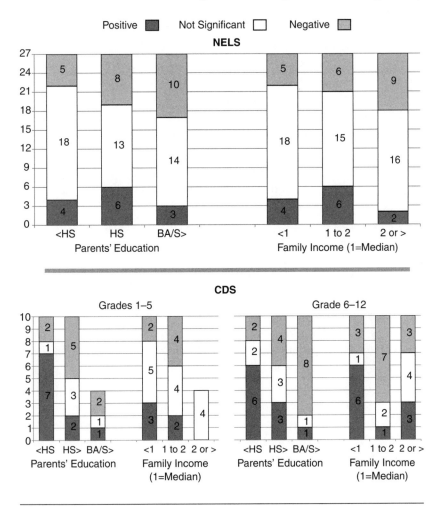

FIGURE 3.6. Number of parental involvement measures that are associated with changes in achievement. *Note:* Insufficient sample size for the top category of social class within the younger CDS subsample did not allow for analyses of the *4-year degree or greater* and the *twice the median income or greater* subsamples for three outcomes. Thus, there are only four estimates obtained for each of these social class groups.

each category of social class. The top panel summarizes the findings for the analyses based on the NELS. Because there are nine measures of parental involvement at home and three achievement outcomes, there are a total of twenty-seven estimates for each class category. The figure shows that most measures of parental involvement are not related to achievement. Out of the 162 total estimates reported for the NELS, 94 are not significant, which equates to 58%. Only 15% of the estimates (25) are positive. More importantly, slightly more than one-quarter are negative (43). In fact, although negligible, the number of negative estimates increases with social class. Thus, although much of our discussion throughout the chapter focuses on the positive estimates, a greater share of parental involvement measures are associated with declines in achievement. The findings are nearly identical for both dimensions of social class.

The same information is displayed in the bottom panel of Figure 3.6 for analyses based on the CDS. Because there are five measures of parental involvement and two achievement outcomes, a total of ten estimates were examined for each class category. Insufficient sample size for the top category of social class within the younger subsample did not allow for analysis of the three parent-child discussion measures. Therefore, a total of four estimates were assessed for each of the top two social class categories for the younger subsample.

The figure shows that most of the benefits of parental involvement are experienced by youth from the lowest social class category. Out of the ten estimates assessed for each group, the number of positive estimates was seven for youth whose parents attained less than a high school education in the younger subsample, and six for adolescents from the low social class category for both parents' education and family income. However, if the findings are summarized in a more holistic manner, out of the 108 total estimates examined using the CDS, 35 are positive (32%), 31 are not significant (29%), and 42 are negative (39%). Thus, similar to the analysis based on the NELS, there are a greater number of negative estimates than positive estimates. This pattern is similar for both the younger and the older subsamples. Specifically, for the former, there are an equal number of positive and negative estimates (15, or 31%), and a greater number of nonsignificant estimates (18, or 38%). For the older subsample, 20 estimates are positive (33%), 27 are negative (45%), and 13 are not significant (22%).

In Figure 3.7, we show the number of positive, nonsignificant, and negative estimates for each measure of parental involvement at home

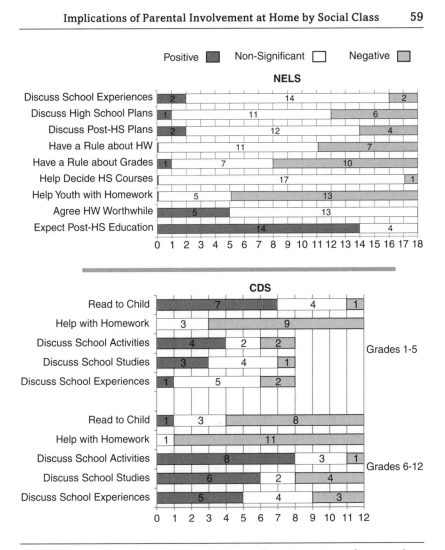

FIGURE 3.7. Number of positive, nonsignificant, and negative estimates for parental involvement measures.

examined in this chapter. This organization strategy makes it easier to identify which forms of parental involvement are associated with gains in achievement for the largest share of youth. Just as importantly, the figure accentuates the measures of involvement associated with declines in achievement. For each measure, the darker bar on the left-hand side of the figure represents the number of positive estimates, the lighter bar in the center represents the number of nonsignificant estimates, and the gray bar on the right-hand side represents the number of negative estimates.

The top panel summarizes the results for each measure of parental involvement based on the NELS. For each of the first seven measures, which capture the things parent do, there are a greater number of negative estimates than positive estimates. In fact, whereas less than 5% of these estimates are positive (6 out of 126), roughly one-third (43) are negative. An overwhelming majority of estimates is not significant (77). In contrast, the final two measures, which capture how parents think, yielded a substantial proportion of positive estimates (52%), and no negative estimates. The bottom panel shows that reading to children earlier in life—prior to them entering grade 1—is more effective for raising achievement than reading to them after they have already entered the first grade. However, parent-child discussions appear to be more effective for older youths. Perhaps the most surprising finding in this chapter is that helping with homework is not associated with increases in reading, math, or grades for any youth in neither the NELS nor CDS. Rather, nearly 80% (33) of the forty-two total estimates for helping with homework in both the NELS and CDS are negative (the rest are not significant).

If the findings for the NELS and CDS are combined, roughly one-fifth of the estimates examined in this chapter are positive (60/270 = 22%). However, nearly one-third are negative (85) and close to half (125) are not significant. These findings challenge the notion that parental involvement has a widespread benefit on children's achievement. The findings discussed in this chapter suggest quite the opposite; to the extent that parental involvement is consequential for achievement, more of the effects seem negative than positive.

To be clear, there are some forms of parental involvement at home that are beneficial to achievement. However, our findings suggest that rather than assuming that any form of parental involvement is a good thing, parents and educators should be aware that some forms of involvement that parents can employ outside of school might actually lead to declines in achievement and, in most cases will not have any effect on achievement. With regard to the measures of parental involvement associated with declines in achievement, we caution against advising parents to become less involved in their children's schooling. Rather, the negative estimates are indicative of forms of involvement that parents need guidance on to become more effective and thus avoid compromising achievement. In the next chapter, we replicate the analysis from this chapter using measures of parental involvement that require parents to come into contact with schools. It could be that parental involvement at schools has a greater connection to children's achievement than forms of involvement at home.

— 4 —

Implications of Parental Involvement
at School by Social Class

The positive association between economic status and parental involvement shown in Chapter 2 indicates that parents will vary in their knowledge about the schooling process and, accordingly, about the opportunities their children have to learn. What it means to participate at school in various ways (e.g., attending parent-teacher meetings or open house) could be fundamentally different for parents from different socioeconomic backgrounds. Compared to more affluent parents, who have an advantage in social capital gained from relationships fostered with teachers and extended networks (Heckman and Peterman 1996; Lareau 1987, 2000), parents from disadvantaged backgrounds have greater challenges negotiating the school environment in ways that positively influence their children's academic outcomes (Coleman 1988; Hango 2007).

In previous chapters, we discussed how parents with different socioeconomic backgrounds may differ in their patterns of involvement because of variations in amounts of cultural capital (Grenfell and James 1998). According to McNeal (1999), the cultural capital possessed by parents from higher social class backgrounds magnifies the effects of their involvement on their children's academic achievement. A concept closely related to cultural capital that sheds further light on why parents from high social class backgrounds might experience greater achievement returns for their children from their involvement at school is "habitus" (Bourdieu 1984).

Whereas cultural capital refers to the constellation of knowledge, preferences, tastes, codes of appropriate conduct, and consumption practices that stem from one's upbringing, habitus is a disposition to act, grasp experiences, and think a certain way with minimal cognitive—or even unconscious—effort (Brubaker 2005). Thus, cultural capital is knowledge about the rules of behavior (e.g., knowing the order in which forks should be used for each course), and habitus is the instinctive enactment of behaviors (e.g., knowing which fork to use without considering that an alternative order is even possible). If cultural capital is analogous to an athlete's knowledge of how to play a particular sport, habitus is the muscle memory that enables the athlete to successfully perform tasks during competition without being conscious of the principles of kinesiology that undergird movements. The more concordance between an individual's habitus and their field (or domain, such as school), the greater social advantage the individual tends to experience within that field (Lareau and Horvat 1999).

Like cultural capital, habitus varies according to socioeconomic background, leading some parents to display different types of involvement at school than others (Grenfell and James 1998). Thus, habitus—or unconscious orientation toward schools—is related to economic resources, educational knowledge, and experiences with and confidence in the educational system (Lee and Bowen 2006). Middle-class parents, on average, are more capable of advancing their children's academic success than lower-class parents as a result of their higher cultural capital and habitus (Hauser-Cram, Sirin, and Stipek 2003). Research has shown that children whose parents share the same values as the school system are perceived by teachers as having advanced academic skills and brighter academic futures (Kim 2009).

In concrete terms, having high levels of cultural capital and the habitus appropriately suited for the academic domain means that parents know the codes of interaction with schools and have the comfort and instinctive disposition to engage in these interactions effortlessly. Parents from higher social class backgrounds tend to demonstrate greater comfort in interacting with their children's teachers, are more proficient at mediating individualized school careers for their children, are more involved with their children's schools and details of schooling, and expend greater efforts in seeking out appropriate educational materials to enhance their children's learning relative to lower-class parents (Cheadle 2008; Lareau 2000). In contrast, sharp differences from their children's teachers in education, income, and occupational status can lead parents with low social class to be hesitant to initiate discussions with educators, be more passive at parent-teacher functions, and view school as an "alien world" (Lareau 2000). When interactions with teachers do arise, disadvantaged parents are less proficient at mediating individualized school careers for their children (Lareau and Horvat 1999; McNeal 1999) and may feel that they do not know enough

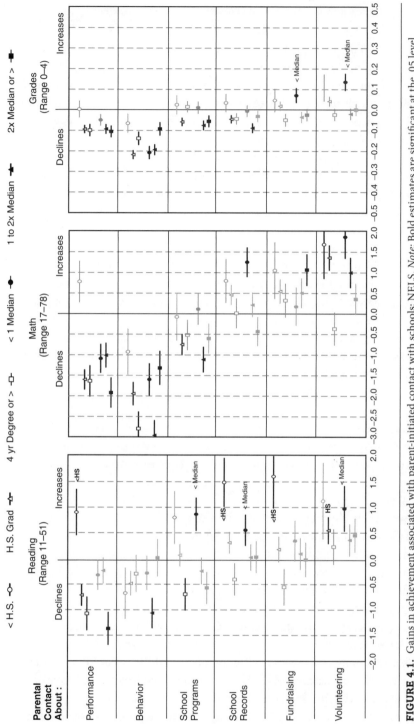

FIGURE 4.1. Gains in achievement associated with parent-initiated contact with schools: NELS. *Note:* Bold estimates are significant at the .05 level. Estimates account for parents' education, household income, family structure, youths' sex, and prior achievement/grades. Achievement was assessed when youth were in grade 12 and the parenting measures were assessed prior to the youth entering high school (grade 8). Every 1-point change corresponds to a percentage change of 3 in reading and 2 in math relative to the mean. For grades, a 0.1 change corresponds to a 5% change relative to the mean.

to ask the right questions, or that their input is not appreciated (Fine 1993; Lott 2002).

It is important to note that although they may highly value education, socioeconomically disadvantaged parents may exhibit less school involvement because they feel less confident in communicating with school staff or less capable of navigating the school system because of their own educational experiences. Thus, parents with lower socioeconomic standing might be less able to convert involvement in school into academic gains for their children. Middle-class parents have the social capital and resources to make their voices heard in school (Lareau and Horvat 1999). Therefore, schools seeking to have an involved base of parents should be aware of the need to empower parents from low social class backgrounds, provide them with more opportunities to participate in school, and allow their voices to be heard (Ballenger 2009).

Parental Involvement with School and Achievement

Our analysis of the effectiveness of parental involvement within schools begins in Figure 4.1, which shows results for the link between six measures of parent-initiated contact with their children's school and achievement. As in Chapter 3, we display the results in a series of estimate graphs that show the gain or loss in achievement attributable to each measure of parental involvement, which are listed along the left-hand side of the graph. Recall that estimates on the negative side of the graph suggest that the measure of parental involvement is associated with a decline in achievement (vice versa for estimates on the positive side of the graph), significant estimates are highlighted (dark, bold line) and nonsignificant estimates are displayed in gray, and six estimates are displayed for each indicator of parental involvement (one for each social class group).

The findings in the left-hand panel of Figure 4.1 show that only a relatively few number of estimates suggest parental involvement raises reading achievement. No form of parental involvement appears to be beneficial for youth across the board. To the extent that a pattern exists, it appears that youth from low social class backgrounds benefit the most from parents initiating contact with schools. Out of the seven positive estimates for reading, three are for youth whose parents have a low level of education and three are for youth from low-earning homes. Youth whose parents contact their school about volunteering have higher math achievement than those

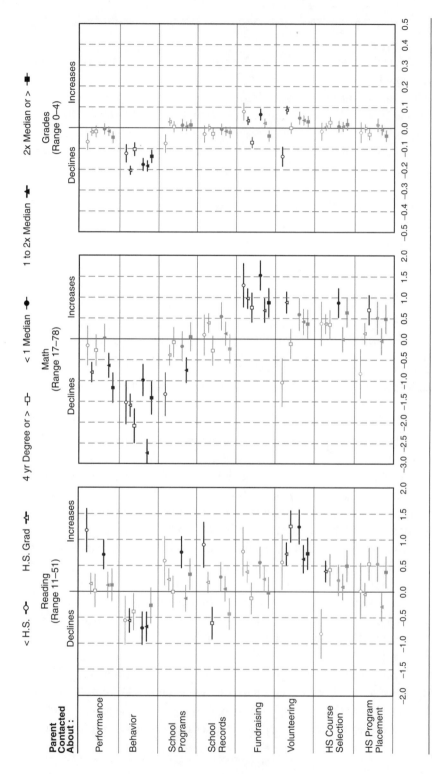

FIGURE 4.2. Gains in achievement associated with school-initiated contact of parents: NELS.

whose parents do not, and this finding extends to four of the six social class groups; the only exception is for youth in the highest social class group. Finally, only two estimates are significant and positive for students' grades. Youth from the low-income group seem to experience an increase in grades when parents contact their school about fund-raising and volunteering. An important pattern shown in Figure 4.1 is that approximately one-third of the estimates for math and grades are negative.

The findings for whether parent-school contact is an important mechanism for raising achievement when the contact is initiated by the school are displayed in Figure 4.2. The results suggest that, with a few exceptions, most youth benefit in reading when their parents are contacted about volunteering and in math when the contact concerns fund-raising. With regard to grades, only three of the forty-eight estimates are positive. The findings in Figures 4.1 and 4.2 suggest parental involvement measures that capture parents' contact with their children's school—whether initiated by them or the schools—are related to increases in achievement in only a small number of cases; the overwhelming majority of estimates are either negative or not significant. We return to this topic in the chapter summary.

In Figure 4.3, we report the findings for parents' engagement with schools by way of the parent-teacher organization (PTO) and by volunteering at school. The figure shows that there is no discernible pattern with regard to positive estimates for reading achievement. Besides the first panel for reading, which suggests that children in the moderate social class category experience gains in achievement if their parents are PTO members, the patterns of positive estimates for the other three measures is random. However, although most of the estimates for reading are not significant, there are no negative estimates. For math achievement, seven of the eight estimates for the moderate social class category are positive. In fact, the moderate social class category accounts for nearly all of the positive estimates for math achievement (7/9). Only two of the twenty-four estimates are negative. Finally, with regard to grades, only three estimates are positive; children from the lowest-earning families benefit from their parents' PTO membership and engagement in PTO activities, and children whose parents are moderate in terms of education benefit from their parents' volunteering at school. Overall, it seems that parental engagement through the PTO and volunteering at school is associated with increases in achievement mostly for math.

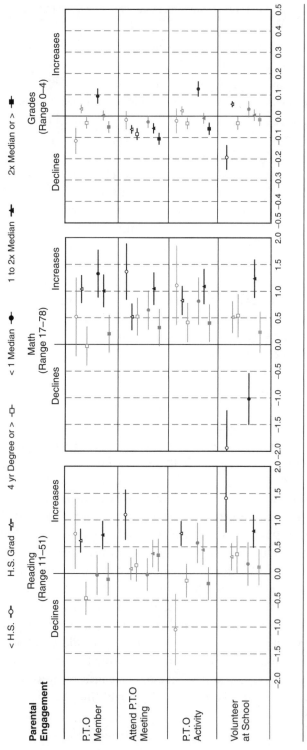

FIGURE 4.3. Gains in achievement associated with parental engagement with schools: NELS. *Note:* Bold estimates are significant at the .05 level. Estimates account for parents' education, household income, family structure, youths' sex, and prior achievement/grades. Achievement was assessed when youth were in grade 12, and the parenting measures were assessed prior to the youth entering high school (grade 8). Every 1-point change corresponds to a percentage change of 3 in reading and 2 in math relative to the mean. For grades, a 0.1 change corresponds to a 5% change relative to the mean.

With the exception of volunteering at school, the measures of parental involvement in Figure 4.3 capture parents' participation with the parent-teacher organization at their children's school. However, there are other forms of engagement aside from participation with PTO. In Figure 4.4, in addition to examining the achievement benefits of parent-teacher organizations and volunteering, we use the CDS to assess whether parents' attendance of school events or their observations of their children's classes are associated with increases in students' achievement. The analyses were conducted for both the younger and older subsamples from Chapter 3.

The findings in the top panel of Figure 4.4 are for the younger sample. Whereas achievement was obtained from the CDS-II, the measures of parental involvement are from the CDS-I. As such, they capture parents' engagement with schools when their children were in early child care, preschool, or kindergarten. Insufficient sample size prevented analysis for the top category of both dimensions of social class within the younger subsample. The findings suggest that these forms of parental involvement very early in children's schooling are not associated with increases in achievement. There are only four positive estimates; parents' attendance of school events is beneficial for both reading and math for youth from the moderate-income category and math for youth from the moderate category in terms of parents' education. Parents' observations of classes are beneficial for the reading achievement of youth from the moderate-income category. The bottom two measures of parental involvement—whether parents met with their parent-teacher association (PTA) and volunteer at school—yield no positive estimates.

In the bottom panel of Figure 4.4, we report the results for the older subsample. The measures of parental involvement for this subsample were assessed when youth were in elementary and middle school. The findings suggest that meeting with the PTA is associated with increases in reading achievement for the largest share of youth. For math achievement, the largest share of youth benefit from their parents' attendance at school events. The estimated gains in achievement are minimal, however, ranging from less than 1 to 3% (with the exception of the nearly 6% gain in math for youth whose parents are college graduates and attend school events). Slightly more than half of the estimates in the bottom panel are negative, which suggests that these forms of parental involvement are associated more with declines in achievement than with increases in achievement. We discuss this topic further in the chapter summary.

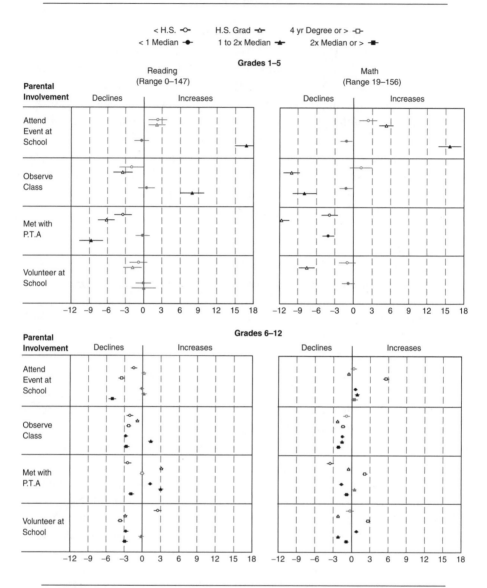

FIGURE 4.4. Gains in achievement associated with parental involvement at school: CDS. *Note:* Bold estimates are significant at the .05 level. Estimates account for parents' education, household income, family structure, youths' sex, grade in school, and prior achievement. Achievement was assessed from CDS-II, and the parenting measures were obtained from CDS-I. Insufficient sample size for the top category for social class within the younger subsample did not allow for analyses of the *4-year degree or greater* and the *twice the median income or greater* subsamples. Every 1-point change corresponds roughly to a 1% change in reading and math relative to their respective means. The estimates predicting math for youth in grades 1–5 in the *1 to 2x the median* category are −21.73 (1.872) and −14.12 (1.82) for *Met with PTA* and *Volunteer at school,* respectively.

The measures of parental involvement that we have examined to this point do not capture parents' level of assertiveness with their children's teachers. Although parent-teacher organizations bring parents into contact with teachers, these meetings typically occur after the school year has already begun. However, in Figure 4.5, we examine whether some of the

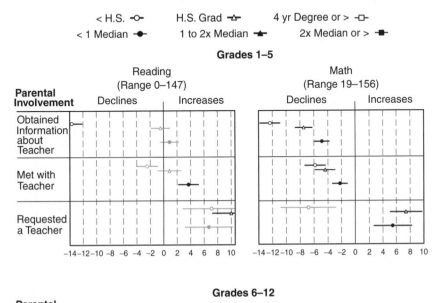

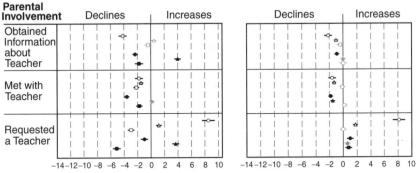

FIGURE 4.5. Gains in achievement associated with parents' assertiveness with teachers: CDS. *Note:* Bold estimates are significant at the .05 level. Estimates account for parents' education, household income, family structure, youths' sex, grade in school, and prior achievement. Achievement was assessed from CDS-II, and the parenting measures were obtained from CDS-I. Insufficient sample size did not allow for analyses of the *4-year degree or greater, 1 to 2x the median* and *twice the median income or greater* subsamples for youth in grades 1–5. Every 1-point change corresponds roughly to a 1% change in reading and math relative to their respective means.

things parents can do with regard to teachers prior to the beginning of the school year is consequential for youths' achievement. Specifically, we examine whether children whose parents obtain information about the teacher, meet with the teacher, or request a particular teacher have higher achievement than children whose parents do not engage in these behaviors prior to the academic year. These measures of parental involvement require a greater initiative on the part of parents.

The top panel shows that obtaining information about the teacher is not associated with increases in achievement early in the schooling process. Meeting with a child's teacher is beneficial only for the reading achievement of the least affluent youth, and requesting a teacher is associated with increases in reading and math for youth in the moderate social class group along the dimension of parents' education and in math for the least affluent youth. The bottom panel shows that most of the estimates for the older subsample are actually negative, particularly for the first two measures of parental involvement (obtaining information about the teacher and meeting with the teacher). On the other hand, requesting a teacher is associated with increases in reading and math for low and moderate social class groups by parents' education, in reading for youth in the moderate social class group based on family income, and in math for the least and most (not moderate) social class groups based on family income. Similar to the results in Figure 4.4, the findings in Figure 4.5 suggest that parental influence declines as children become older, as the estimated effect sizes are smaller for the older subsample. The variation in these results further highlights the need to consider the effects of parental involvement by youths' stage of development and social class background.

We consider more measures of parental involvement that require parents to be assertive in Figure 4.6. Specifically, we examine whether parents' interactions in the form of formal conferencing or casual conversation with their children's teacher and principal are associated with increases in achievement. The top panel shows that most of the estimates for these forms of involvement are positive for reading achievement; a large share of youth seem to benefit in reading the more their parents interact with important school personnel early in the schooling process. For math achievement, the advantages appear to be limited to informal conversations between parents and school personnel. Also, the gains in achievement associated with these forms of involvement are substantial, ranging from 3% to roughly 14%. The results are different for older youth, which are reported in the bottom panel. Nearly

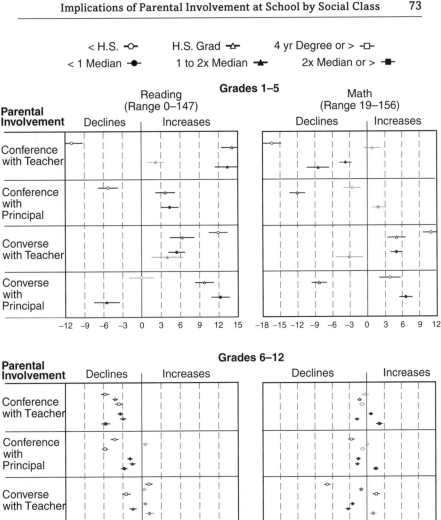

FIGURE 4.6. Gains in achievement associated with parental-teacher interaction: CDS. *Note:* Bold estimates are significant at the .05 level. Estimates account for parents' education, household income, family structure, youths' sex, grade in school, and prior achievement. Achievement was assessed from CDS-II, and the parenting measures were obtained from CDS-I. Every 1-point change corresponds roughly to a 1% change in reading and math relative to their respective means. The estimate predicting reading for youth in grades 1–5 in the *median to 2x the median* category is −17.46 (2.322) for *Conference with principal*. The estimate predicting math for youth in grades 1–5 in the *median to 2x the median* category is −41.69 (2.051) for *Conference with principal* and −26.959 (1.895) for *Converse with principal*.

all of the estimates for reading achievement for parents who have a conference with teachers and principals are negative, and informal conversations
with these educators are beneficial for only a few groups. For math achievement, there are slightly more negative estimates (10) than positive estimates
(7), with youth from the top social class category (by parents' education or
family income) accounting for most of the latter. Furthermore, the estimated
effect sizes are substantially smaller for the older youth than those observed
for the younger subsample in the top panel.

We present the findings for the final set of parental involvement measures
in Figure 4.7. These measures capture whether parents met with the school

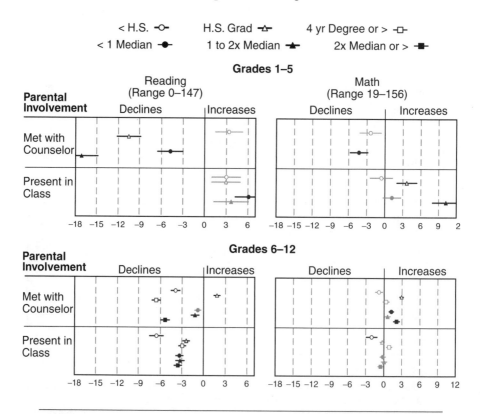

FIGURE 4.7. Gains in achievement associated with parents' meeting with counselor and
making class presentation: CDS. *Note:* Bold estimates are significant at the .05 level.
Estimates account for parents' education, household income, family structure, youths' sex,
grade in school, and prior achievement. Achievement was assessed from CDS-II, and the
parenting measures were obtained from CDS-I. Every 1-point change corresponds roughly
to a 1% change in reading and math relative to their respective means. The estimates for
met with counselor predicting math for youth in grades 1–5 in the *high school grad* and
median to 2x the median categories are −25.49 (1.459) and −40.71 (2.027), respectively.

counselor and presented in their child's class. There is no discernible pattern for the younger subsample in the top panel. However, the bottom panel shows that for the older subsample, most of the estimates for both measures are negatively related to reading achievement. With regard to math, achievement is higher for three of the six social class categories for youth whose parents have met with the school counselor than for those whose parents have not.

Parental Involvement and Achievement Gaps by Social Class

The first set of findings for the achievement-gap analysis is based on the NELS and presented in Figure 4.8. The gaps are assessed by examining the achievement of the low and moderate social class groups relative to the higher social class group under five scenarios. As such, there are five bars for each social class group.

The first bar shows the raw differences in achievement relative to the higher social class group; it represents the point disadvantage between youth in the group to which the bar corresponds and those from the highest social class group. This is the baseline gap (BL) against which the other bars are compared. The second and third bars show the achievement gap after accounting for parental involvement at home (Hm) and school (Schl), respectively. The change in the bars can be interpreted as the portion of the gap that can be attributed to the factors labeled above the bars. The fourth bar shows the gap after simultaneously accounting for all twenty-seven measures of parental involvement at home and at school. The final bar shows the gap after accounting for youths' socioeconomic background (parents' education/income, family structure, and youths' sex). In sum, the next set of figures display the proportion of the achievement gaps by social class that can be attributed to parental involvement at home, at school, both, and to socioeconomic background. The left-hand side of the graph shows findings by parents' education, and the right-hand side shows findings by family income.

The top panel of Figure 4.8 contains the findings for reading achievement. The first set of bars in the left-hand panel shows the gap analysis for youth whose parents have less than a high school diploma relative to those whose parents have a college degree. The first bar shows that the baseline gap in reading between these groups is 8.2 points. The second bar shows

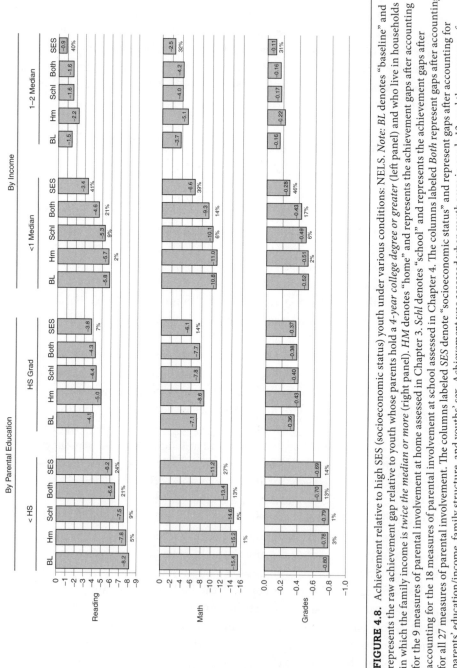

FIGURE 4.8. Achievement relative to high SES (socioeconomic status) youth under various conditions: NELS. *Note: BL* denotes "baseline" and represents the raw achievement gap relative to youth whose parents hold a *4-year college degree or greater* (left panel) and who live in households in which the family income is *twice the median or more* (right panel). *HM* denotes "home" and represents the achievement gaps after accounting for the 9 measures of parental involvement at home assessed in Chapter 3. *Schl* denotes "school" and represents the achievement gaps after accounting for the 18 measures of parental involvement at school assessed in Chapter 4. The columns labeled *Both* represent gaps after accounting for all 27 measures of parental involvement. The columns labeled *SES* denote "socioeconomic status" and represent gaps after accounting for parents' education/income, family structure, and youths' sex. Achievement was assessed when youth were in grade 12, and the measures of parenting and SES were assessed prior to the youth entering high school (grade eight).

that parental involvement at home accounts for 5% of the gap; the gap reduces from 8.2 to 7.8 points. Parental involvement at school explains slightly more of the lower class group's disadvantage (roughly 9%) than involvement at home. The next bar suggests that when both sets of parental involvement measures are taken into account, the gap reduces by 21%. However, although one-fifth of the achievement gap between these groups can be attributed to parental involvement, even more of the gap (24%) can be explained by students' socioeconomic backgrounds. Thus, the twenty-seven measures of parental involvement account for less of the gap than the three measures of socioeconomic background.

The next set of bars in the top panel is for the achievement gap between youth whose parents have a high school diploma and those whose parents have a college degree. The gap is substantially smaller between these groups (4.1 points). The next three bars suggest that parental involvement does not account for any portion of this gap. In fact, the gap either widens slightly or remains unchanged after accounting for parental involvement. The final bar shows that socioeconomic background explains 7% of the gap. Thus, similar to the previous set of findings for the low social class group, socioeconomic background accounts for more of the achievement gap than parental involvement.

The findings in the right-hand side of the graph show the gap analysis by family income. With the exception of the size of the achievement gaps by family income, which are substantially smaller than the achievement gaps when social class is measured by parents' education, the findings are essentially the same. Socioeconomic background accounts for more of the achievement gaps than does parental involvement. Aside from slightly smaller percentage declines, this pattern is similar for math achievement (center panel) and grades (bottom panel). Thus, the extent to which parental involvement explains the achievement gaps by social class is rather limited.

The same information is displayed for the achievement gaps in reading and math for the younger subsample of the CDS in Figure 4.9. The substantive conclusion is similar to that based on the NELS. Youths' socioeconomic background explains a greater share of the achievement disadvantage for the low and moderate social class groups relative to the higher social class group than parental involvement both at home and at school. The primary difference from the findings based on the NELS is that parental involvement at home accounts for more of the achievement gaps than parental

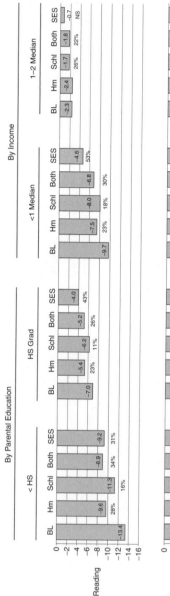
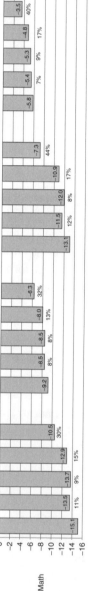

FIGURE 4.9. Achievement relative to high SES youth under various conditions for youth in grades 1–5: CDS. *Note: BL* denotes "baseline" and represents the raw achievement gap relative to youth whose parents hold a *4-year college degree or greater* (left panel) and who live in households in which the family income is *twice the median or greater* (right panel). *HM* denotes "home" and represents the achievement gaps after accounting for the 5 measures of parental involvement at home assessed in Chapter 3. *Schl* denotes "school" and represents the achievement gaps after accounting for the 13 measures of parental involvement at school assessed in Chapter 4. The columns labeled *Both* represent gaps after accounting for all 18 measures of parental involvement. The columns labeled *SES* denote "socioeconomic" and represent gaps after accounting for parents' education/income, family structure, youths' sex, and grade in school. Achievement was assessed from CDS-II, and the measures of parenting and SES were assessed from CDS-I.

involvement at school. It seems that parental involvement at home is more critical for addressing class-based achievement gaps early in children's schooling careers than involvement at school.

The final set of findings from our achievement-gap analysis is for the adolescent subsample from the CDS and is displayed in Figure 4.10. For youth whose parents hold less than a high school diploma, the full set of parenting measures accounts for slightly more of their academic disadvantage both in reading and in math than socioeconomic background. However, the rest of the gap comparisons yield patterns similar to those observed previously; socioeconomic background appears to play a larger role in achievement differences than parental involvement.

Chapter Summary

In this chapter, we examine the connection between parents' school involvement and children's achievement by social class. The analyses mirrored those from Chapter 3. These assessments were made for youth from low, moderate, and higher social class backgrounds by both parents' education and family income. The involvement-achievement relationship was assessed for each form of involvement by comparing the achievement of children whose parents typically engage in the involvement measure to those whose parents do not typically engage in the measure.

Much of our analyses can be summarized as follows: most of the ways in which parents can be involved have little impact on children's gains in reading and math achievement. A key finding is that many of the parental measures we examine are *negatively* related to achievement. For example, for the results displayed in Figure 4.4 in which we examine the link between four measures of parental involvement at school from the CDS to achievement for youth in grades 6–12, slightly more than half of the estimates are negative. In fact, there are more than twice as many negative estimates as positive estimates. The findings in Figure 4.4 suggests that—on average—when parents attend events at school, observe class, meet with PTA, and/or volunteer at school, it helps children's achievement gains *less* compared to children whose parents do not perform the given involvement activity.

In the second part of this chapter, we try to explain achievement differences by social class by comparing the achievement of youth with low and moderate social class backgrounds to that of their more advantaged counterparts. The comparisons are made after accounting for parental involvement

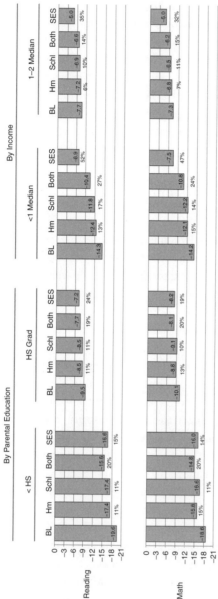

FIGURE 4.10. Achievement relative to high Socioeconomic Status youth during adolescence under various conditions: CDS. *Note: BL* denotes "baseline" and represents the raw achievement gap relative to youth whose parents hold a *4-year college degree or greater* (left panel) and who live in households in which the family income is *twice the median or more* (right panel). *HM* denotes "home" and represents the achievement gaps after accounting for the 5 measures of parental involvement at home assessed in Chapter 3. *Schl* denotes "school" and represents the achievement gaps after accounting for the 13 measures of parental involvement at school assessed in Chapter 4. The columns labeled *Both* represent gaps after accounting for all 18 measures of parental involvement. The columns labeled *SES* denote "socioeconomic" and represent gaps after accounting for parents' education/income, family structure, youths' sex, and grade in school. Achievement was assessed from CDS-II, and the measures of parenting and SES were assessed from CDS-I.

at home, school, and both. Our analyses begin with a baseline gap, which show that youth in the low and moderate social class groups have lower achievement in reading, math, and grades than youth from the highest social class group. Then we add a set of home and school involvement measures, first separately and then simultaneously, to assess the portion of the achievement gap explained by all measures of involvement at home and at school—a total of twenty-seven parental involvement measures in the NELS and eighteen in the CDS. We find that the importance of parent involvement for closing achievement gaps depends upon social class comparisons. For example, the full set of parental involvement measures in the NELS explains roughly one-fifth of the gap in reading and roughly 13% of the gap both in math and in grades between youth whose parents have less than a high school education and those with college-educated parents. However, when we compare youth with high school–educated parents to those with college-educated parents we find that parental involvement does not account for any differences in achievement; in some cases, the gap is larger or remains unchanged after accounting for parental involvement. Also, with the exception of youth with the least educated parents in the CDS, children's socioeconomic background explains a greater share of achievement differences than parent involvement.

Another major pattern that our findings uncover is that one size does not fit all when it comes to the benefits of parental involvement. Some forms of parental involvement might be beneficial to the achievement of youth in one group, but be detrimental to the achievement of youth who belong to another group. In fact, only one out of thirty-one forms of involvement examined in this chapter is beneficial for achievement across the board for youth in all groups; youth whose parents are contacted by schools about fund-raising have higher math achievement than those whose parents are not contacted about fund-raising.

In Figure 4.11, we provide a useful summary of the findings based on the NELS that identify which forms of involvement "work" for each social class group. Recall that the NELS captures parental involvement for children in middle school, which we relate to their high school academic outcomes. The measures of parental involvement from this and the previous chapter are listed along the top of the figure, and the social class groups are listed along the left-hand side of the figure. These cross-tabulations allow one to follow the column of a particular form of involvement to see whether the measure is associated (positively or negatively) with achievement for each social class grouping.

Positive Estimate ●   Negative Estimate ⊗

FIGURE 4.11. Positive and negative associations for parental involvement and achievement by class: NELS.

		Involvement at Home									Contact School						Contacted by School								PTO				TOTALS		
		Regularly talk / school exp.	Regularly talk / HS plans	Regularly talk / post-H.S.	Have a rule about HW	Have a rule about GPA	Parent decide HS Courses	Help youth with Homework	Agree HW is worthwhile	Expect post-HS education	Academic Performance	Behavior	Academic Program	Info on School Records	School Fundraising Activity	Volunteering	Academic Performance	Behavior	Academic Program	Info on School Records	School Fundraising Activity	Volunteering	Course Selection for H.S.	Program Placement for H.S.	P.T.O. Member	Attend P.T.O. Meeting	Participate in P.T.O. Activity	Volunteer at School	Positive Estimates	Negative Estimates	Non-Significant Estimates
Reading	< H.S.			●					●	●	●		●	●			●		●					●				●	9	0	18
Reading	H.S. Grad		●		⊗			⊗	●	●	⊗			●				⊗			●	●			●	●	●		8	4	15
Reading	BA/S or >		⊗	⊗	⊗	⊗	⊗	⊗		●		⊗	⊗			●		⊗			●								2	8	17
Reading	< 1 Median				⊗					●				●	●	●	●	⊗			●				●				7	2	18
Reading	1-2 Median		●					⊗	●	●		⊗			●	●		⊗			●				●			●	6	3	18
Reading	2x Median or >		⊗			⊗		⊗		●	⊗							⊗			●						●		2	3	22
Math	< H.S.	⊗				⊗				●						●	⊗	⊗			●				●			⊗	4	5	18
Math	H.S. Grad				⊗	⊗				●	●	⊗	⊗			●	⊗	⊗			●	●	●		●	●	⊗		7	7	13
Math	BA/S or >			⊗		⊗				●		⊗						⊗		●	●			●					3	4	20
Math	< 1 Median		●		⊗	⊗		⊗	●	●	⊗	⊗				●		⊗			●	●			●		●	⊗	7	6	14
Math	1-2 Median					⊗		⊗	●	●	⊗	⊗	●		●	●	⊗	⊗		⊗	●	●			●	●	●	●	8	7	12
Math	2x Median or >	⊗		⊗		⊗		⊗		●		⊗					⊗	⊗			●								2	6	19
Grades	< H.S.	⊗	⊗			⊗		⊗		●								⊗			⊗							⊗	1	6	20
Grades	H.S. Grad	●	⊗		⊗	⊗		⊗		●	⊗	⊗	⊗	⊗				⊗			●	●			⊗			●	5	10	12
Grades	BA/S or >		⊗	⊗	⊗	⊗				●	⊗	⊗						⊗				●			⊗				1	9	17
Grades	< 1 Median				⊗			⊗	●		⊗	●			●	●		⊗				●	●	●			●		6	4	17
Grades	1-2 Median	●	⊗		⊗	⊗		⊗			⊗	⊗	⊗	⊗				⊗							⊗				1	10	16
Grades	2x Median or >	⊗	⊗	⊗	⊗			⊗			●	⊗	⊗					⊗							⊗	⊗			1	11	15
TOTALS	Positive	2	1	2	0	1	0	0	5	14	1	0	1	3	3	7	2	0	1	1	8	7	2	1	6	4	4	4	80		
TOTALS	Negative	2	6	4	7	10	1	13	0	0	12	11	6	2	0	0	3	15	2	1	1	1	0	0	0	4	1	3		105	
TOTALS	Non-Significant	14	11	12	11	7	17	5	13	4	5	7	11	13	15	11	13	3	15	16	9	10	16	17	12	10	13	11			301

For example, the measure *regularly talked about school experiences* shows a positive connection to grades for two groups (the moderate social class category based on parents' education and income) and two negative connections—youth whose parents hold less than a high school diploma appear to experience declines in math and grades when parents talk to them regularly about school experiences. This pattern suggests that parents belonging to this group could benefit from an adjustment in how they employ this form of involvement. Finally, the other fourteen links between this form of involvement and achievement are not significant; there is no difference in achievement between the youth of parents who regularly talk to their child about their school experiences and those whose parents do not. The numerical totals for positive, negative, and nonsignificant links are summarized along the bottom of the figure. Similarly, following along

Positive Estimate ●   Negative Estimate ⊗

Grades 1 - 5

		Positive Estimates	Negative Estimates	Non-Significant Estimates
Reading	< H.S.	4	5	9
	H.S. Grad	6	5	7
	BA/S or >	1	0	1
	< 1 Median	7	2	9
	1-2 Median	5	5	8
	2x Median or >	0	0	2
Math	< H.S.	6	5	7
	H.S. Grad	5	11	2
	BA/S or >	0	2	0
	< 1 Median	4	6	8
	1-2 Median	2	10	6
	2x Median or >	0	0	2

TOTALS (Grades 1-5):

	Read to Child	Help with Homework	Discuss School Activities	Discuss School Studies	Discuss School Experiences	Attend Events at School	Observe Class	Met with P.T.A	Volunteer at School	Obtained Info on Teacher	Met with Teacher	Requested a Teacher	Conference with Teacher	Conference with Principal	Converse with Teacher	Converse with Principal	Met with Counselor	Presented in Class	Total
Positive	7	0	4	3	1	3	1	0	0	0	1	3	2	2	6	4	0	3	40
Negative	1	9	2	1	2	0	3	7	2	4	3	0	4	4	0	3	6	0	51
Not Significant	4	3	2	4	5	5	4	1	6	4	4	5	2	2	2	1	2	5	61

Grades 6 - 12

		Positive Estimates	Negative Estimates	Non-Significant Estimates
Reading	< H.S.	6	11	1
	H.S. Grad	5	7	6
	BA/S or >	0	16	2
	< 1 Median	5	9	4
	1-2 Median	4	9	5
	2x Median or >	0	12	6
Math	< H.S.	4	7	7
	H.S. Grad	5	10	3
	BA/S or >	6	4	8
	< 1 Median	8	9	1
	1-2 Median	2	9	7
	2x Median or >	8	4	6

TOTALS (Grades 6-12):

	Read to Child	Help with Homework	Discuss School Activities	Discuss School Studies	Discuss School Experiences	Attend Events at School	Observe Class	Met with P.T.A	Volunteer at School	Obtained Info on Teacher	Met with Teacher	Requested a Teacher	Conference with Teacher	Conference with Principal	Converse with Teacher	Converse with Principal	Met with Counselor	Presented in Class	Total
Positive	1	0	8	6	5	3	1	4	3	1	0	7	2	1	2	5	4	0	53
Negative	8	11	1	4	3	4	10	6	7	6	9	3	8	8	6	3	4	6	107
Not Significant	3	1	3	2	4	5	1	2	2	5	3	2	2	3	4	4	4	6	56

FIGURE 4.12. Positive and negative associations for parental involvement and achievement by class: CDS.

the rows allows one to identify which measures of parental involvement are associated with increases or decreases in achievement for each social class group. For example, the first row, which is for parents with less than a high school diploma, shows that nine measures of parental involvement are associated with increases in reading achievement for youth who belong to this group. In contrast, none of the measures are associated with declines in reading for this group, and eighteen measures are not systematically related to reading.

The two measures for which the greatest number of positive estimates is observed are parents' educational expectations for their youth (14), school-initiated contact of parents in regard to fund-raising (8), and parent-school contact about volunteering (7), whether the contact is initiated by the parent or by the school. Parents' post–high school expectations appear to be important regardless of social class background and achievement outcome. What is telling about this figure is that far more of the estimates are negative than positive. Collectively, parent involvement is positively associated with reading, math, and grades in only 16% of relationships we test (80/486 = .16). In contrast, a higher percentage of the estimates (22%) are negatively related to achievement. However, the overwhelming majority of connections we examine between parental involvement and achievement are not significant (62%).

We display the same information for the CDS in Figure 4.12. Whereas the patterns in the top panel are for the younger subsamples (children in grades 1–5), the patterns for the older subsamples (children in grades 6–12) are shown in the bottom panel. Only one-quarter of the estimates are positive (26% for the younger subsample and 25% for the older subsample), which is slightly higher than the 16% observed in the NELS. However, one-third of the estimates for the younger subsample are negative (34%), and half of the estimates are negative for the older subsample. Both the NELS and CDS yield patterns that are consistent with the notion that the positive benefits of parental involvement for children's academic achievement are overstated. In fact, the findings from this chapter suggest that a greater number of the actions that parents take to improve achievement actually compromise academic outcomes. Even nonsignificant estimates are observed more frequently than positive estimates in both the NELS and CDS. In the chapters that follow, we shift the focus of this study to parental involvement and race.

— 5 —

Academic Orientation among Parents at Home by Race

If we were to conduct a national poll of the U.S. population asking people to rank whites, Asians, Hispanics, and blacks in terms of parental involvement in children's schooling, it is likely that the majority of people would place whites and Asians at the top and Hispanics and blacks at the bottom. This arrangement would be consistent with the widely held notion that Asian parents have raised model children with respect to education (Osajima 2005) and the contrasting view that Hispanic and black parents are unconcerned with their children's education. The latter view is related to a wider narrative that claims that members from disadvantaged minority groups resist assimilation into mainstream American ideals crucial for upward socioeconomic mobility and, instead, cling to an oppositional culture largely responsible for persistent racial inequalities within the United States (McWhorter 2000; Ogbu 1978; Steele 1990).

The term "model minority" has been used extensively in this country to pay tribute to the variety of academic successes Asian children have attained (Chua 2011; Kao 1995; Osajima 2005). The term also credits Asian parents for raising high-achieving children and "successfully" assimilating into mainstream American society. One could argue that the model minority label is not helpful to minority groups. The presumption this stereotype carries—if Asians can raise high-achieving children, so can every other racial/ethnic group—often leads to the idea that poverty, low-socioeconomic status, discrimination, and neighborhood segregation do not pose significant obstacles to some minority parents who are trying to raise high-achieving children.

When held against the model minority perspective, the comparative lack of educational success among black and Hispanic students might be attributed to laziness, lack of appreciation for opportunity, or lack of determination. Because parents are youths' primary socializing agents, black and Hispanic parents might be viewed as indifferent about the importance of educational success. There is some evidence to suggest that this belief is not uncommon among educators. Souto-Manning and Swick (2006) report that teachers they interviewed attributed the lower achievement of English language learners (ELLs) and black children relative to whites to "lack of parent involvement" or "no parent investment." Their analysis of word collocation of interview transcripts shows that *parent involvement* was closely located with deficit words, such as *lack, low,* and *no* when teachers spoke about parents of minority backgrounds. In fact, they find that many teachers blamed the low achievement of Hispanics and blacks relative to whites on their parents' "not caring."

Similarly, DeCastro-Ambrosetti and Cho (2005) show evidence that preservice and in-service teachers have negative attitudes toward parents of ethnic minority groups. The majority of the teachers in their sample exhibited negative perceptions toward the value ethnic minority parents place on education and attributed children's low achievement to factors at home and a lack of value their parents place on education. Perhaps what makes these findings more alarming is that the teachers in their study were enrolled in a teacher credentialing program that had cultural diversity concepts embedded within the curricula. In fact, the general belief that some minorities prefer failure to upward mobility is somewhat prevalent among teachers. Based on data from the General Social Survey, a major source of nationally representative trend data on attitudes since the mid-1970s, Lucas (2008, 32) shows that roughly one-third of teachers believe that blacks' long-standing socioeconomic disadvantage relative to whites persists because blacks "just don't have the motivation or willpower to pull themselves up out of poverty." This finding suggests that the assumption of blacks as unmotivated or lacking a desire to be upwardly mobile is so prevalent that it extends beyond the domain of schooling even for many teachers. It is reasonable to expect that this belief stems from teachers' experiences with (or stereotypes and assumptions of) both black youth and their parents.

In Figure 5.1 we highlight the framework that guides our analysis of parental involvement and race in chapters 5–8. In this chapter, we determine whether parents from the major racial groups within the United States differ in their orientation toward their child's education by comparing them on a series of parental practices that they can engage in at home with their child (path *f*). We examine the implications of these practices for achievement in Chapter 6. Although socioeconomic resources and human capital can be determining factors in parents' ability to engage in some of these practices, the constraints are most tempered for forms of involvement that can occur outside of school. Parental involvement at school is likely to be driven more by parents' level of cultural and social capital, relating to parents' level of comfort in interacting with educators in schools and authority figures in general. We examine parental involvement at school by race in Chapters 7 and 8. In contrast, parents have greater autonomy in how they choose to be involved in their children's education at home. Parental involvement at home relies less on resources available to parents and therefore taps into the value parents attribute to their children's education. In the following section, we discuss factors that give reason to expect racial variation in parental involvement.

For the purposes of reorientation, recall that we focus on aspects of parental involvement that can be *directly* linked to achievement. Thus, there are forms of parental involvement that might be beneficial to youths' social and emotional development, psychological well-being, or general enrichment that we do not consider. As we discussed in Chapter 1, this study is not about parenting or about whether parents should be more (or

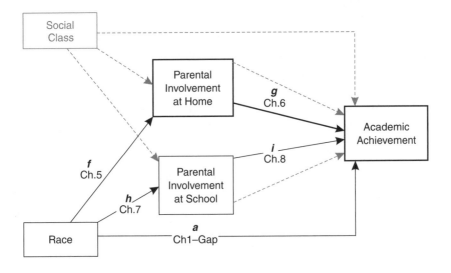

FIGURE 5.1. Focus of Chapters 5–8.

less) involved in their children's lives. Rather, this study is about parental involvement *to increase academic outcomes.* Although some forms of general parenting, such as visits to museums, travel, and extracurricular activities, might be beneficial for achievement, these are not things parents do *only* to improve academic achievement. As the previous three chapters have shown, the forms of parental involvement that we focus on are parent-child communication about education, parents' beliefs or behaviors that have *direct* implications for children's academic outcomes, and parental engagement with schools and school personnel.

Theories about Group Differences in Education

Most theories on group differences in education propose factors that contribute to the persistence of group differences in academic outcomes. These theories propose factors that range from group variation in genetic makeup (Herrnstein and Murray 1994; Jensen 1969) and various types of socio-economic characteristics (Brooks-Gunn, Klebanov, and Duncan 1996; Duncan, Brooks-Gunn, and Klebanov 1994; Massey and Denton 1993; Moynihan 1965; Wilson 1987, 1996), to racial bias in standardized testing (Kozol 2000; Meier 2000; Sacks 1999) and schools' reinforcement of existing patterns of inequality (Bourdieu and Passeron 1977; Bowles and Gintis 1976;). Although these theories are useful for understanding racial differences in achievement, they are more concerned with explaining why achievement gaps persist than explaining group differences in academic orientation, which is more relevant to our discussion on racial differences in parental involvement at home.

Cultural theory is perhaps the most relevant for understanding racial differences in the extent to which parents value education. In addition to addressing group differences in resources, cultural explanations speak to value systems in general and are more geared toward understanding the value that different racial groups attribute to schooling. The same applies to theories about the assimilation experiences of immigrant groups, which also employ some form of cultural explanation for understanding the experiences of groups with an immigrant background. Thus, cultural and assimilation theories place greater emphasis on attitudes and beliefs than on group variation in resources related to genetics, socioeconomic factors, and power and privilege. For this reason, they give more insight into what one should expect with regard to racial differences in parental involvement at home than other popular frameworks within sociology of education. In the next section, we discuss popular cultural and assimilation theories that speak to group variation in the value attributed to education and provide guidance in the development of hypotheses regarding race and levels of parental involvement at home.

Culture and Minority Educational Investment

Cultural explanations were popularized in the 1960s to explain persistent patterns of racial inequality across nearly every life-chance outcome. These frameworks view culture, rather than societal conditions, as responsible for persistent inequality as disadvantaged groups are posited to have a "culture of poverty" (Lewis 1961, 1968). Based on ethnographic studies of Latin American poverty, Lewis argued that prolonged exposure to factors prevalent in disadvantaged communities, such as unemployment, low income, lack of home ownership, and chronic shortage of basic necessities (food and health care), promotes behavioral patterns that compromise upward socioeconomic mobility. Specifically, these conditions promote feelings of marginality and helplessness and contribute to a lack of impulse control or ability to defer gratification and plan for the future. Lewis argued that despite emerging in response to constrained opportunities, this culture of poverty becomes entrenched and self-sustaining and serves as a primary factor in the persistence of disadvantage. Once the values and attitudes that comprise this culture of poverty are absorbed, people "are not psychologically geared to take full advantage of changing conditions or increased opportunities which may occur in their life-time" (Lewis 1968, 188).

The cultural thesis was also applied to black Americans during the same time period. In fact, this line of thinking gained notoriety in the political arena in the mid-1960s with the release of *The Negro Family: A Case for National Action* (1965), a report commissioned by President Lyndon B. Johnson and authored by sociologist and Assistant Secretary of Labor Daniel Moynihan. Moynihan presented a sharply pointed argument that existing and prospective government economic and social welfare programs should be designed to encourage the stability of the Negro family, which he claimed was unstable and thus a central feature of "the tangle of pathology" of life in the ghetto. He warned that the disintegration of the black family was a result of the lack of employment opportunities in black communities, which also compromised the academic outcomes of black youth.

The cultural explanations advanced by Lewis and Moynihan suggest that cultural behavioral patterns are strategies for coping with feelings of hopelessness and despair that arise from depressed socioeconomic conditions. However, the structural (societal) component occupies a subordinate status to the cultural aspect of their thesis. Both Lewis and Moynihan view racial inequality as maintained by an autonomous culture of poverty among the disadvantaged minority groups. In fact, their work fueled the cultural side of the structure versus culture debate within the scientific community, the political arena, and popular culture that began in the 1960s and continues into the twenty-first century. Critics of this perspective argue that new generations of blacks and other disadvantaged groups are viewed as sharing cultural behavioral patterns with their predecessors because they experience similar economic conditions and constraints to upward social mobility (Massey and Denton 1993; Wilson 1987, 1996); norms, aspirations, and patterns of behavior are not seen as intractable and undergo change or "rise and fall with changes in situations" (Gans 1968, 211).

Whereas the culture of poverty thesis as described by Lewis and Moynihan was intended to explain racial inequality in life-chance outcomes, the cultural narrative became popular within the educational arena with the introduction of the oppositional culture theory (or resistance model) (Ogbu 1978), which was intended to explain group differences in academic orientation. Thus, the oppositional culture thesis provides guidance on what to expect regarding racial differences in the value attributed to schooling. A key concept underlying the resistance model is the system of social mobility, which reflects the arrangements within any society by which people gain (or lose) resources that allow them to move up the socioeconomic ladder. Accordingly, the resistance model posits that racial differences in academic outcomes result from the belief among minorities that the system of social mobility is rooted in educational and occupational discrimination based on race. Members of groups who perceive themselves as targets of discrimination adopt counterproductive schooling behaviors. Although the theory is intended to explain racial differences in academic achievement, some of the underlying tenets are applicable for understanding racial variation in the academic orientation of parents. The intergenerational transmission of beliefs about schooling as a mechanism for achieving upward socioeconomic mobility is an important component of the resistance model; youth are posited to acquire their beliefs about opportunities from their parents.

An important component of the theory for understanding why groups differ in academic orientation is Ogbu's minority classifications: voluntary or immigrant, and involuntary (Ogbu and Simons 1998).[1] Voluntary minorities are groups who willingly move to the United States seeking better opportunities (e.g., employment, greater political or religious freedom). They view education as the primary mechanism for achieving opportunities that led them to the United States. For this reason, they fail to develop identities in opposition to the dominant group or adopt counterproductive schooling behaviors, often overcoming experiences of discrimination and difficulties to do well academically. They attribute the barriers they initially experience to cultural differences and interpret them as temporary obstacles to overcome. With little history of being targeted for oppression by the dominant group, they are trusting of them and their institutions for upward mobility. Furthermore, their immigration status provides them with the opportunity to compare their educational opportunities with their counterparts from their sending country, and these comparisons are usually favorable. Thus, as a voluntary minority group, Asian Americans should have a favorable academic orientation toward schooling.[2]

In contrast, involuntary minorities are groups who have been historically enslaved, colonized, or conquered, and interpret their group's incorporation into the United States as forced by white Americans. Relative to other groups, involuntary minorities experience greater and more persistent forms of discrimination (i.e., job ceiling) leading them to perceive barriers to success with regard to future employment and earnings. Members of these groups are precluded from competing for the most desirable roles in society on the basis of individual training and abilities. Even after a society abandons formal mechanisms responsible for the unequal treatment of minority groups, vestiges of past discriminatory policies in the labor market and education remain in effect. Thus they become disillusioned about the future and doubt the value of education. Mexican Americans and black Americans are regarded as examples of involuntary minorities.

Whereas the designation of Asians as voluntary minorities is rather clear, Ogbu makes the case that Mexican Americans should be considered involuntary minorities because Mexican Americans—who comprise nearly two-thirds of the Hispanics living in the United States (U.S. Census 2000)—feel alienated from American society stemming from bitter memories of their incorporation into the United States via American imperialistic expansion in the 1840s. Furthermore, Ogbu and Matute-Bianchi (1986) argue that Mexican Americans behave more like involuntary minorities because they have experienced considerable discrimination within the United States, and therefore do not have the same expectations as other voluntary minorities.

Although there is some empirical evidence for some aspects of the resistance model (Farkas, Lleras, and Maczuga 2002; Fordham and Ogbu 1986; Fryer and Torelli 2010; Mickelson 1990; Ogbu 2003), it is important to note that many of the theory's tenets have been heavily contested. Several studies fail to find support for the notion that members from disadvantaged ethnic minority groups value school less than white Americans using both quantitative (Ainsworth-Darnell and Downey 1998; Cook and Ludwig 1997, 1998; Harris 2006, 2008; Harris and Marsh 2010; Harris and Robinson 2007) and qualitative (Akom 2003; Carter 2005; Horvat and Lewis 2003; O'Connor 1997; Tyson 2002; Tyson, Darity, and Castellino 2005) methodology. In fact, nearly every claim within the framework was tested and rejected in two recent books on the resistance model—one qualitative (Tyson 2011) and the other quantitative (Harris 2011). Nevertheless, the belief that members of disadvantaged ethnic minority groups have lower academic orientation than their white counterparts is widely held by teachers (Bol and Berry 2005; Diamond, Randolph, and Spillane 2004; Downey and Pribesh 2004; McKown and Weinstein 2008; Neal et al. 2003; Tyler, Boykin, and Walton 2006). Furthermore, most studies examine the academic orientation of youth; it is still quite possible that the communities the minority groups described within the theory came from have the academic orientation attributed to them within the framework.

In the following section, we provide a discussion on how the experiences of minority groups within the United States seem consistent with tenets of the resistance model. Specifically, we discuss how the assimilation experiences of Asians and Hispanics perpetuate the perception that Asians are the model minority and that, like blacks, Hispanics care little about schooling. We also discuss how the experiences of black Americans make aspects of the resistance model seem plausible. It should be noted that the following discussion of Asian and Hispanic immigrants[3] contains some generalizations. Although there are broad similarities in the assimilation processes immigrants face, the wide diversity across racial/ethnic groups, within racial/ethnic groups, and within individual families renders it impossible to speak in terms of a unified immigrant experience. We seek to limit these generalizations as much as possible and we realize that a proper discussion of each racial/ethnic group's immigrant experience requires substantially more pages than the focus of this book permits.

Experiences of Minority Groups within the United States

Asian Americans

In general, the assimilation into the United States of immigrants from Asia has perhaps been the most successful of all immigrant groups. Asian populations tend to be more highly educated than the average American population. For example, the percentage of people age 25 and older who have a bachelor's degree or higher is 29% for all Americans, but 52% for Asian Americans (U.S. Census 2008). Additionally, only 10% of all Americans have a graduate (e.g., master's or doctorate) or professional degree compared to 20% percent of Asians. It is important to note that the Asian population is quite diverse in their demographic characteristics. For example, approximately 70% of Asian Indians age 25 and over held a bachelor's degree or higher in 2008, and 38% held either a graduate or professional degree. Comparatively, 28% of Vietnamese-Americans held a bachelor's degree or higher, and 9% held a graduate or professional degree (U.S. Census 2008). Median income differs across Asian ethnic groups as well. Although still greater than the median income of whites in 2007, Asian Indians held the highest median income at $83,820, whereas Vietnamese-Americans held the lowest at $54,048 (U.S. Census 2009). Nevertheless, as a group Asian-Americans had the highest educational attainment and median income in 2008 among all race groups within the United States (U.S. Census 2008).

The upward assimilation of Asians is consistent with the experiences attributed to them by the resistance model and has reinforced the notion that some members of this group are model minorities. As prominent economist Thomas Sowell (1981, 284) notes, "Groups that arrived in America financially destitute have rapidly risen to affluence, when their cultures stressed the values and behavior required in an industrial and commercial economy. Even when color and racial prejudice confronted them—as in the case of the Chinese and Japanese—this proved to be an impediment but was ultimately unable to stop them." As voluntarily immigrants to the United States, they often have stronger beliefs that hard work will pay off (also see Kao and Tienda 1995 for a review), and Asian parents are more apt to cultivate pro-school attitudes such as being attentive, applying diligent effort, and limiting social activities in order to secure social mobility for their children (Matthews 2002).

Louie (2001) shows that Asian immigrant parents' educational expectations are shaped by structural conditions in the destination country. For example, the immigrant parents she interviewed from Hong Kong, Taiwan, and China were struck by the availability of low-cost, high-quality public universities in the United States. In contrast, they often described institutions of higher education in their native countries as closed to both them and their children. Louie's study attributed the wide availability of higher learning opportunities in the United States to Asian parents' decision to immigrate and found that these opportunities drove parents' educational expectations for their children regardless of social class background. It should be noted that a high value on education can encourage migration, so that Asians within the United States are "selected" on this characteristic and are not random samples from Asian countries.

Hispanics

In contrast to Asians, Hispanic immigrants (particularly Mexicans) are often incorporated into lower sectors of the American status system. For example, only 12% of Hispanics hold a bachelor's degree or higher (U.S. Census 2008). Similarly, the median household income of foreign-born Hispanics is substantially lower ($35,734) than that of their Asian counterparts ($68,094). Furthermore, one-fifth of foreign-born Hispanics live below the poverty line compared to only one-tenth of foreign-born Asians (U.S. Census 2006). These education and economic indicators illustrate the vast differences in levels of human and financial capital between the two groups.

The education and economic indicators for Hispanics are primarily driven by immigrants of Mexican descent, the largest Hispanic group within the United States. Portes and Rumbaut (2001) note that to a large extent Mexican immigrants experience a "downward assimilation" toward the underclass. Mexican immigrants are more likely than many other Hispanic immigrants to experience poverty. This status is related to low educational attainment, inadequate English proficiency, and low rates of Mexican mothers having full- or part-time employment. Portes and Rumbaut (2006) argue that the limited English skills and limited human capital (education and work experience) of some Mexican immigrants leads to a decline in educational attainment across generations. The inclination for foreign-born Hispanics to settle into high-density immigrant neighborhoods also contributes to a fair degree of social isolation. Tienda and Mitchell (2006) report that immigrant Hispanics tend to reside in neighborhoods where more than one-third of their neighbors are also foreign-born and where less than half their neighbors speak English at home. In general, limited English skills, social isolation, and a prevailing economic market that demands low-wage, low-skilled labor virtually assures that a significant number of Hispanics (particularly Mexicans) will be incorporated into lower sectors of the American status system.

In the broadest sense, the Asian assimilation experience has been an upward asymptotic trajectory similar to that of early twentieth-century European immigrants; after an initial adjustment period with varying degrees of challenges and obstacles to upward mobility, a level of assimilation that successfully approximates (or even surpasses) mainstream middle-class values and qualities are attained. In contrast, there are some important distinctions between the paths of assimilation European immigrants underwent in the first half of the twentieth century and the path taken by recent Hispanic immigrants. Most European immigrants experienced "straight-line assimilation" into the American mainstream, in which their use and proficiency of English increased from generation to generation. Eventually, many European immigrants ceased using their native language and gave up many of their native traditions (Rumberger and Larson 1998).

Black Americans

The popular narrative regarding the parental involvement of black parents in the schooling of their children is couched in the academic orientation attributed to the wider black community. Numerous scholars argue that the larger black community has an antagonistic relationship with education, which stems from a cultural norm of underachievement in response to inequitable educational opportunities and discriminatory social and employment policies experienced within the United States (Fordham and Ogbu 1986; Ogbu 1978, 2003; Steinberg, Dornbusch, and Brown 1992). Black Americans experience barriers toward advancement not just in education but in other realms such as the labor and housing markets (Baldi and McBrier 1997; Bertrand and Mullainathan 2004; Elliott and Smith 2004; Goldsmith, Hamilton, and Darity 2006; Pager 2007; Smith 2005;

Tomaskovic-Devey, Thomas, and Johnson 2005; Zhao, Ondrich, and Yinger 2006). Although these experiences were particularly acute prior to the civil rights movement, racial disparities persist on numerous life-chance outcomes.

Given that blacks have historically had challenges in education and the labor market, it is reasonable to expect that the values and norms black parents impart to their children—particularly around education—will be different from other racial groups. Parents are major conduits for children's knowledge about the opportunity structure—the configuration of resources that determine opportunities important for upward socioeconomic mobility. Black parents' experiences with an unfair opportunity structure and a system of social mobility in which blacks' educational accomplishments are under-rewarded relative to whites are posited to compromise black children's academic motivation (Fordham and Ogbu 1986; Mickelson 1990; Ogbu 1978, 2003). According to Ogbu (1978) and Fordham and Ogbu (1986), parental experiences with discrimination limit children's confidence in the system of social mobility, thereby instilling a negative attitude towards future opportunities and diminished appreciation for education. As Mickelson (1990, 59) notes, "Young blacks are not bewitched by the rhetoric of equal opportunity through education; they hear another side of the story at the dinner table."

Should the Narratives about Race and Parental Involvement Change?

The resistance model attributes a general culture of academic pursuit to Asian Americans and an oppositional culture characterized by the resistance to academic goals to the wider black and Hispanic communities. The upward assimilation of Asians and the downward assimilation of most Hispanics are consistent with the experiences attributed to them by the resistance model. These assimilation patterns, discussed in the previous section, might give rise to invidious comparisons of the cultures and the success of different immigrant groups. However, some scholars suggest that the worse life-chance outcomes of some Hispanics and blacks relative to whites might be due to factors other than culture.

With regard to immigrant groups, Portes and his colleagues provide a framework for understanding the different assimilation patterns between (and within) Asians and Hispanics. They argue that the degree to which members of U.S. society and government are receptive to immigration from a particular country contributes significantly to whether immigrants from that country will successfully assimilate into the United States (Portes and MacLeod 1996; Portes and Rumbaut 2001, 2006; Portes and Zhou 1993). The reception context includes the political relations between the sending and receiving countries; the values and prejudices against the sending country and its members; and the size, structure, and resources of a group's preexisting co-ethnic communities (Portes and Rumbaut 2001). Portes and Rumbaut (2006) identify four conditions for immigration that influence the context of reception, each with different legal statuses and levels of human capital: labor, professional, entrepreneurial, and refugee or asylees.

Labor migrants move in search of low-wage jobs and are often illegal immigrants, which precludes them from access to public services given to legal immigrants. Professional migrants are often legal immigrants who migrate because of a lack of professional occupations in their home country and to attain higher levels of education in the United States. Thus they rarely work in low-wage occupations. Entrepreneurial immigrants have business expertise and access to sources of capital and labor, often within ethnic enclaves, which enables them to collaboratively maintain businesses. Most rely on transnational ties that facilitate the importation of goods from their native countries. Finally, refugees or asylees immigrate in an attempt to escape persecution or physical harm in their home countries. They often receive several benefits such as welfare assistance, the right to work, and most importantly, legal status, which allows them to assimilate into American society in a much more effective manner than labor migrants.

Although the four immigration conditions Portes and Rumbaut (2006) identify can apply to immigrants from any country, the relationship between the United States and other countries determines the proportion of immigrants in each of the four conditions from each country. For example, whereas Mexican immigrants tend to be labor migrants, Filipino and Indian immigrants tend to be professional immigrants. Examples of entrepreneurial immigrants include migrants from Korea, Pakistan, and Iran, while refugees or asylees tend to be from Communist countries, Southeast Asia, or Eastern Europe. The different legal statuses afforded to each of these immigrant groups combined with the varying levels of human and social capital determine how an immigrant group will assimilate into the United States.

Portes and MacLeod (1996) also show that the designation of Asians as one type of immigrant group and Hispanics as another is not entirely accurate. For example, as products of Communist takeovers, Cuban and Vietnamese immigrants are often considered political refugees, which results in them being treated sympathetically. They are able to draw on various forms of federal assistance and private resources to create solidarity and close-knit entrepreneurial communities that view schooling as the primary reason for their upward mobility. In contrast, Haitian and Mexican immigrants are primarily "economic" immigrants rather than "political" immigrants and are therefore viewed less sympathetically and are ineligible for federal assistance granted to refugees. Many are unauthorized immigrants who are subject to deportations and are routinely denied refugee status; they experience pervasive discrimination even if the immigration is legal. Thus there is heterogeneity in immigration type within the racial groups that we examine.

By emphasizing the importance of social incorporation and the context of reception, Portes and his colleagues go beyond theories that merely stress the role of culture and socioeconomic background for educational attainment. Portes and MacLeod (1996) note that "the factors that account for the significant differences among these groups have to do with the human capital that immigrants bring with them from their countries of origin and the social context that receives them and shapes their adaptation in the United States" (271). Inequalities in the *situation* of various immigrant national-origin groups influence the academic success of their youth, indicating that the transmission of both class and ethnic privilege from generation to generation is not entirely due to culture.

With regard to blacks, it is important to reiterate that extensive assessments of the resistance model have not found support for the theory's tenets (for a more thorough review, see Harris 2011). In fact, the position that blacks have historically possessed a cultural resistance to schooling is altogether indefensible; a long line of work by historians suggests blacks had a reverence toward education during periods in U.S. history in which racial barriers were blatant and overwhelming, such as the eras of slavery (pre-1865), Reconstruction (1865–77), and Jim Crow (1876–1965) (Anderson 1988; Litwack 1998; Williams 2005). Nevertheless, the black cultural deficiency narrative gained traction within the educational community during the latter part of the twentieth century coinciding with the work of Lewis (1961, 1968), Moynihan (1965), and Ogbu (1978). More importantly, many of the framework's tenets remain popular among educators and policy makers (Bol and Berry 2005; Delpit 1995; Diamond, Randolph, and Spillane

2004; Ferguson 2000; Lopez 2003; Morris 2005). Similarly, the notion that Asian parents raise model children with respect to education is also popular (Osajima 2005). These group-specific narratives lead to the hypothesis that, relative to whites, parental involvement at home is greater among Asians and lower among Hispanics and blacks.

Does Parental Involvement at Home Vary by Race?

Although the narrative that academic orientation among parents varies greatly by race remains popular, the evidence in support of this claim is surprisingly lacking. In this section, we provide racial comparisons for parents' academic orientation using data from the NELS and CDS. Regarding our analysis, three points are worthy of note. First, we are not testing the resistance model. A test of the resistance model would require a racial comparison of youths' academic orientation. We draw on the oppositional culture theory because it is perhaps the most popular cultural framework about racial differences within the domain of education. Given that parental involvement at home is more within the purview of parents than parental involvement at school and that we consider forms of involvement open to parents of all socioeconomic backgrounds, it is reasonable to believe that parental involvement at home—as defined in this study—is driven by parents' academic orientation in general. Whereas theories that invoke parent-school cultural incongruence are useful for understanding racial differences in parental involvement at school, the resistance model provides some insight into the potential link between parental involvement at home and racial differences in academic orientation.

Second, for our analysis based on the NELS, we account for some of the variability that exists within the immigrant minority groups. Subgroups within the Asian category vary considerably in immigration histories (Hirschman and Wong 1986; Zhou 1997), assimilation patterns (Fuligni 1997), language and economic status (Bankston and Zhou 1995; Zhou and Bankston 1998), and opportunities for social mobility (Chen and Stevenson 1995; Goyette and Xie 1999; Kao 1995; Zhou 1997). The same can be said for Hispanics, whose members have roots in eighteen sovereign nations and one U.S. commonwealth (Puerto Rico). These countries include Argentina, Bolivia, Colombia, Costa Rica, Cuba, Chile, the Dominican Republic, Ecuador, El Salvador, Guatemala, Honduras, Mexico, Nicaragua, Panama, Paraguay, Peru, Uruguay, and Venezuela. Members from each of these countries have their own unique culture, history, indigenous language(s), religions, and individual philosophies (Novas 2008). The terms "Asian American" and "Hispanic" encompass numerous ethnic groups with distinct histories, cultures, assimilation patterns, socioeconomic status, and educational outcomes. Therefore, we sort Asian parents into two groups: Asians A and Asians B. Whereas the former category comprises groups that are commonly considered part of the "model minority," the latter group comprises socioeconomically disadvantaged Asian groups (see Appendix B for further details). Similarly, we disaggregate Hispanics into two groups: non-Mexicans and Mexicans. Although these classifications are not perfect, we believe these distinctions allow us to better see within-group differences that may be masked by aggregation.

Third, in conducting our assessment of whether racial differences exist in parental involvement at home, we decided to display the unadjusted values for each group because teachers, other school personnel, and the general public typically do not cognitively adjust for social class or assimilation factors when they develop perceptions about the level of parental involvement across racial groups. It is important to highlight any evidence that lends credibility to arguments that are part of a popular national narrative. This "stacking of the deck" in favor of finding support for the narrative is helpful for identifying the narrative's origin. Accounting for background factors could explain away the racial differences posited by some people within the wider population. Furthermore, we believe it is important to establish what the baseline levels of parental involvement are across racial groups to provide a sense of the general state of parental involvement within the United States. Only after findings show differences consistent with the dominant narrative does it become necessary to explain the pattern by accounting for background factors.

We begin our assessment in Figure 5.2 by showing the proportion of parents from each racial group who discuss various aspects of schooling with their child and who have rules regarding their child's academic performance (see Appendix C for a detailed description of measures). The top panel suggests that the aspects of schooling that parents discuss with their children vary by race. Nearly 85% of white parents report regularly discussing schooling experiences with their children, a clear advantage compared to Asian, Hispanic, and black parents. Roughly three-fourths of non-Mexican Hispanics and blacks regularly discuss schooling experiences with their child, followed by both Asian groups (about 65% each) and Mexican parents (63%). However, when it comes to regular discussions about future educational plans (both high school and post–high school), Hispanic and black parents hold an advantage relative to the other racial groups. Surprisingly, white parents and those in the Asian A category appear to be the least likely to discuss future educational plans with their child on a regular basis. The findings in the bottom panel suggest that the proportion of parents who set rules for maintaining a certain GPA and homework completion and the proportion who expect their child to attend college are similar across the racial groups.

We determine the value parents attribute to their child's education using a different set of factors in Figure 5.3. Specifically, we show the proportion of parents in each racial group who reported (1) that they would be influential in decisions regarding the courses their child will take during high school and (2) that they believe homework is worthwhile, as well as (3) the

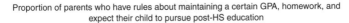

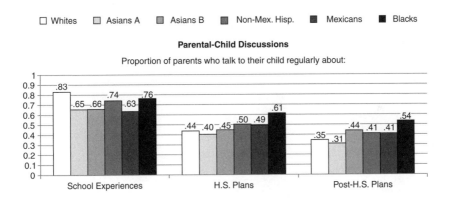

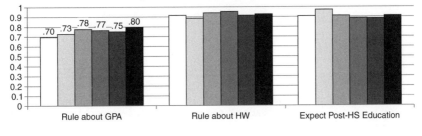

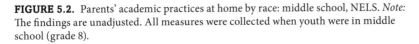

FIGURE 5.2. Parents' academic practices at home by race: middle school, NELS. *Note:* The findings are unadjusted. All measures were collected when youth were in middle school (grade 8).

frequency with which they help their child with homework. It appears that a similar proportion of parents from each racial group perceive themselves as influential for their child's course selection during high school. The racial groups are separated by a modest 5%. When it comes to parents' belief about the importance of homework, blacks and Asians A demonstrate the highest proportion of parents who feel homework is worthwhile. However, Asians B and both Hispanic groups also affirm this belief more than whites.

The bottom panel shows a fair amount of similarity among parents across all racial/ethnic groups in the frequency with which they help their child with homework. Most questions asking individuals to self-report their behaviors will contain a degree of bias. It is probable in this case that some parents are overstating the extent to which they help with homework. Whether this is the case or not, all parents appear to offer infrequent help on homework to their middle school children. Despite the relative similarity in the amount of help parents offer on homework, the more

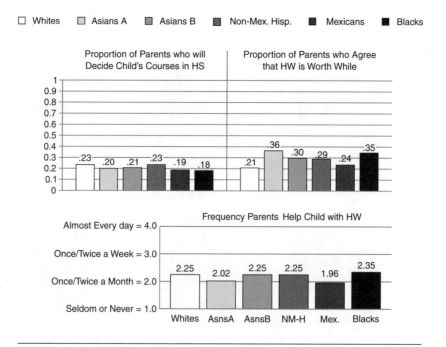

FIGURE 5.3. Parents' value of schooling by race: Middle school, NELS. *Note:* The findings are unadjusted. All measures were collected when youth were in middle school (grade 8).

likely source of variation among parents is the quality of help they provide, which our measure does not assess.

Figures 5.2 and 5.3 capture the extent to which parents are involved with their adolescent children's education during middle school. Do the patterns we observed remain relatively stable if the assessment is made when youth are in high school? We supplement the analysis based on the NELS using data from the Educational Longitudinal Study (ELS) to assess parents' involvement through interactions with their children in the later stages of schooling. In Figure 5.4, we show the proportion of parents who often provide advice to their high school children on current schooling, future schooling, and life affairs. The general patterns appear to be consistent with those in Figures 5.2 and 5.3.

The top panel of Figure 5.4 shows that Hispanic and black parents are on par with white and Asian parents in providing advice on courses and

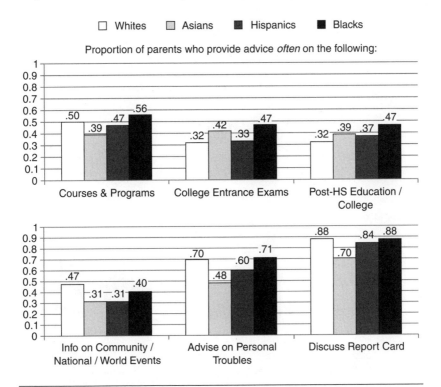

FIGURE 5.4. Parent-child interactions during high school by race: ELS. *Note:* Estimates are unadjusted. All measures are from the first wave of data collection, which occurred when youth were in grade 10.

programs, college entrance exams, and college. Interestingly, the proportion of black parents who interact with their child about college entrance exams and college plans is greater than that observed for any other group. The bottom graphs show that white parents appear to advise their children more often on general life affairs than other racial/ethnic groups, but are equal in proportion with black parents in providing advice on youths' personal troubles and in discussing youths' report cards. Asians actually have the lowest proportion of parents who provide youth with general advice and engage in discussions about report cards.

We employ data from the CDS to determine whether the patterns observed in the NELS and ELS also occur at an earlier period in children's schooling. The CDS does not disaggregate Hispanics (Asians are excluded due to insufficient sample size). This analysis is shown in Figure 5.5, which contains racial comparisons on the frequency with which parents read to their child and work on homework with their child. The data show that Hispanic and black parents read less to their child prior to the child entering

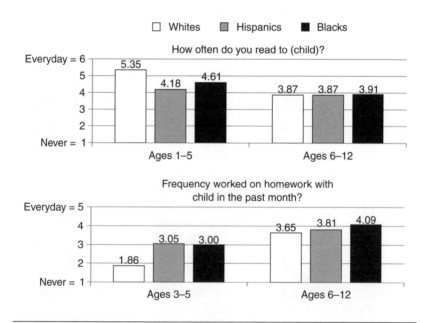

FIGURE 5.5. Parental involvement at home by race: CDS-I. *Note:* Estimates are unadjusted. The left panel filters on youth in elementary school (grades 1–5) during CDS-II, and the right panel filters on youth during adolescence (grades 6–12) in CDS-II. Thus, the ages listed represent the age range during CDS-I for the bulk of youth (roughly 90% or greater) for the given filter.

school than white parents. However, the bottom panel suggests that Hispanic and black parents spend more time helping on academic work before their child begins the first grade than their white counterparts.

The findings in the right-hand side of Figure 5.5 show that once youth are of school-age, parents are relatively similar with regard to both of these forms of involvement. Note that our figures do not permit us to distinguish parents' reasons for helping. Thus, the higher reported frequency of homework help by Hispanic and black parents early on might reflect a response to their child's academic struggles. Nevertheless, the findings do not appear consistent with the popular narrative of parental involvement attributed to each group.

Although the findings in Figures 5.2 through 5.5 challenge the notion that Hispanic and black parents are less involved in their children's academic lives, the findings in Figure 5.6 are consistent with the aforementioned narrative. Figure 5.6 shows the proportion of parents from each racial group who regularly discuss various aspects of schooling with their child. A lower proportion of Hispanic and black parents regularly discuss school activities, things studied in class, and general schooling experiences with their child prior to and during adolescence than white parents.

Chapter Summary

The assumption that racial differences exist in the extent to which parents are concerned with their children's schooling is widespread. Whereas white and Asian parents are perceived as caring about their children's education, many Hispanic (particularly Mexican) and black parents are characterized as disinterested about the schooling of their children (Bol and Berry 2005; DeCastro-Ambrosetti and Cho 2005; Souto-Manning and Swick 2006). We documented the reasons behind the persistence of this belief within the national narrative on parental involvement. Specifically, these racial groups have unique background experiences that make it logical to expect wide variation in how parents from these groups view their child's academic success within the larger context of this society and in the ways they express their involvement in children's education. We find that although racial groups might have reasons to differ in the importance they attribute to education for their children (e.g., an immigration experience, history of oppression), most of the actual differences do not coincide with the popular narratives about each group.

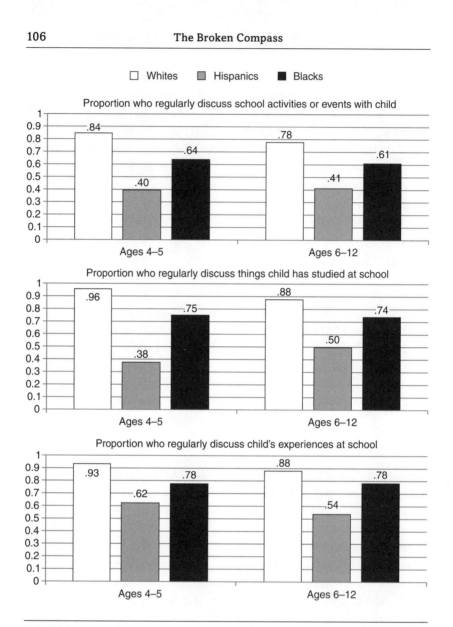

FIGURE 5.6. Parent-child discussions of schooling by race: CDS-I. *Note:* Estimates are unadjusted. The left panel filters on youth in elementary school during CDS-II, and the right panel filters on youth during adolescence (grades 6–12) in CDS-II. Thus, the ages listed represent the age range during CDS-I for the bulk of youth (roughly 85% or greater) for the given filter.

Parents appear quite similar in their home involvement across the three nationally representative data sets we examined. It is important to reiterate that the findings we present do not account for background factors, which suggests that despite the vast difference in the experiences of these racial groups, the importance parents attribute to schooling is rather stable across racial groups. That is, one's assimilation history for example, might provide one with a view of schooling that is different from someone else's view, but in the end the importance they place on schooling may be largely similar to others whose assimilation histories might be quite different. The main findings of this chapter suggest that Hispanic and black parents do value schooling and are generally just as involved in their children's education as white parents. Thus, it appears that the superior value of education attributed to Asian parents and the disregard for the importance of schooling attributed to the parents of Hispanic and black youth are overstated.

The findings from this chapter are similar to other studies that examine the academic orientation of Hispanic parents. In a study on the challenges of improving literacy in America, Morrison, Bachman, and Connor (2005) suggest that immigrant Hispanic parents place high value on educational attainment as a ticket to financial security and greater opportunity. They note that the ways in which Hispanic parents value education remains stable as length of residency in the United States (in years) increases and in the face of perceived discrimination. Studies have shown that even poor, immigrant Hispanic mothers tend to believe that education provides the most direct pathway to social mobility and tend to hold strong educational goals for their elementary school children despite feeling inadequate in helping with school assignments (Stevenson and Baker 1987). Furthermore, Hispanic parents have been shown to express greater concern about their children's kindergarten readiness than white parents (Diamond, Reagan, and Bandyk 2000).

Hispanic parents' beliefs about their children's education are intricately linked to more basic beliefs about children's moral development (Valdes 1996). Reese and colleagues (1995) interviewed Hispanic parents of preschoolers and found that many parents were concerned that in the United States their children are more prone to bad influences than in their home countries. Hispanic parents tended to believe that they had a small window prior to adolescence to instill proper moral values into their children. These parents had developmental goals for their children that related to moral development within schooling, general goals for their children's futures, and specific beliefs about the challenges their children would experience while trying to lead a good life.

The findings in this chapter for blacks are also consistent with those of other studies. For example, Harris (2011) finds that despite believing their children will experience discrimination and that race serves as an encumbrance for their children, black parents still expect their children to attain more education than their white counterparts. This reinforces the results of a national poll commissioned by the National Center for Public Policy and Higher Education, which found that black parents place higher value on obtaining an education as a means for advancement than whites (Public Agenda 2000). Research shows that this pattern extends even to blacks with lower social class backgrounds. Working-class black parents are more likely to discuss their children's school experiences and plans, restrict television on school nights, set rules about grades, and help with homework than their Asian and white counterparts (U.S. Department of Education 1992).

MacLeod's (2009) ethnographic study of low-income youth yields similar results. He found that the "Hallway Hangers" (white youth) expressed limited belief in opportunities for upward mobility, which was driven by their parents' experiences. Their parents were "hesitant to encourage hefty ambitions in their children. . . . As the Hallway Hangers tell it, there is little stimulus from home to raise their aspirations" (2009, 58). In contrast, the parents of the "Brothers" (black youth) expected them "to perform up to a certain standard at school, both in terms of academic achievement and discipline" (2009, 59). MacLeod's narratives suggest that black parents project their frustrated and unfulfilled educational and occupational ambitions onto their children by cultivating in them high hopes for the future.

Despite the similarity across race on the parental involvement activities that we assessed in this chapter, all of these measures have the potential to enhance children's academic performance. Furthermore, some activities might matter more for children from some racial groups than those of others. We are also mindful that some activities have the potential to explain the racial achievement gap; although the groups are similar across the majority of parental involvement activities we assessed in this chapter, there are some measures for which Asians B, both Hispanic groups, and blacks—groups with an achievement disadvantage relative to whites—report to engage in less than whites.

We highlight the factors that have the potential to explain the achievement disadvantage that children from these groups have relative to whites in Table 5.1. All twenty parental measures assessed in this chapter from Figures 5.2 to 5.6 are listed along the left-hand side of the table. A "yes" in the first column indicates that a racial disadvantage exists relative to whites on both achievement and the particular parental involvement activity for at least one group. The four columns on the right identify the particular racial group(s) for which this disadvantage exists (Asians A are excluded because they do not trail whites in achievement).

Note that we highlight only those parental activities for which the disadvantage relative to whites is *meaningful*. By meaningful we do not mean statistically significant. Instead, we made reasonable assessments regarding which factors could contribute to explaining a substantial proportion of the achievement gap for a particular group relative to whites. For example, if the proportion of parents that engaged in a particular involvement activity was .81 for whites and .79 for blacks, we would not consider the difference between these groups to be substantial. However, if the proportion for blacks were .74, then it would be reasonable to expect that statistically controlling for the parental activity in question could explain some portion of the black-white achievement gap. We chose to consider only differences of .07 or greater as meaningful. There are three measures for which this standard does not apply because they are measured in scales rather than proportions (*frequency with which parents help their child with homework* in both the NELS and CDS, and *frequency with which parents read to their child*). Among these measures there was only one activity for which Hispanics and black parents substantially trailed whites in their frequency of participation. For this measure—reading to child prior to school age—we made an arbitrary decision to consider a disadvantage of .50 or greater to be meaningful.

Table 5.1 highlights that the parents whose youth have an achievement disadvantage relative to whites do not have lower levels of participation on thirteen of the twenty measures of parental involvement at home than white parents. It appears that the racial differences exist on parental involvement that requires parents to discuss the more daily aspects of schooling with their child. It is important to note that we do not account for factors that might explain these differences, such as parents' educational attainment, family structure, and English language ability, which are particularly important for immigrant groups such as Asians B and Hispanics. Similarly, we

TABLE 5.1. Parental measures for which meaningful racial differences exist

Parental measure	Potential mechanism for gap convergence	Meaningful disadvantage in level of involvement relative to whites[a]				
		Asian B	Non-Mexican Hispanic	Mexican	Black
NELS						
Regularly talk/school experiences	**Yes**	Yes	Yes	Yes	Yes
Regularly talk/high school (HS) plans	No	No	No	No	No
Regularly talk/post-HS plans	No	No	No	No	No
Have a rule about GPA	No	No	No	No	No
Have a rule about homework	No	No	No	No	No
Expect post-high school education	No	No	No	No	No
Parent will decide HS courses	No	No	No	No	No
Agree homework is worthwhile	No	No	No	No	No
Help youth with homework	No	No	No	No	No
ELS		Hispanic	Black		
Advice/courses and programs	No	No	No	—	—
Advice/college entrance exams	No	No	No	—	—

		Pre-school		School-age	
		Hispanic	**Black**	**Hispanic**	**Black**
Advice/post-HS education or college	No	No	No	—	—
Discuss/community/national event	**Yes**	Yes	Yes	—	—
Advice/personal troubles	**Yes**	Yes	No	—	—
Discuss report card	No	No	No	—	—
CDS					
Read to child	**Yes**	Yes	Yes	No	No
Worked on homework	No	No	No	No	No
Discuss school activities	**Yes**	Yes	Yes	Yes	Yes
Discuss things studied	**Yes**	Yes	Yes	Yes	Yes
Discuss school experiences	**Yes**	Yes	Yes	Yes	Yes

Note: Because our interest is in identifying the parental factors that could potentially explain low achievement relative to whites, we present only the groups that have lower achievement than whites. Therefore, Asians A are excluded from the NELS, and Asians are excluded from the ELS.

a. By "meaningful difference," we do not mean "significant." We made reasonable assessments regarding which factors could contribute to explaining the achievement gap for each group if held constant based on the racial differences observed in Figures 5.2 to 5.6.

do not highlight those parental involvement activities for which a greater proportion of parents of youth from the lower-achieving racial groups employ relative to white parents. Thus, although fewer parents from the racial minority groups interact with their child about schooling than whites, the lack of controls and the relative similarities across most of the parental involvement activities should temper the conclusion that these parents do not care about their children's education. So besides the obvious factors such as English language proficiency and socioeconomic status, what might account for the differences we report in this chapter? Furthermore, given the lack of overwhelming support for the notion that minority parents (excluding Asians) do not care about schooling, why is this belief so widespread?

From recent surveys, we have learned that Asian, Hispanic, and black parents tend to value involvement in their children's academic learning. Yet wide racial differences exist both in the nature and frequency of help parents provide. Although part of this variation is owed to differences in economic resources, trust and confidence in the educational system and parental knowledge about schooling are also integral to parents' involvement practices. Parents from immigrant groups tend to have different beliefs about teaching and learning than parents from nonimmigrant groups. For example, some Asian and Hispanic parents feel that respect is shown to teachers by not interfering in education, and they may not become involved in certain ways as a result (Yan and Lin 2005).

With regard to black parents, research suggests that they tend to administer home involvement in ways meant to protect their children from racism found in the larger society (Bowman and Howard 1985; Cross, Parham, and Helms 1991; Jarrett 1995; Taylor et al. 1990), which might lead them to engage less in traditional forms of academic involvement. However, studies consistently show that they view education as a major path to opportunity for their children in a world where they are confronted with racism (Suizzo, Robinson, and Pahlke 2007). Thus, the differences that we report should not be taken as an indication that minority parents care less about their children's future; recall that Figure 5.2 shows that a greater proportion of Hispanic and black parents regularly discuss future educational plans with their child than white parents. It seems that conveying the importance of long-term educational achievement is a critical socializing goal for parents in these groups.

It is unlikely that the parental involvement activities in this chapter for which a lower share of parents from racial minority groups employ relative to whites fuels the widespread perception that these parents are less involved in their children's education. These forms of involvement are likely to occur during more private family moments (e.g., over dinner, transportation). What then perpetuates the perceptions that minority parents (excluding Asians) are less involved in their children's education? For one, many prior studies on black parents have focused mainly on low-income populations or largely ignored the in-group variation that exists among black families. A host of recent studies find that when social class is taken into account, black parents report the highest frequency of home-based involvement practices and the highest aspirations for their children's educational attainment (Fan 2001; Jeynes 2003; Suizzo, Robinson, and Pahlke 2007).

We suspect that these perceptions remain strong for two reasons. The first is the intuitiveness of the notion that "parents matter." Because parents are important determinants of student achievement, and minority parents care about their children's education just as much (if not more) than white parents, then why do minority youth underperform relative to whites? The logical answer must be that these minority groups do not truly value education. Second, the indicators for parental involvement that most people can observe are those that occur in and around schools rather than in the more private home domain.

Many teachers (and parents) often report that minority parents are less visible at school than their white counterparts. We will explore the evidence behind these reasons in Chapters 7 and 8. In Chapter 6, we turn our attention to whether the forms of involvement examined in this chapter have implications for children's academic outcomes for each racial group.

— 6 —

Effectiveness of Parental Involvement at Home by Race

The belief that parental involvement works is deeply ingrained in the American educational system ethos. An online search of parental involvement will take you to the websites of numerous organizations, coalitions, and various other entities that make strong calls for parents to become more involved at home and for schools to develop partnerships with parents to assist child learning. Yet, many of the academic benefits they purport children will receive from home involvement are unattached to empirical evidence. As discussed in the previous chapters, some evidence supports the belief that high-achieving students are more likely to have active, interested, and involved parents compared to low-achieving students (Crosnoe 2001; Marjoribanks 1979; Muller 1995, 1998; Rivera and Nieto 1993; Sui-Chu and Willms 1996; Topping 1992). However, the findings reported in Chapters 3 and 4 regarding the link between parental involvement and achievement by social class suggest that not all forms of parental involvement are beneficial for all groups. It is possible that variation exists in the forms of involvement that are effective by race.

Although cumulative evidence supports the theoretical link between parents and academic performance (Amato and Fowler 2002; Dornbusch et al. 1987; Steinberg, Dornbusch, and Brown 1992), it is unclear whether a blueprint exists for effective home involvement that is specific to each racial group. In the last chapter, we found little variation between minority and nonminority parents in the extent to which they are involved in their children's schooling at home. The next pressing question is "Which at-home involvement activities impact children's academic performance for each racial group?"

Evidence suggests that the effects of home involvement are not consistent across families of different racial backgrounds (Yan and Lin 2005). For example, in a meta-analysis of the impact of parental involvement on minority students' achievement, Jeynes (2003) reports that several forms of involvement, including communicating with the school, checking homework, and encouraging reading, benefits black and Hispanic students more than Asian students. Similarly, whereas some research has shown that black youth do not benefit in terms of achievement from parental involvement and encouragement (Steinberg, Dornbusch, and Brown 1992), parent-child discussions about school have been found to increase science achievement for white and black adolescents but not for Hispanic or Asian youth (Mc-Neal 1999). Racial variation in effects seems to extend even to parenting styles; white and Hispanic youth experience increases in grades from authoritative parenting, which is not the case for Asian or black adolescents (Dornbusch et al. 1987; Steinberg et al. 1991). These studies make it reasonable to expect that some forms of parental involvement are associated with increases in achievement for some groups but not others.

Data that we have presented in previous chapters also give reason to expect that the effects of parental involvement differ by race. For example, as we find in Chapter 5, Asians and whites have greater academic achievement than Hispanics and blacks despite not having a substantial advantage in parental involvement at home. If we take as givens that parental involvement at home is consequential for achievement but does not vary much by race, then we can assume that the effects should be greater for the racial groups with greater achievement. Research on parental expectations for children's education among Asians suggests that this finding might be the case. Although parents from all racial groups have high educational expectations for their children, Asian parents often send the message to children that high achievement is more than just about academic success; it is a reflection of their self-worth (Chao 2000a, 2000b; Ho 1994; Kim and Chun 1994). Asian children are often raised to honor their parents and family by succeeding in school. Exemplary performance in school is a means through which familial obligation and respect are conveyed in Chinese families (Bempechat, Graham, and Jimenez 1996; Kim and Chun 1994). Indeed, for many Chinese parents academic excellence is considered the most important socializing goal along with respecting parents (Chao 2000a, 2000b; Ho 1994). These studies suggest that expectations may carry a unique aspect that is specific to Asian families (or to some Asian families) because of their cultural practices or their lived experiences within the United States, which differs from that of other racial groups. Our analyses were conducted with the consideration that sociodemographic differences in students' backgrounds prevent the one-size-fits-all model of involvement.

In this chapter, we examine the implications of parental involvement at home on achievement for youth from *each* racial group separately, which allows us to determine which parental involvement factors from Chapter 5 are associated with increases in achievement for each group. We begin by presenting the findings for analyses similar to those employed in Chapters 3 and 4 by race. This strategy allows us to show the individual estimated effect of each involvement activity for each racial group. We also present findings for scales created from the individual activities, which estimate the effectiveness of a more holistic approach to parental involvement.

The Implications of Parental Involvement at Home for Achievement by Race

We present the findings for our analysis on the association between parental involvement at home and academic achievement for each racial group in a series of estimate graphs similar to those displayed in Chapters 3 and 4. These graphs show the gain or loss in achievement (along with the margin of error) attributable to each measure of parental involvement examined in Chapter 5. The estimates account for family income, parents' education, marital status, youths' sex, and prior academic skills (see Appendix B for analytic details and sample sizes). Thus, the estimates represent the difference in achievement between children whose parents engage in or affirm the parental involvement measure and those whose parents do not, after accounting for background factors. Recall that we highlight estimates for which a significant relationship exists (either positive or negative) and display nonsignificant estimates in gray. We focus more of our discussion on forms of involvement that are beneficial to students' achievement.

The first set of findings, which are based on the NELS, are contained in Figure 6.1. We display six estimates for each indicator of parental involvement; an estimate is displayed for the following racial groups: whites (open circle), Asians A (open triangle), Asians B (full triangle), non-Mexican Hispanics (open square), Mexicans (full square), and blacks (full circle).

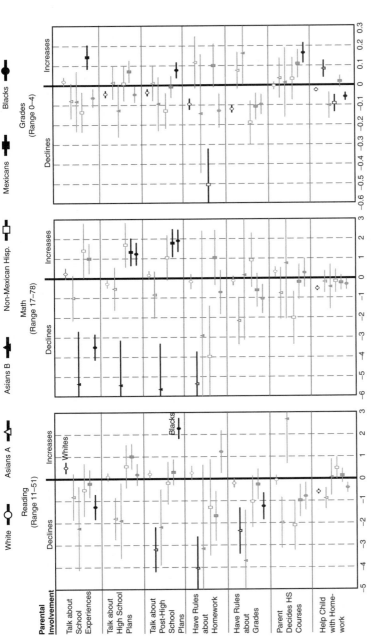

FIGURE 6.1. Gains in achievement associated with parental involvement at home by race: NELS. *Note:* Bold estimates are significant at the .05 level. Estimates account for parents' education, household income, family structure, youths' sex, and prior achievement/grades. Achievement was assessed when youth were in grade 12, and the parenting measures were assessed prior to the youth entering high school (grade 8). Unlike the other parenting factors, *Help with homework* is measured along a 4-point scale: 1 = seldom or never to 4 = almost every day. Every 1-point change corresponds to a percentage change of 3 in reading and 2 in math relative to the mean. For grades, a 0.1 change corresponds to a 5% change relative to the mean.

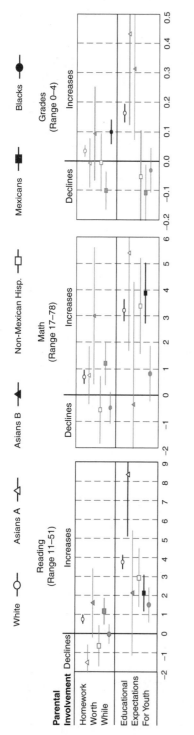

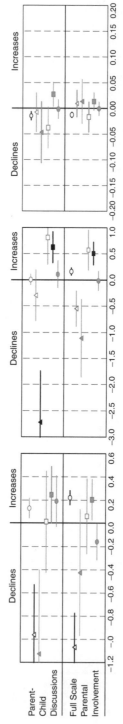

FIGURE 6.2. Gains in achievement associated with parents' views about homework and education expectations by race: NELS. *Note:* Bold estimates are significant at the .05 level. Estimates account for parents', education, household income, family structure, youths' sex, and prior achievement/grades. Achievement was assessed when youth were in grade 12, and the parenting measures were assessed prior to the youth entering high school (grade 8). Every 1-point change corresponds to a percentage change of 3 in reading and 2 in math relative to the mean. For grades, a 0.1 change corresponds to a 5% change relative to the mean. In "Scales of parental involvement at home," *Parent-child discussions* is the sum of *Talk about school experiences, Talk about high school plans,* and *Talk about post–high school plans* (mean = 1.63, SD = 1.07; unweighted n = 10,062; Cronbach's alpha = .657). *Full-scale parental involvement* is the sum of all parental measures of home involvement in Figures 6.1 and 6.2 except *Help with homework* (0 = affirm none, 8 = affirm all; mean = 4.64, SD = 1.59; unweighted *n* = 9,555; Cronbach's alpha = .530).

The most striking aspect of Figure 6.1 is that most parental involvement measures do not appear to lead to real gains in achievement. The left-hand panel shows that there are only two positive estimates for reading; white youth appear to benefit from parent-child discussions about school experiences, and black youth seem to benefit from discussions about their post–high school plans. The center panel shows that positive estimates exist in math achievement only for Mexican and black youth, who benefit from parent-child discussions about high school and post–high school plans. With regard to grades, the right-hand panel suggests that Mexican youth benefit from regular discussions about their schooling experiences, black youth benefit from regular parent-child discussions about post–high school education and from their parents' involvement in their course selections, and youth in the Asian A group benefit from help with homework.

Whereas the findings displayed in Figure 6.1 are for more behavioral forms of involvement, the top panel of Figure 6.2 contains findings for two measures of parental involvement that tap into parents' views about education. Parents' estimate about the usefulness of homework appears to raise reading and math achievement for white youth and grades for black youth. Parents' educational expectations are associated with increases in all three measures of achievement for whites, reading and math achievement for Mexicans, and reading for youth in the Asian A group. The findings in Figure 6.1 and the top panel of Figure 6.2 show that only two forms of involvement are associated with increases in all three measures of achievement for any group; parent-child discussion about post–high school plans for blacks and educational expectations for whites. In sum, most of the findings by race appear to be random.

The bottom panel of Figure 6.2 contains the results for parental involvement in the form of scales. The first scale, *Parent-child discussions*, was constructed from the first three measures of parental involvement listed in Figure 6.1: (1) *Talk about school experiences*, (2) *Talk about high school plans*, and (3) *Talk about post–high school plans*. This measure is associated with increased achievement only for Mexicans in math. The second scale, *Full-scale parental involvement*, is the sum of all parental involvement measures listed in Figure 6.1 and the top panel of Figure 6.2 with the exception of the frequency with which parents *Help youth with homework*, which is coded differently than the other measures. The estimates for *Full-scale parental involvement* can be interpreted as the change in achievement associated with each additional activity (within the scale) that parents

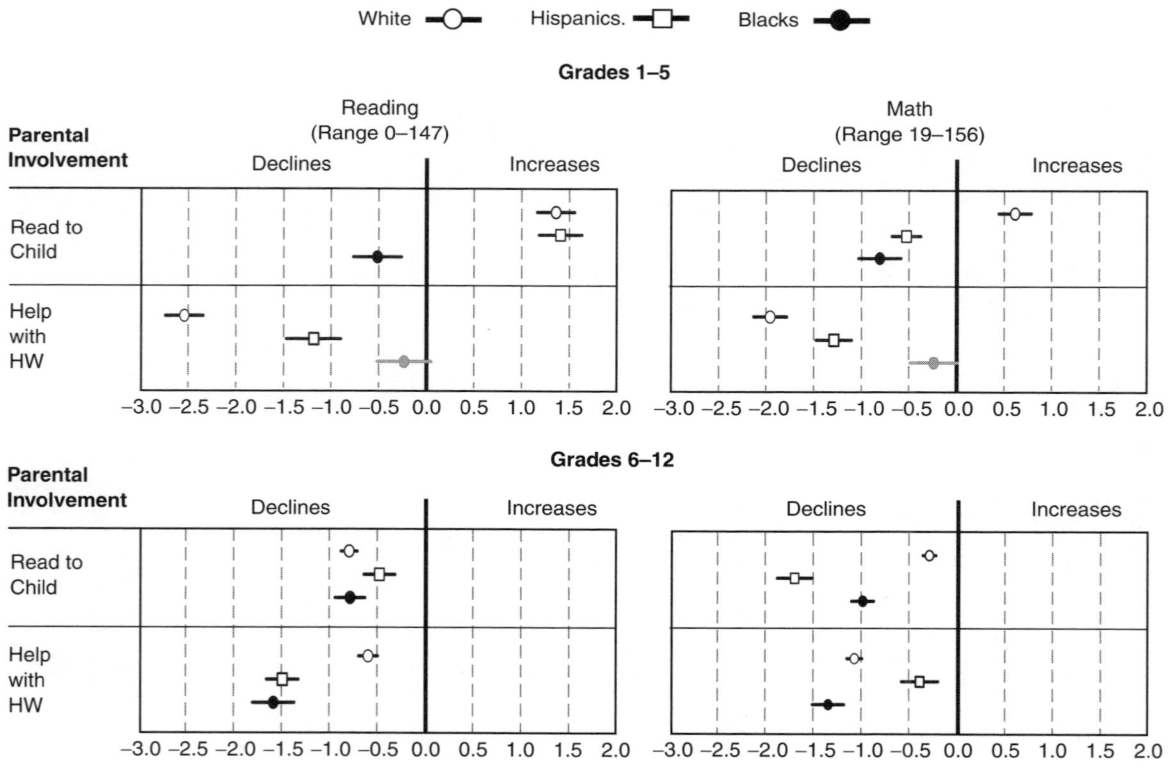

FIGURE 6.3. Gains in achievement associated with parental involvement at home by race: CDS. *Note:* Bold estimates are significant at the .05 level. Estimates account for parents' education, household income, family structure, youths' sex, grade in school, and prior achievement. The findings for Hispanics in the younger subsample do not account for prior achievement. Achievement was assessed from CDS-II, and the parenting measures were obtained from CDS-I. Every 1-point change corresponds to roughly a 1% change in reading and math relative to their respective means.

employ or affirm. The *Full-scale* is associated with increases in reading and math for whites and increases in math for Mexicans.

A question that remains is whether the patterns observed in Figures 6.1 and 6.2, for which measures of parental involvement were assessed when youth were in middle school, are similar for younger students. We address this question by repeating these analyses using the CDS, which captures parental involvement from before youth enter school through elementary school. Recall that for the subsample of youth in grades 1–5, parental involvement was measured prior to youth entering the first grade. For youth in the older subsample, parental involvement was measured while the youth were in elementary school. Given that the CDS does not contain a sufficient sample size for Asians and does not allow for the same level of racial disaggregation as the NELS, our analysis is restricted to whites, Hispanics, and blacks. These findings are presented in Figure 6.3.

The top panel contains estimates that represent the change in achievement that can be attributed to parents reading to their child and helping with homework for youth in grades 1–5. Similar to the analytic strategy employed for the previous analyses, we show the association between each measure of parental involvement at home and achievement after accounting for family socioeconomic background factors. Reading to children is associated with increases in both reading and math for white youth and in reading for Hispanic youth. In contrast, helping with homework is associated with declines in both reading and math for whites and Hispanics. The findings for older youth in the bottom panel of Figure 6.3 are striking; every single estimate is negative. It seems that both reading to children and helping with homework are associated with declines in achievement for all three racial groups. Recall that negative estimates cannot be attributed to parents responding to poor academic performance; the findings account for student quality by including prior achievement in the analysis and thus represent the change in achievement that can be attributed to each measure of parental involvement.

In Figure 6.4, we show findings for analyses on the link between parent-child discussions about various aspects of schooling and achievement for whites, Hispanics, and blacks. The primary pattern from these analyses is that every estimate for Hispanics in Figure 6.4 is significant and positive, which indicates that Hispanic youth benefit in reading and math from parent-child discussions about schooling, regardless of grade level. Among the younger subsample, the only other significantly positive estimate is for whites, who appear to benefit in reading from parent-child discussions about school activities. The bottom panel also suggests that whites and blacks experience increases in reading from parent-child discussions about school activities, and whites benefit in math from all forms of discussions we examined. Interestingly, the estimated effect sizes are smaller for the older subsample, which is consistent with the notion that the effect of parental involvement declines with youths' age.

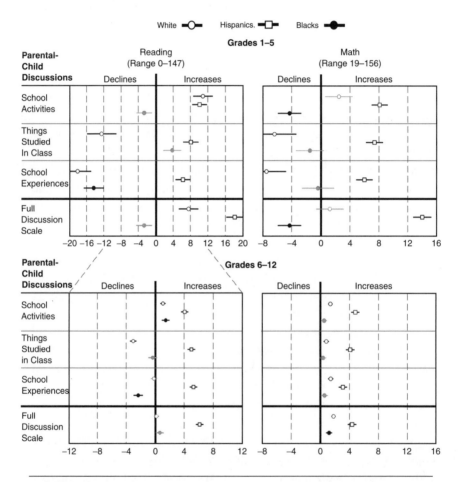

FIGURE 6.4. Gains in achievement associated with parental-child discussions by race: CDS. *Note:* Bold estimates are significant at the .05 level. Estimates account for parents' education, household income, family structure, youths' sex, grade in school, and prior achievement. The findings for Hispanics in the younger subsample do not account for prior achievement. Achievement was assessed from CDS-II, and the parenting measures were obtained from CDS-I. Every 1-point change corresponds roughly to a 1% change in reading and math relative to their respective means.

Chapter Summary

In this chapter, we set out to assess the importance of parental involvement at home for the academic lives of youth from different racial groups. We were interested in determining whether parents have been an effective force in the learning process for students within the United States. Our assessment considered that white, Asian, Hispanic, and black families each have different lived experiences within the United States, which poses unique challenges to the "one-size-fits-all" model of home involvement. Thus, we examined whether parental involvement at home is associated with increases in achievement for each racial group. In specific terms, the findings can serve as a diagnostic assessment of parental involvement as they provide parents and educators with some insight on where to focus. We highlighted the forms of involvement that are associated with increases in academic outcomes and those that appear to be ineffective, or even harmful. These results can serve as *one* resource for educators to provide parents with guidance about which forms of involvement need to be implemented in a better (or different) fashion. Also, analyzing data separately for each racial group proved to be useful and uncovered interesting patterns.

We provide a summary of the general link between parental involvement and achievement for each racial group in Figure 6.5. Specifically, the figure shows the number of positive, nonsignificant, and negative estimates for each group in both the NELS (top panel) and CDS (bottom panel). The NELS contained twenty-seven possible "effects" for each group—nine measures of parental involvement by three academic outcomes (reading and math achievement, and grades). Most of the estimates for each group are not significant. Only six estimates are significant in the positive direction for whites and blacks, followed by five for Mexicans. What is even more surprising is that only two positive estimates are observed for Asians A, and there were no measures of parental involvement associated with increases in achievement for Asians B and non-Mexican Hispanics. There are actually more negative estimates than positive estimates for whites (7), Asians A (4), Asians B (3), and non-Mexican Hispanics (2).

The bottom panel contains the same information for children in elementary school and in adolescence. There are ten estimates for each racial group among both the elementary school and adolescent samples—five measures of parental involvement by two academic outcomes (reading and math). For the elementary school sample, there are three positive estimates

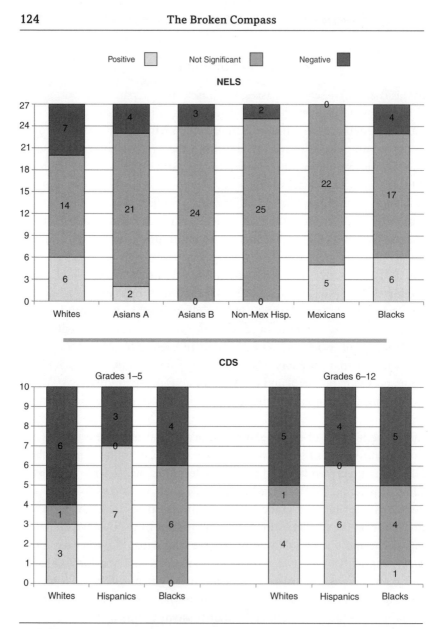

FIGURE 6.5. Number of parental involvement measures associated with changes in achievement by race.

for whites and seven for Hispanics. There are no positive estimates for blacks. For the adolescent sample, the number of positive estimates was four for whites, six for Hispanics, and one for blacks. Thus, it seems that Hispanic youth benefit the most from parental involvement prior to their entering schooling, which is when parental involvement was measured for the younger subsample, and from involvement during elementary school, which is when involvement was measured for the older subsample. In contrast, there are a greater number of negative estimates than positive estimates for whites and blacks, regardless of subsample.

In Figure 6.6, we show the number of positive (dark bar on the left), nonsignificant (light bar in the center), and negative (gray bar on the right) estimates for each measure of parental involvement examined in this chapter. The top panel contains the summary for the NELS. There are 18 links between each parental factor and achievement across all racial groups (3 achievement outcomes by 6 groups). With regard to the big picture, the figure shows that out of the 162 total estimates, only 19 are positive, 20 are negative, and 123 are not systematically related to achievement. Thus, only 12% of the estimates are positive. The nearly equal numbers of positive and negative estimates suggest that parents enact these forms of involvement in ways that are just as counterproductive as they are helpful for achievement. In contrast, 76% of the estimates are not significant.

The bottom panel shows that parental involvement earlier in the academic process is more beneficial for achievement than involvement during middle school. One-third of the estimates for the CDS are positive for both the younger (10 of 30) and older (11 of 30) subsamples. However, nearly half of the estimates for both subsamples are negative (13 for the younger subsample and 14 for the older subsample). The greater percentage of positive estimates for the CDS (35%) relative to the NELS (12%) partially reflects the difference in the types of involvement being assessed; all of the parental involvement measures from the CDS require direct interaction between parents and their child (reading to child, help with homework, and three measures of parent-child discussions). In contrast, the NELS includes measures that do not require ongoing direct parent-child interaction (e.g., rules about GPA and homework, educational expectations, belief that homework is worthwhile).

Several useful interpretations can be made from the patterns of specific measures of parental involvement. For example, regular conversations with children about their post–high school plans and parents' educational

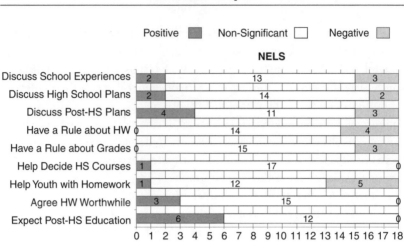

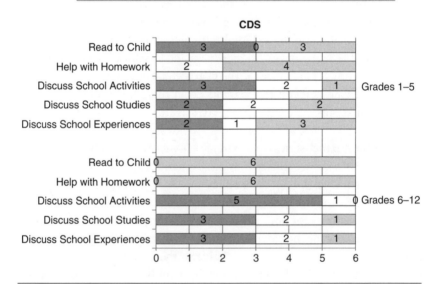

FIGURE 6.6. Number of positive, nonsignificant, and negative estimates for each measure.

expectations show the most associations with increased achievement (4 and 6, respectively). It seems that, in general, parents can do more to increase their children's achievement by focusing on post–high school education (either through conversations or expectations), than they can by helping with homework or setting rules about homework or grade point averages. In the bottom panel, discussing school activities with children seems to provide positive benefits for achievement more than any other form of parental involvement. In contrast, helping children with homework is not related to increased achievement for any racial group during elementary school or during adolescence. Figure 6.6 drives home the point that very few measures of parental involvement at home are linked to increases in grades and test scores.

The results presented in this chapter show that parental involvement at home is systematically related to increases in achievement in only 18% of the total comparisons made in this chapter (40 of 222). In contrast, a greater percentage of links we assessed suggest that parental involvement at home is associated with declines in achievement (47 of 222, or 21%). From this basic tally method, one could conclude that there is not an unequivocal systematic relationship between parental involvement at home and students' achievement. Furthermore, there are far more nonpositive estimates (82%) than could reasonably be attributed to chance, particularly given the expectation that parental involvement "works." We recognize that our tally method is crude and implies that all forms of parenting carry the same weight. Nevertheless, it allows us to provide a general sense of the relationship between parental involvement at home and academic achievement.

It is important to note that some forms of involvement are detrimental for the achievement of *some* groups. Furthermore, educators should consider the possibility that the negative estimates for some forms of involvement might reflect an ineffective or flawed mode of implementation of the given form of involvement by parents rather than an actual negative association between the form of involvement and achievement in theory. Some of these measures might actually be beneficial for achievement if parents made adjustments in how they employ the behavior described by the parental involvement measure.

A common interpretation is that negative associations between involvement and achievement reflect parents' attempts to address poor achievement. Thus, students' achievement might be driving parental involvement. There are a number of reasons to think parents' investments in children's academic success will be determined by child performance. Parents might be willing to invest more effort in a child who shows academic promise. It might also be the case that parents become most involved when their child is struggling academically. McNeal (1999) concluded that parental involvement was mainly a reaction to children's poor performance. Milne and colleagues (1986) studied the effects of family structure on reading achievement and found a negative relationship between parents helping their children with homework and achievement among whites. These studies suggest that parents' influence is correlational rather than causal. However, the findings we present in this chapter account for students' prior achievement levels, and thus reflect the change in students' achievement that can be attributed to parental involvement.

Our findings should not be interpreted as causal. We cannot say definitively that parental involvement does or does not lead to improved student outcomes. What we provide is an extensive account of the association between what parents do at home to facilitate learning and children's academic outcomes, rather than an assessment of causal effects. To establish a causal link, the following criteria need to be met: (1) the factors purported to be the cause should be related to the factors being affected; (2) the cause must precede the effect in time; and (3) alternative explanations should be ruled out. Although our findings do not establish causality, they are suggestive of where causality might exist. Our findings meet the first two conditions by establishing associations and ensuring that our predictors are measured at a time prior to the outcomes. However, we fall short on the third criteria. Although we control for key background factors, we are aware that these are not a perfect or an exhaustive set of controls.

Nevertheless, in a more general sense, the findings in this chapter should serve as caution for educators and policy makers to avoid putting the bulk of their eggs in the parental involvement basket. The preponderance of evidence from the analyses we conducted in this chapter suggests that although parental involvement has some effect on children's schooling for *some* groups, particularly the way they think about academic tasks, the connection between home involvement and academic achievement is modest; the overwhelming majority of parental involvement measures that we examined show no relationship to achievement. More importantly, parental involvement might be more effective if it is applied in a more directed, rather than blind, manner.

— 7 —

Parental Involvement at School by Race

> Washington Avenue Elementary School's parent liaison Carmen
> Torres was selected as New Jersey's delegate to attend the Emerg-
> ing Minority Leaders Conference, which will coincide with the
> 115th Annual National Parent Teacher Association Conference . . .
> Now in its sixth year, the EML conference is designed to build the
> leadership skills of ethnic minority parents, caregivers and
> advocates at every level of PTA as well as to offer anyone working
> in minority communities usable information and take-away
> resources to help them better engage in communities of color.
> —*Shore News Today*, May 26, 2011

Having outlined the ways parents can promote educational success in the
home, we turn our attention in this chapter to parents' involvement at
school by race. Despite the lack of overwhelming support in Chapter 5 for
the notion that minority parents are less involved in their children's education, the perception that minority parents—mostly Hispanic groups and
blacks in particular—care less about their children's schooling still persists.
This belief might be driven by patterns of involvement at school rather than
at home. The opening epigraph partially captures this sentiment. Essentially, the pervasive belief of teachers and school administrators is that
programs need to be established to increase minority parents' low levels of
involvement in their children's schooling.

Despite the importance placed on parents' participation at school, there
is a sentiment in America's schools that many parents are not as involved
as often as they could and should be. Our main objective in this chapter is
to examine the extent to which parents of different racial backgrounds differ in the types of school involvement activities they employ. The aim is
simply to provide a survey of the state of parental involvement at school
across racial groups within the United States. The findings we show are
mainly descriptive and are not designed to answer why parents of different

racial backgrounds vary in the ways they participate at school. Teachers, other school personnel, and the general public typically do not cognitively adjust for social class when they develop perceptions about race and parental involvement based on their observations within schools. Therefore, we believe it is important to display the raw averages for each racial group during racial comparisons of parental involvement because the findings might lend credibility to educators' real-time assessments of the level of involvement for parents from the various racial groups.

In the following section, we discuss the reasoning behind the push for parents to become more involved with their children's schools. We then turn our attention to the factors that might contribute to racial differences in parental involvement at school, which could be responsible for perpetuating the popular conception that Hispanic and black parents are less involved in their children's education than white and Asian parents. Specifically, we discuss how parents' patterns of involvement might be partially determined by how they construct their roles with regard to their child's academic lives, the experiences related to being members of an immigrant group, and the opportunities for involvement they encounter at schools. These factors account for how *both* parents and schools structure the process of parental involvement at school.

Parental Involvement with Schools

As previously discussed, school participation on the part of parents is encouraged by schools as a means of boosting academic outcomes for children and enhancing the educational effectiveness of schools. It is believed that activities at school such as fund-raising, volunteering for school programs, and attending open-house sessions positively impact academic outcomes (Marzano 2003). Additionally, a parent who actively participates at school communicates to teachers that the child's education is being taken seriously (Bol and Berry 2005; Souto-Manning and Swick 2006). Teachers recognize this parental interest and may come to feel that the student is equally as interested, which is commonly known as the halo effect. Teachers also know that parents who are involved at school are easily accessible to address or to circumvent any potential problems in the child's education (Steinberg 2001). Parental involvement at school might send a message to children that their parents believe education is important, which can strengthen the child's own belief in the importance of schooling.

Although the enactment of parental authority occurs mostly within the home, parents have the potential to reinforce the educational process that takes place at school. Parents and teachers have a mutual dependence on each other to help educate students. Teachers need parents' expertise about their particular child, whereas teachers' expertise in child development, curriculum, and instruction is important for informing parents on how to support children's education. Because school is one of the two main arenas in which children are educated (the other being family), regular participation at school can allow parents, teachers, and children to develop a common language, perhaps giving children a sense of cohesion between the two learning arenas. Therefore, it is reasonable to expect parent-school relationships to be central to the push for increasing parental involvement.

Parents as Initiators of Involvement with Schools

A major factor governing parents' involvement in their child's education is their construction of the parental role (Hoover-Dempsey and Sandler 1997). Parents' beliefs regarding appropriate roles direct their child-rearing practices and how they interpret their children's behaviors. Some parents hold high regard for conformity and obedience (e.g., some Asian, black, and Hispanic parents) (Mau 1997). These parents tend to believe that learning is best fostered in environments high in external control (e.g., directives, punishment, demands) and are apt to construct their parental role around pressuring their child through coercion to attend to their schoolwork. Because the feasibility of employing practices consistent with this view of parenting is greater at home than at school, these parents might invest a greater portion of their involvement outside of schools. Others place a high value on self-dependence, an individualistic characteristic more commonly associated with European-American parents and schools (Trumbull, Rothstein-Fisch, and Hernandez 2003). Parents who hold the latter values tend to view their roles as academic tutor and to be outspoken advocates for their children at school.

Examining the efforts that parents make to engage with their child's school is one way to determine if racial differences exist in how parents view their role. We do so in Figure 7.1, which displays the proportion of parents who contact schools about various matters for each racial group. Parents of youth from racial groups that have lower academic performance than whites—Asians B, both Hispanic groups, and blacks—contact schools less (by at

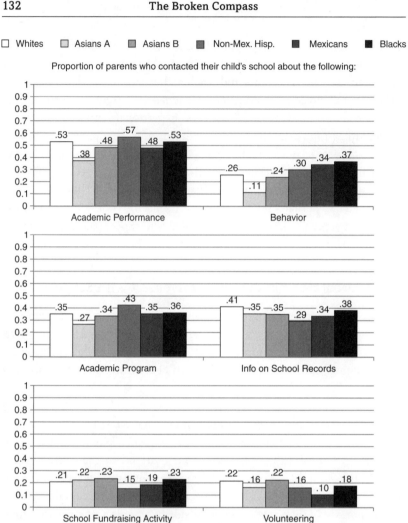

□ Whites   ☐ Asians A   ▣ Asians B   ▨ Non-Mex. Hisp.   ■ Mexicans   ■ Blacks

Proportion of parents who contacted their child's school about the following:

FIGURE 7.1. Parent-initiated contact during middle school by race: NELS. *Note:* The findings are unadjusted. All measures were collected when youth were in grade 8.

least 7% or more) than their white counterparts on only two of the six measures for parent-initiated school contact. Specifically, the proportion of parents who contact schools about school records is lower for both Hispanic groups, and the proportion who contact schools about volunteering is lower for Mexicans. Parents from the Asians B and black groups are similar to whites on all six measures. In contrast, parents from the Asians A group contact school less than whites on three of the six measures: academic performance, child's behavior, and academic programs. The former two measures might reflect that the child is having academic difficulty at school. However, collectively, the measures in Figure 7.1 to some extent capture parents' comfort levels for initiating contact with their child's school. These findings suggest that minority parents are just as concerned with their children's academic outcomes as white parents, and more importantly, are just as willing to put forth the effort to show their concern.

The similarities between whites and racial minorities on the proportion of parents that contact schools observed in Figure 7.1 is surprising given the lower socioeconomic background of Hispanics and blacks. Educators have labeled low-income parents as hard to reach, uncooperative, and a hindrance to educating children. Though studies continue to show that low-income parents value their children's education and seek ways to become involved (Lott 2001; Shannon 1996), the stereotypes that they are apathetic, unconcerned about their children's education (Bol and Berry 2005; Souto-Manning and Swick 2006), and not competent to help with homework persist (Davies 1993; Lott 2002). These views have changed very little over the past several decades (Lott 2001). Educators often perceive low-income parents as reluctant to accept school efforts to involve them, infrequent in their participation at school events, and uncommitted to their child's academic success. However, the fact that minority parents in general face greater constraints to their involvement yet appear to be involved at similar rates as other parents may signal that minority parents are even *more* concerned with their children's schooling.

An important factor that must be considered when interpreting the patterns observed for Asian and Hispanic groups is immigration status. These groups contain a greater share of the immigrant population within the United States, and immigration status is a determining factor in parents' involvement patterns. Scholars have documented that the extent to which immigrant parents advocate for their children at school (e.g., attending school meetings or parent-teacher conferences) is complex, relating to a host of socioeconomic, cultural, language, employment, and school-family relationship factors. In general, immigrant parents tend to view themselves as socializing agents whose primary obligation is to make sure their child is displaying the proper conduct at school. Initiating discussions with teachers or attending classroom learning sessions may be viewed as inappropriate to many immigrant parents, in part because of the belief that teachers and administrators hold the primary responsibility for educating children (Lee and Manning 2001; Trumbull, Rothstein-Fisch, and Hernandez 2003).

Trumbull et al. (2001) provides an example of this based on a California Department of Education study, which found that involvement attitudes for some Vietnamese-American parents in California appear passive to teachers and administrators. These parents rarely joined parents' advisory committees and rarely participated in school programs and activities even though they placed a high value on education. They were reluctant to voice concerns and engage teachers in discussions about educational issues. One explanation for this reticence is provided by Lee and Manning (2001), who note that Asian parents highly value nonverbal communication and pay close attention to teachers' tone of voice, facial expressions, gestures, and treatment of time and space in order to understand how teachers feel about them and their children. Certain cues, such as a fast walk or slumped posture could be perceived as the teacher wanting a short interaction (Lee and Manning 2001). Furthermore, studies show that many Asian American parents prefer indirect types of support to foster learning, such as controlling children's time outside of school, purchasing extra textbooks and assigning extra homework, hiring tutors, and enrolling children in music or language lessons (Sui-Chu and Willms 1996).

For some Hispanic parents, particularly those with strong ties to their native country or limited English skills, viewing themselves in a partnership with schools to improve their children's education is a strange concept. These parents perceive themselves as responsible for getting their children to school and consider it appropriate to let teachers and administrators handle educational matters (Rivera and Nieto 1993). Valdes (1996) describes what it means for Hispanic parents to raise an educated child by saying that English speakers conceive "education" to be school or book learning. Spanish speakers view "education" in a broader sense encompassing both manners and moral values. Raising an educated child means involving oneself as a parent in ways that teach the rules of conduct that need to be followed to attain success in school, in the family, and in the community.

Carger's (1996) study of Mexican-Americans and their educational experiences in the United States provides an example of how this sentiment plays out among immigrant Hispanic groups. He describes the case of a Mexican mother named Alba who despite being unable to help her son with school encouraged him to work hard and behave in class. She also directed her involvement to giving her son daily lessons about avoiding gangs and how to navigate racism in the community. Being raised to respect others, to handle racial conflict appropriately, and to be a respectable member of the community are considered to make the child *bien educado,* or well educated, by many Hispanic parents. Furthermore, research suggests that Hispanic parents feel intimidated by teachers and are discouraged from becoming involved by unwelcoming school environments (Hyslop 2000).

A factor related to immigration that serves as a barrier to involvement for some Hispanic and Asian parents is limited English proficiency. A significant amount of attention has been given to language as a barrier to school involvement, particularly for immigrant parents or parents with English difficulty (Pena 2000). It can be quite challenging for parents and teachers to have productive interactions about students' grades, behavior, progress, and homework when the two parties are comfortable with different languages. Most public school teachers have little to no formal training in teaching English as a second language, and many of these teachers are not likely to speak the immigrant parents' language (Valdes 1996). Moreover, schools rarely employ interpreters to help facilitate these discussions (Tinkler 2002).

The issue of language is related to how schools generally communicate with parents. Schools often communicate the ways they want parents to be involved at school through notices sent to family residences. If these notices are not drafted with concerns for native languages, attempts to increase school participation could be futile. Communication issues can also surface if schools do not provide culturally appropriate ways to share information about children. McCaleb (1997) interviewed parents of first graders in a Spanish emersion program that was 43% Spanish-language dominated and had 37% African-American students. Parents expressed frustration about not being provided enough information from teachers about how to be involved at their children's schools. One parent claimed that schools needed to improve their contact with families and offer them more ways to participate. Connors and Epstein (1995) claim that it is very difficult for a parent unfamiliar with U.S. schools to lead the charge when the school environment includes an unfamiliar language and different norms of communication. Valdes (1996) found that immigrant parents in the small community she studied were too embarrassed to attend their child's school. Even parents who highly valued education reported that they were reluctant to speak with teachers directly.

The Role of Schools for Parental Involvement

Both schools and parents share the responsibility of forging relationships that benefit children's achievement. Schools must provide opportunities for parents to engage in dialogue with teachers. They must effectively manage the flow of information between the school and children's homes, ensuring that information regarding children's progress and ways parents can help children improve academically is regularly disseminated. Schools are also responsible for creating a school environment that makes parents feel comfortable enough to become involved. Although parents receive the lion's share of the focus in discussions of parental involvement at school, schools play an important part in structuring parents' involvement opportunities.

Some studies suggest that teachers do not always welcome parental efforts to be involved at school. Lewis and Foreman (2002) illustrate this point in their qualitative analysis of parent-school relations in elementary schools. They report that teachers may view highly involved parents as intruding upon their workspace. Interviews with teachers revealed elaborate systems to *limit* parental involvement in the school. One such strategy involved staying away from their classrooms from 8 a.m. until just before school started at 8:30 to avoid parents who may want to converse about their child as they dropped them off at school. Lewis and Foreman (2002) noted that one of the inexperienced teachers was given advice by senior colleagues on how to manage or control parental participation.

Lewis and Foreman (2002) provide a telling example of this feeling of intrusion in describing efforts made by "Ms. Cone," a first-grade teacher at the middle-class elementary school they observed. Ms. Cone planned special activities over a two-week period where parents could come to the school and participate in the classroom. These activities were arranged for preestablished times on Tuesdays, Wednesdays, or Thursdays. One child's father preferred Fridays, much to the chagrin of Ms. Cone who then had to plan something special for his visit. In fact, she viewed his visit as an imposition. It was not convenient for her to accommodate his participation outside of the carefully confined boundaries she had established. Ms. Cone expressed her frustration in saying that parents often think they are qualified to do teachers' jobs and that "sometimes it's better for the kids without them" (Lewis and Foreman 2002, 10). Lewis and Foreman found this feeling of intrusion to be common among teachers at the middle-class elementary school.

Lewis and Foreman's (2002) findings are particularly interesting be-cause educators and schools have relied on middle-class parents to actively participate in their children's schools (Kim 2009). The involvement of middle- and upper-class parents tends to be the model to which involve-ment from lower-class parents is compared. Indeed, it has been suggested that schools with larger numbers of middle-class parents are effective in part because these parents are powerful advocates for, and assets to, public schools (Cucchiara and Horvat 2009). Moreover, it is often said that the aggressive participation from middle-class parents is tolerated by teachers, whereas minority parents' involvement is generally ignored and perceived as irrational (Kim 2009; Shannon 1996).

Given the important role that schools play in forging a relationship with parents and families, we examine the extent to which schools reach out to parents from each racial group. Figure 7.2 shows the proportion of parents from each racial group that have been contacted by their child's school about various aspects related to their child's schooling. Although the measures we examine do not tap into the involvement climate created by schools, they do capture the initiative schools show in obtaining involvement from parents.

The top panel of Figure 7.2 shows that a greater proportion of white par-ents are contacted about their child's academic performance than any other racial group. Also, despite the lower school performance of Mexican youth, Mexican parents are contacted about their child's performance less than whites. When it comes to being contacted about youths' behaviors at school, a substantially greater proportion of black parents are contacted than the other racial groups. These reasons for being contacted might re-flect an attempt by schools to have parents address difficulties that their child is experiencing. The other measures for school-initiated contact cap-ture schools' efforts to involve parents more generally or to keep them in-formed about their child's schooling. Using the same 7% criteria (relative to whites) that we have employed throughout this study, schools appear to reach out less to Hispanic parents. Schools contact a smaller share of par-ents from both Hispanic groups about their child's school records, fund-raising activities, and volunteering at school. Mexicans are additionally disadvantaged in being contacted about their child's course selection and program placement for high school.

Whereas Hispanics appear to be contacted less by their child's school, parents of youth from the other two racial groups with lower achievement than whites are contacted at rates similar to whites across measures with

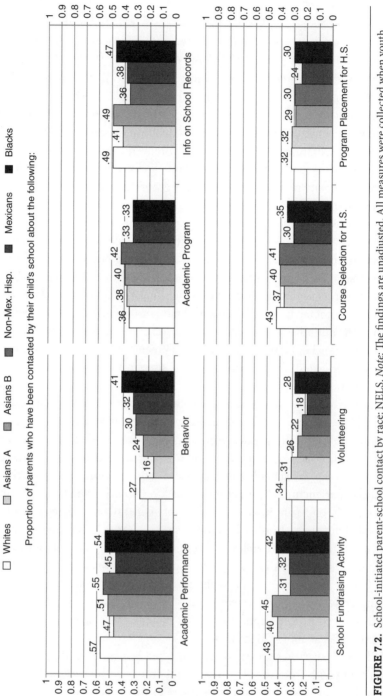

FIGURE 7.2. School-initiated parent-school contact by race: NELS. *Note:* The findings are unadjusted. All measures were collected when youth were in middle school (grade 8).

one exception for each group: Asians B are contacted less about volunteering at school, and blacks are contacted less about their child's course selection for high school. The findings in Figure 7.2 touch directly on whether minority parents are isolated from teachers and schools to a greater extent than their white counterparts. Isolation from teachers appears to be the case more for Hispanics than the other racial minority groups.

Research suggests that school personnel often have a negative perception of Hispanic parents, particularly those with an immigrant background. In a study on the academic experiences of youth from immigrant groups, Suarez-Orozco, Suarez-Orozco, and Todorova (2008) find that although teachers might be positive toward these youth, they tend to view their parents as uninterested in the child's welfare. They show that teachers' judgments of these parents are often harsh. In general, they perceive that these parents have already accomplished their primary goal of entering the United States and that they do not consider education to be a priority. The narratives provided by Suarez-Orozco and colleagues' research might help explain the patterns observed for Hispanic parents in Figure 7.2.

Parental Involvement at School by Race

As we have previously discussed, a major challenge educators face in getting parents to be more involved in schools is that parents vary in the forms of involvement prescribed by their cultural backgrounds. Therefore, what it means to be involved in children's education can differ quite dramatically across racial, ethnic, and cultural groups. To some parents, it can mean advocacy in the form of joining councils and committees, or participating in school operations and decisions. To others, it can mean serving as classroom aides, assisting teachers, or volunteering at school events. Parental involvement at home may also mean improving children's school performance through such activities as reading to children, helping with homework, or discussing current events.

Wide variation in what it means to be involved exists even in high-performing schools. In interviews with teachers from high-performing predominantly Hispanic schools in Texas, Scribner, Young, and Pedroza (1999) show that teachers consider parental involvement to be participation in school events and meetings or working as a teacher assistant or tutor. In contrast, parents define involvement as participating in home activities, such as reviewing homework assignments, reading to children, providing nurturance, and ensuring children are fed and well rested. Thus, teachers' conceptions of involvement have more to do with helping children improve academically, whereas parents conceive of involvement as a means for improving children's total well-being. The disjuncture in meaning parents and teachers assign to involvement can make it difficult to develop cooperative relationships centered on improving children's education.

We show the proportion of parents that engage in various forms of involvement for each racial group in Figure 7.3. The NELS asks parents whether they (1) are members of their school's parent-teacher organization, (2) attended a PTO meeting, (3) participated in a PTO sponsored activity, and (4) volunteered at school. The latter three forms of involvement are not conditional on being a PTO member; PTO meetings and activities are not limited to PTO members. The top panel shows that a smaller proportion of parents from Asians B and both Hispanic groups are members

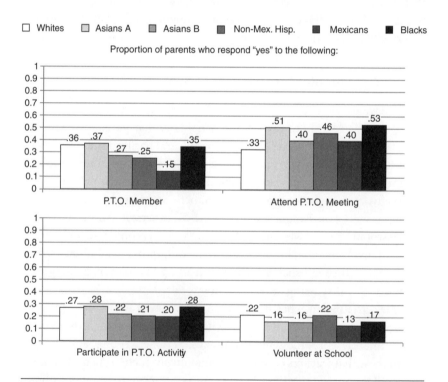

FIGURE 7.3. Parents' participation at school by race: Middle school, NELS. *Note:* The findings are unadjusted. All measures were collected when youth were in middle school (grade 8).

of their school's PTO than their white counterparts. However, whites have the lowest proportion of parents to attend PTO meetings. The bottom panel shows that parents are relatively similar with regard to their participation in PTO activities and volunteering at school with one exception: a lower proportion of Mexican parents engage in each of these forms of involvement. Finally, blacks have the highest proportion of parents who attend PTO meetings and participate in PTO activities.

The findings in Figure 7.3 are for the parents of eighth graders, who are typically thirteen-year-old students. We provide racial comparisons on another set of parental involvement activities in Figure 7.4 using the CDS, which allows us to examine patterns of involvement for parents of younger children. The top panel shows that for youth between the ages of 4 and 8 (those who were in elementary school during CDS-II), a substantially greater proportion of white parents volunteer at school and attend school events than parents from the racial minority groups (Asians are excluded because of insufficient sample size). However, Hispanics have the greatest proportion of parents to observe their child's class and meet with the parent-teacher association at their child's school. White and black parents are relatively similar on these forms of involvement.

The bottom panel of Figure 7.4 shows that the patterns observed in the top panel are similar for youth between the ages of 9 and 12. Specifically, whites still maintain an advantage in terms of volunteering at school and of attending school events, though their rate of volunteering is lower than the rate observed in the top panel. The proportion of parents who attend school events is substantially higher than observed in the top panel for the racial minority groups. Hispanics have the highest proportion of parents who observed their child's class, whereas the proportion of parents that met with the PTA is similar across race. Figures 7.3 and 7.4 suggest that parental involvement at school is greatest for younger children, and that most parents are not involved at school (regardless of race), as evidenced by the prevalence of proportions below 50% across racial groups.

Most of the measures in Figures 7.3 and 7.4 capture forms of involvement that allow parents to interact with other parents rather than just with teachers. These forms of involvement are important because they offer parents avenues for participation at schools that do not require direct one-on-one interaction with teachers. In addition to low socioeconomic status, language barriers, job constraints, and low education levels, studies have shown that discomfort towards direct contact with school staff and

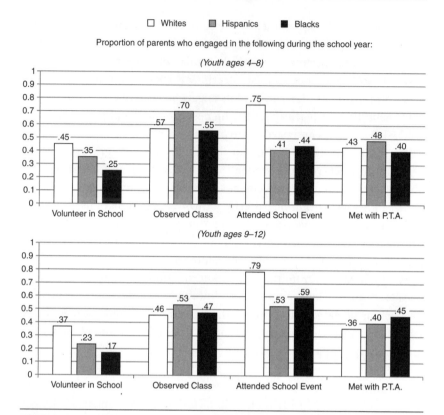

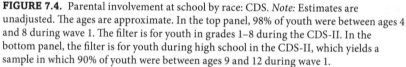

FIGURE 7.4. Parental involvement at school by race: CDS. *Note:* Estimates are unadjusted. The ages are approximate. In the top panel, 98% of youth were between ages 4 and 8 during wave 1. The filter is for youth in grades 1–8 during the CDS-II. In the bottom panel, the filter is for youth during high school in the CDS-II, which yields a sample in which 90% of youth were between ages 9 and 12 during wave 1.

personnel is a major barrier preventing some minority parents from being involved at their children's schools (Daniel-White 2002; Fantuzzo, Tighe, and Childs 2000; Grolnick et al. 1997; Gutman and McLoyd 2000).

The discomfort felt by racial minorities in their interactions with teachers and school personnel has been documented in previous studies. In interviews with Hispanic parents and parents in two low-income Anglo neighborhoods, Finders and Lewis (1994) find that for many parents, their own experiences with education create a mistrust which prevents them from fully participating at their children's school. One father spoke of the lack of regard shown for his attendance years ago. He ultimately dropped out of school and cited his experience as a main reason he does not feel confident at his son's school. The authors point out that this father's reluctance to participate at school should not be interpreted as a lack of concern about his son's education. Rather, schools need to hear the concerns of parents whose voices are rarely heard.

Studies on black parents also lend credence to the notion that discomfort can serve as a barrier to parental involvement at school. Black parents often express a high interest in their children's education but lack the necessary conditions to support their involvement (Chavkin and Williams 1993). Studies suggest that black parents' perceptions of racism are negatively related to school involvement, perhaps because these perceptions dissuade some black parents from engaging in relations with teachers or staff or from attending school events (McKay et al. 2003). McKay and colleagues (2003) suggest that interventions aimed at increasing parental involvement at home and at school for blacks need to explore associations between perceptions of racism and opportunities for involvement at school.

The discomfort felt by parents from racial minority groups can occur for several reasons. The parent-teacher dyad is imbued with a power dynamic that can be intimidating for some minority groups. Addi-Raccah and Ainhoren's (2009) research probes teachers' attitudes toward parental involvement in schools and suggests that whereas teachers are empowered to be involved in school processes and policy, interactions with parents present an opportunity for challenges to their professional position and for redesigning their work. Teachers are required to be responsive to their parents' concerns, and parents are encouraged by schools and policy makers to be active participants in school affairs. Some argue that this empowerment has intensified conflicts between parents and teachers (Lieberman and Miller 1999), which can create a context in which racial minorities do not feel comfortable.

Another factor that might contribute to this discomfort is the cultural discontinuity between Hispanic and black families and the institutionalized structure of schools, which value cultural norms of "mainstream" white middle-class society. Numerous studies show that minority groups experience greater difficulty in converting cultural resources into cultural capital in schools (Lareau and Horvat 1999; Roscigno and Ainsworth-Darnell 1999). Lareau and Horvat (1999) find that the possession and activation of capital (both social and cultural) in schools vary by race. As such, ethnic minorities face greater challenges in gaining social inclusion in school settings.

This cultural discontinuity seems to be most compromising for the academic success of Hispanics and blacks. Fordham (1988, 1996) notes that the collective ethos held by the black fictive kinship system—a kinship-like connection and sense of peoplehood or collective social identity resulting from similar social, political, and/or economic status—conflicts with the individualistic ethos sanctioned by the school context. Fordham (1988, 55) states that black children are forced to "unlearn or, at least, to modify their own culturally sanctioned interactional and behavioral styles and adopt those styles rewarded in the school context if they wish to achieve academic success." The same can be said for many Hispanic parents, for whom the concept of "familism," or *familismo*—having foremost devotion to the welfare of the family—has held prominence because it is thought to underlie many parenting decisions (Esparza and Sanchez 2008). This core cultural value cultivates the desire to maintain strong family bonds, creates a deep feeling of loyalty to the family, and engenders strong obligation to the family above the self.

Cultural discontinuity also applies to many Asian groups. Studies have shown that Asian children are often raised to honor their parents and family by succeeding in school (Desimone 1999; Mau 1997). These familial obligations, which are tied to school success, inevitably drive how parents structure the child's learning environment and their involvement in the child's schooling. An interesting disconnect seems to be present in Asian families regarding the involvement-achievement link in that Asian parents tend to be less involved on most involvement indicators, yet their children tend to have high achievement. What appears to be different about Asians is that their efficacy in parenting is judged by how well their children do in school rather than by their actual levels of involvement.

Given the findings from previous studies that document the discomfort in schools felt by most parents from racial minority groups, it is reasonable to expect that as a group, these parents will be less assertive in their involvement with schools. We examine this supposition in Figure 7.5, which shows the proportion of parents from each racial group that are assertive with regard to their child's teacher using the CDS. We elicit the term "assertive" to refer to efforts made by parents prior to the start of the school year to obtain information on their child's teacher, to meet personally with their child's teacher, or to request that their child be taught by a particular teacher. Whereas the top panel shows findings for parents with children ages 4–8, the bottom panel shows the findings for parents of slightly older children (ages 9–12).

Both panels in Figure 7.5 show that whites have the highest proportion of parents who obtain information about their child's teacher and request a particular teacher for their child. On the former measure, four-fifths of white parents obtain information about teachers compared to a little more than two-thirds of Hispanic and black parents. Only 20% of white parents request a particular teacher for their child, and the proportions on this measure are substantially lower for parents from the racial minority groups. This pattern is the same in both panels. However, a greater proportion of Hispanics and blacks met with their child's teacher prior to the start of the school year compared to whites for both the younger and older samples. Interestingly, meeting the teacher seems to be less important for white,

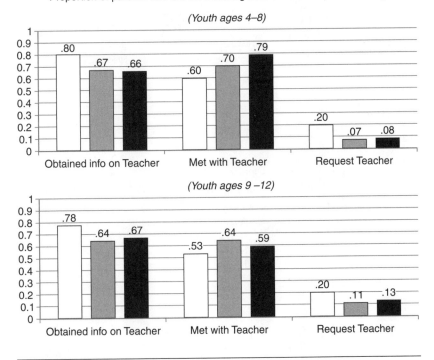

FIGURE 7.5. Parents' assertiveness regarding teachers by race: CDS. *Note:* Estimates are unadjusted. The ages are approximate. In the top panel 98% of youth were between ages 4 and 8 during wave 1. The filter is for youth in grades 1–8 during the CDS-II. In the bottom panel, the filter is for youth during high school in the CDS-II, which yields a sample in which 90% of youth were between ages 9 and 12 during wave 1.

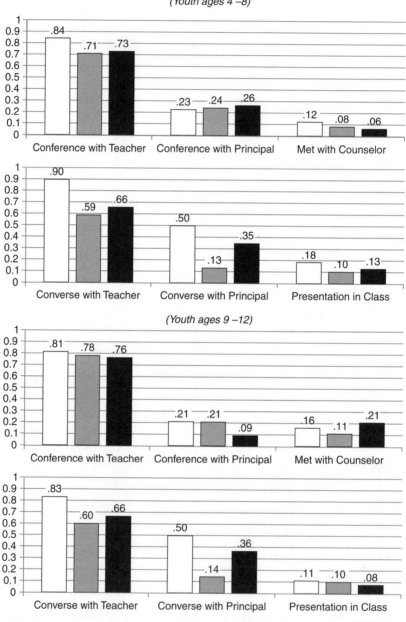

FIGURE 7.6. Parental involvement at school by race: Assertive, CDS. *Note:* Estimates are unadjusted. The ages are approximate. In the top panel 98% of youth were between ages 4 and 8 during wave 1. The filter is for youth in grades 1–8 during the CDS-II. In the bottom panel, the filter is for youth during high school in the CDS-II, which yields a sample in which 90% of youth were between ages 9 and 12 during wave 1.

Hispanic, and black parents of 9–12 year olds than their younger counterparts in the top panel.

These findings should not be viewed as identifying whether parents either care or do not care about their child's education. Parents vary in the ways they choose to participate as a result of differences in economic circumstances, parental education, and perspectives on the roles of parents and teachers as educators. As a quick example, parents who work full-time and/or do not have much flexibility in their jobs may not participate as much at school. Stay-at-home parents, on the other hand, will have greater opportunity for school involvement, and some may even view school involvement as part of their role as a stay-at-home parent. A limitation of these measures is that the precise nature of the visit cannot be ascertained. They do not tell us, for instance, whether a meeting with a teacher was to help a child who is struggling academically or if parents were simply being proactive in their child's schooling.

We compare the racial groups on another set of assertive forms of parental involvement in Figure 7.6. The first two panels show the levels of involvement across racial groups for parents with young children (ages 4–8). Larger proportions of white parents report that they communicate with their child's teacher in the form of a conference or during informal conversation than their Hispanic and black counterparts. The racial groups are similar with regard to holding a conference with the school principal and meeting with the school counselor. A greater share of white parents engaged in informal conversation with the principal of their children's school than the other racial groups. The bottom panel shows that the patterns for the parents of slightly older youth are relatively similar to those in the top panel. The primary exception is that the rates at which parents have a conference with teachers are similar across the racial groups.

Chapter Summary

Our analyses reveal substantial differences by race in parents' school involvement behaviors. This contrasts with findings from Chapter 5, which indicate that minority and nonminority parents are fairly similar in the ways they are involved at home. It appears that the comparatively lower school involvement of minority parents that educators have long observed is reflected in the national data sets we explored.

We summarize the findings from this chapter in Table 7.1. The table highlights that parents of youth from racial groups with an achievement

TABLE 7.1. Parental measures for which meaningful racial differences exist

Parental measure	Substantial difference by race	Meaningful disadvantage in level of involvement relative to whites[a]			
		Asian B	Non-Mexican Hispanic	Mexican	Black
NELS					
Parent-initiated contact					
Academic performance	No	No	No	No	No
Behavior	**Yes**	No	No	yes	yes
Academic program	No	No	No	No	No
Information on school records	**Yes**	No	yes	yes	No
School fund-raising activity	No	No	No	No	No
Volunteering	**Yes**	No	No	yes	No
School-initiated contact					
Academic performance	**Yes**	No	No	yes	No
Behavior	**Yes**	No	No	No	yes
Academic program	No	No	No	No	No
Information on school records	**Yes**	No	yes	yes	No
School fund-raising activity	**Yes**	No	yes	yes	No
Volunteering	**Yes**	yes	yes	yes	No
Course selection for high school	**Yes**	No	No	yes	yes
Program placement for high school	**Yes**	No	No	yes	No
Participation at school					
Parent-teacher org. (PTO) member	**Yes**	yes	yes	yes	No
Attend PTO meeting	No	No	No	No	No
Participate in PTO activity	No	No	No	No	No
Volunteer at school	**Yes**	No	No	yes	No

CDS	Younger		Older	
	Hispanic	**Black**	**Hispanic**	**Black**
Involvement at school				
Volunteer at school	**Yes**	Yes	Yes	Yes
Observed class	No	No	No	No
Attended school event(s)	**Yes**	Yes	Yes	Yes
Met with parent-teacher assoc.	No	No	No	No
Assertiveness with teachers				
Obtained information on teacher	**Yes**	Yes	Yes	Yes
Met with teacher	No	No	No	No
Requested teacher	**Yes**	Yes	Yes	Yes
Involvement at school: Assertiveness				
Conference with teacher	**Yes**	Yes	No	No
Conference with principal	**Yes**	No	No	Yes
Converse with teacher	**Yes**	Yes	Yes	Yes
Converse with principal	**Yes**	Yes	Yes	Yes
Met with counselor	No	No	No	No
Presented to class	**Yes**	No	No	No

Note: Because our interest is in identifying the parental factors that could potentially explain low achievement relative to whites, we present only the groups that have lower achievement than whites. Therefore, Asians A are excluded from the NELS, and Asians are excluded from the CDS.

a. By "meaningful difference," we do not mean "significant." We made reasonable assessments regarding which factors could contribute to explaining the achievement gap for each group if held constant based on the racial differences observed in Figures 7.1 to 7.6.

disadvantage relative to whites are lower on twenty-one of the thirty-one measures of school involvement compared to white parents. For the 18 parental involvement measures from the NELS, Mexican parents appear to have the lowest levels of involvement, as they have a substantially lower rate of involvement than whites on the most factors (11), followed by non-Mexican Hispanics (5), blacks (only 3) and Asians B (only 2). The differences are particularly notable for measures of school-initiated contact in the NELS and assertive forms of involvement in the CDS. The disadvantages for minority parents on the former should not be considered as lower involvement, however; they reflect that schools seem to reach out to minority parents less than they do to white parents.

Although racial differences exist on many measures of parental involvement at school examined in this chapter, the findings do not show large racial variations in the proportion of parents that are involved in their children's schools. This observation is surprising given that numerous studies, both qualitative and quantitative, suggest that minority parents are more isolated from their children's schools. Nevertheless, to the extent that these measures are important for improving children's academic outcomes, finding solutions for lower minority participation could prove important for reducing achievement gaps.

The finding that meaningful racial differences exist on most measures for parental involvement at school could lead one to expect that racial differences exist among parents in their beliefs about the quality of education their children are receiving. We examine whether this supposition is the case using four outcomes that measure parents' perceptions of the quality of their eighth-grade child's school. The results for this analysis are displayed in Figure 7.7. The findings show that parents are astonishingly similar in the belief that their children are receiving a quality education. This congruity of belief could signal that minority parents, whose children are more likely to be in lower quality schools, have less awareness of the curricular rigor of their children's schools. Another explanation could be that some minority parents have blind faith in the school's ability to properly educate children.

The racial variation we observed may relate to the fact that parent-school involvement is largely dependent on the relationship parents have with schools and teachers. At present, this relationship is often inefficient, which can be a source for variation among racial groups in their school-involvement behaviors. Lareau (2000) notes that educators frequently behave as if there is only one proper form of parental involvement in school. In two elementary

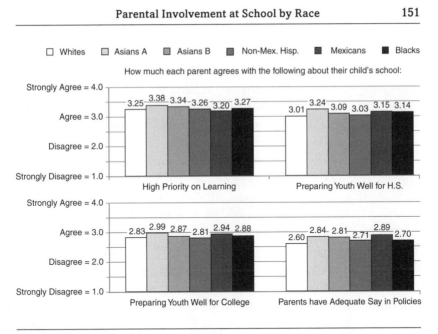

FIGURE 7.7. Parents' perceptions of the quality of youths' school by race: NELS. *Note:* The findings are unadjusted. All measures were collected when youth were in middle school (grade 8).

schools that differed considerably in school resources, she found that educators in both schools promoted only one type of family-school relationship. Parents may wish to be involved at school but lack clarity on how to effectively participate. Finders and Lewis (1994) found that many parents wanted teachers to clarify exactly how they can help. This uncertainty led many parents to feel that they were not a critical part of their children's education. This sentiment could lead parents to be less involved by reducing their own sense of self-efficacy, or the degree to which they believe their involvement can positively impact their child's education.

Not all parents are ready, willing, or able to serve as teacher aides at school (volunteering in the classroom) or participate in school–decision making processes. Yet those who choose not to be involved in ways the school or teachers deem appropriate often face sanctions. Some have pointed out that the institutional perspective makes implicit judgments regarding parents who either do not participate or are ineffective in the ways they are involved at school. The way nonparticipating parents are viewed remains based on a deficit model (Finders and Lewis 1994). Parents who provide little to no involvement in school activities tend to be viewed as impediments to their children's academic success. This view of parents could lead teachers to invest less time and energy in encouraging these parents to participate. One could imagine that teachers give up on parents who are perceived as not pulling their weight. In fact, the idea that teachers prefer to invest their efforts to involve those parents who already have high levels of involvement is supported by previous research (Epstein 1987).

So often in research we base our discussion of parent-teacher relationships on what educators can do to encourage parents to support institutional agendas. This "institutional perspective" of parental involvement places great importance on creating a two-party system of educators—teachers being one and parents the other. Each party is expected to bring their unique knowledge of children and their skills to the enterprise of educating students. Teachers can utilize their professional wisdom to appraise students' learning receptivity; parents can rely on their life experience as well as the accumulated knowledge of their child to make appraisals regarding his/her learning responsiveness. It is clear that the parent-teacher partnership could be reformed to encourage more equitable participation among parents of all racial groups. Nonetheless, to say that schools are correct to be concerned about minority participation would require that we know something about school involvement's role in affecting academic outcomes for these groups. Seeking this knowledge is the logical next step, which we pursue in the next chapter.

— 8 —

Implications of Parental Involvement at School by Race

Throughout this book, we have discussed that advocates of school involvement believe that students gain in academic development when their parents show that they value education on a regular basis. Parent involvement at school has been identified as a key promoter of achievement, and as De Carvalho (2001) notes, educational policy has turned previously informal and limited parental involvement into a mandate. We show in Chapters 2 and 7 that not all parents will be involved with school-related activities to the same extent. But we argue that an important question still remains: Which forms of parental involvement at school are associated with increases in children's achievement for each major racial group within the United States? This chapter is designed to discover whether parents' school involvement is associated with increases in achievement across racial groups.

In this chapter, we also examine whether parental involvement is a potential source for reducing racial achievement disparities, an issue that has received surprisingly little attention from scholars, yet is incredibly important within the context of education. Specifically, we estimate whether a greater share of racial achievement gaps for each group (relative to whites) can be attributed to parental involvement or basic socioeconomic factors. In combination with the parental involvement measures at home assessed in Chapters 5 and 6, this analysis can be informative on several fronts. In particular, it allows us to estimate if parental involvement—whether at home, school, or both—matters more for the racial achievement gap than the socioeconomic resources parents possess.

Previous Research

Previous studies suggest that parents who participate at school tend to enhance their children's achievement. Epstein (1985) found that when teachers see parents who are more involved, they take more time with these children in developing their skills. Pomerantz, Moorman, and Litwack (2007) note that parental involvement at school is important for enhancing children's academic motivation. Children receive "motivational resources" (e.g., intrinsic reasons for pursuing academics, a sense of control over academic performance, positive perceptions of academic competence) from their parents' involvement at school, which fosters their school engagement.

A number of national studies have sought to determine what forms of parental activities at school promote child success. These studies have examined involvement at school for children of different racial/ethnic groups (d'Ailly 2003; Hill and Craft 2003), and at various stages of schooling (Grolnick and Slowiaczek 1994; Stevenson and Baker 1987). However, findings thus far have resulted in few concrete answers. Instead, they vary widely depending on the stage of schooling, the types of parental activities being examined, and the characteristics of parents and children.

For example, Gutman and Eccles (1999) find that parents' school involvement (e.g., attend open houses, volunteering in the classroom) influences grades among European and African American children two years later, controlling for earlier grades. Hill and Craft (2003) find that among middle-class African American families, increased school involvement predicts grades for kindergartners. However, in a study using a large sample of high school students, Steinberg, Dornbusch, and Brown (1992) find that parent-school involvement improves the academic performance of Asian, white, and Hispanic students, but has no effect on black students. Comer (1988) finds that black parents who are active participants at their children's schools are successful in improving academic achievement, but this effect applies to low-income black families with elementary school children, which suggests a more nuanced effect of school involvement within black families. Armor and colleagues (1976) report that parents who are active school participants contribute to large achievement gains for black students, but not Mexican American students. Thus, it is unclear which forms of parental involvement at school are beneficial for different racial groups. We address this issue in the following section by replicating the analysis we conducted in Chapter 4 by race.

Parental Involvement at School and Achievement by Race

We report the findings from our first set of analyses of the link between parental involvement at school and achievement for each racial group in estimate graphs in Figure 8.1, which shows the gains or losses in achievement associated with each form of parental involvement from the NELS examined in Chapter 7. Three general patterns emerge. First, there does not seem to be overwhelming support for the notion that parent-initiated contact of schools is beneficial for achievement. Of the 108 estimates, only 10 are significant and positive, half of which are for reading, three for math, and two for grades. Blacks account for the bulk of these estimates, as black youth appear to benefit in reading when their parents contact schools about their behavior, school programs, school records, and volunteering. Non-Mexican Hispanics benefit in reading and grades when their parents contact schools about volunteering, and in grades when the contact is about fund-raising. White youth appear to experience gains in math when their parents contact schools about fund-raising and volunteering. The second major pattern is that no form of involvement in Figure 8.1 is associated with increases in achievement for Asians or Mexican American youth. Finally, twice as many estimates are negative (21), and the vast majority are not related to achievement. Even if the measures are combined into a scale of the weighted sum of all measures, the findings remain the same; the scale was positively associated with achievement only for blacks in reading.

Perhaps the reason that most of the findings in Figure 8.1 do not show many positive connections between parental involvement and achievement is because the measures capture parent-school contact initiated by parents. Perhaps more positive estimates could emerge if we employ measures that capture contact initiated by schools. We examined this possibility and display those results in Figure 8.2. The findings for school-initiated parent-school contact are substantively similar to those based on parent-initiated contact shown in Figure 8.1. Specifically, the vast majority of estimates are not positively associated with gains in achievement; only 17 of 144 estimates are positive. Most of these estimates are for whites (9) and blacks (5). White youth experience gains in all three forms of achievement when their parents are contacted by schools about fund-raising and volunteering, and they appear to benefit in grades when schools contact their parents about school programs and in math when the contact concerns school records and course selection.

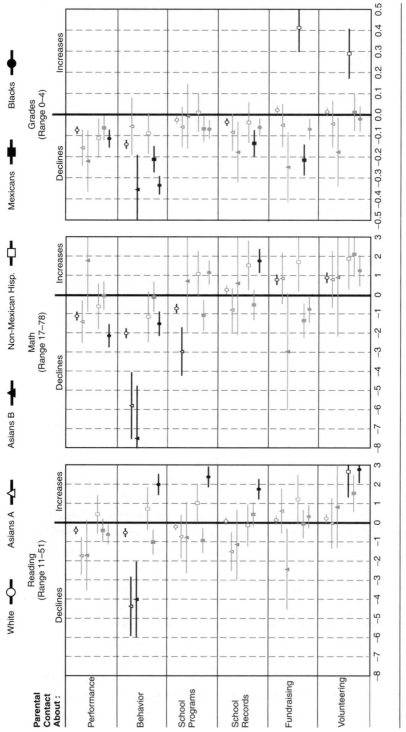

FIGURE 8.1. Gains in achievement associated with parent-initiated contact with schools by race: NELS. *Note:* Bold estimates are significant at the .05 level. Estimates account for parents' education, household income, family structure, youths' sex, and prior achievement/grades. Achievement was assessed when youth were in grade 12, and the parenting measures were assessed prior to the youth entering high school (grade 8). Every 1-point change corresponds to a percentage change of 3 in reading and 2 in math relative to the mean. For grades, a 0.1 change corresponds to a 5% change relative to the mean.

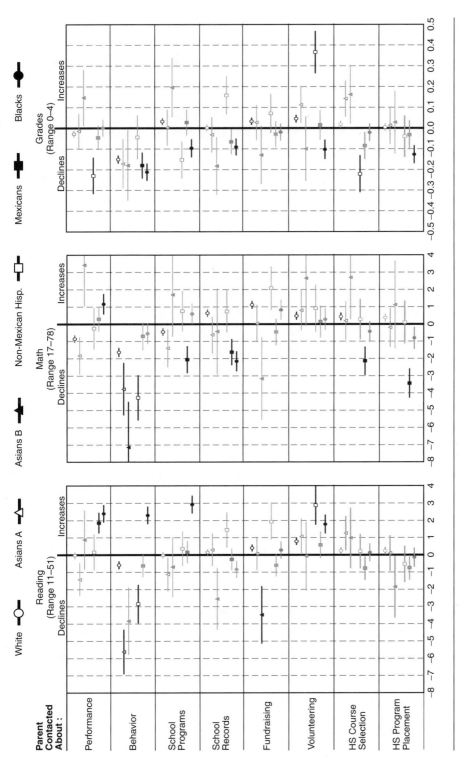

FIGURE 8.2. Gains in achievement associated with school-initiated contact of parents by race: NELS.

With regard to black youth, school-initiated contact about their performance is associated with increases in reading and math, and their reading
appears to increase when their parents are contacted about their behavior,
school programs, and volunteering. The final three positive estimates are
for non-Mexican Hispanics, who experience gains in reading and grades
when their parents are contacted about volunteering, and Mexican American youth benefit in reading when their parents are contacted about their
performance. Similar to the findings in Figure 8.1, there are more negative
estimates (24), and most of the estimates are not significant. Thus, Figures
8.1 and 8.2 suggest that parent-school contact—whether initiated by parents or schools—is associated with increases in achievement in only a
small number of cases, and in most cases, is unrelated to achievement.

In Figure 8.3, we report the findings for analysis on the implication of
parents' engagement with schools through parent-teacher organization and
volunteering for youths' achievement. There are a total of twelve positive
estimates, six of which correspond to whites and five that correspond to
blacks. For whites, all three PTO-related measures—whether parents are
members, attend meetings, or attend activities—are associated with increases in math, and the latter two are associated with increases in reading.
Black youth appear to experience increases in reading and math when their
parents are members of the PTO and when they attend PTO meetings. They
also seem to benefit in reading, along with Mexican youth, when their parents volunteer at school. In contrast to the previous set of analyses for parent-
school contact, the set of measures in Figure 8.3 yield more positive (12)
than negative (3) estimates. However, similar to the findings for the measures of parent-school contact, the majority of estimates (57, or 79%) are not
significant. Furthermore, also similar to the previous results in this chapter,
most of the significant estimates appear to be limited to whites and blacks.

We determine whether the link between parental involvement at school
and achievement is similar at earlier stages of schooling using the CDS.
These findings are reported in Figure 8.4 for whites, Hispanics, and blacks.
In general, the results in the top panel for youth in grades 1–5 are mixed;
although three-fourths of the estimates are significant, an equal number
of these estimates are positive and negative (9). Also, some of the effect
sizes are rather large, ranging from a 5 to 27% change in achievement. Parents' attendance of school events is associated with increases in both reading
and math for whites and Hispanics. These groups also benefit in reading
(and in the case of Hispanics, also math) when their parents observe their
class. For black youth, only one measure is associated with increases in

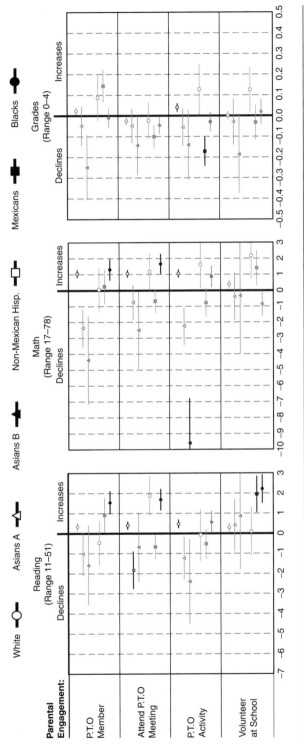

FIGURE 8.3. Gains in achievement associated with parental engagement with schools by race: NELS. *Note:* Bold estimates are significant at the .05 level. Estimates account for parents' education, household income, family structure, youths' sex, and prior achievement/grades. Achievement was assessed when youth were in grade 12, and the parenting measures were assessed prior to the youth entering high school (grade 8). Every 1-point change corresponds to a percentage change of 3 in reading and 2 in math relative to the mean. For grades, a 0.1 change corresponds to a 5% change relative to the mean.

achievement, as they appear to benefit in reading and math when their parents volunteer at school.

In the bottom panel of Figure 8.4, we report the results for the older subsample. The measures of parental involvement for this subsample were assessed when youth were in elementary and middle school. Similar to the results for the younger subsample, the findings are mixed. For white youth, with the exception of PTA meetings, which is associated with increases in reading and math, the other three measures are associated with declines

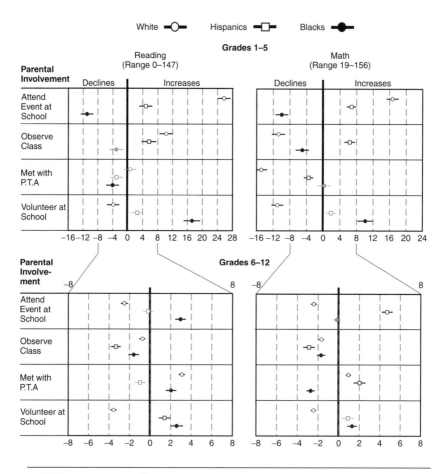

FIGURE 8.4. Gains in achievement associated with parental involvement at school by race: CDS. *Note:* Bold estimates are significant at the .05 level. Estimates account for parents' education, household income, family structure, youths' sex, grade in school, and prior achievement. The findings for Hispanics in the younger subsample do not account for prior achievement. Achievement was assessed from CDS-II, and the parenting measures were obtained from CDS-I. Every 1-point change corresponds roughly to a 1% change in reading and math relative to their respective means.

in both forms of achievement. Parents' observing their child's classrooms is associated with declines in achievement for all three groups. Another consistent pattern in Figure 8.4 is that black youth appear to benefit in both forms of achievement when their parents volunteer at school. This pattern is the case for both the younger and older subsamples, and for black youth in reading in the NELS, which suggests that parental volunteering is beneficial for black youth throughout their schooling careers.

In Figure 8.5, we show findings for the assessment of the link between parents' assertiveness with teachers and achievement. The top panel suggests that the more active forms of assertiveness—meeting with teachers and requesting particular teachers—are associated with higher achievement for more youth within the younger subsample than the more passive form

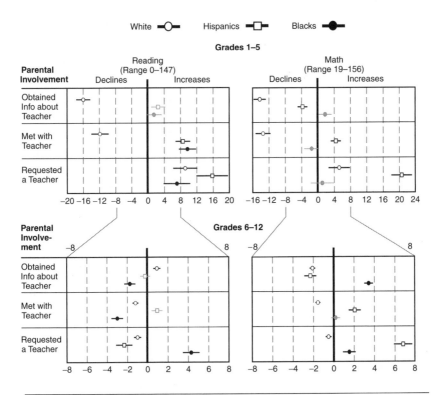

FIGURE 8.5. Gains in achievement associated with parents' assertiveness with teachers by race: CDS. *Note:* Bold estimates are significant at the .05 level. Estimates account for parents' education, household income, family structure, youths' sex, grade in school, and prior achievement. The findings for Hispanics in the younger subsample do not account for prior achievement. Achievement was assessed from CDS-II, and the parenting measures were obtained from CDS-I. Every 1-point change corresponds roughly to a 1% change in reading and math relative to their respective means.

of assertiveness—obtain information about the teacher. Whereas obtaining information about teachers is not related to increases in achievement for any group, parents' requesting a particular teacher appears to lead to increases in reading for all three groups, and in math for two of the three groups. The bottom panel of Figure 8.5 shows that the patterns observed for the younger subsample are not present for older youth. There are only two positive estimates for reading achievement—whites seem to benefit when their parents obtain information about their teachers, and blacks seem to benefit when their parents request a teacher. Hispanics benefit in math from the two active forms of parental assertiveness with teachers. Finally, there are a greater number of negative estimates for these measures, which suggests that the benefits to achievement of parents' assertiveness with teachers decline as youth become older.

In Figure 8.6, we consider more measures of parental involvement that require parents to be assertive through formal conferences and casual conversation with key school personnel—teachers and principals. There are two consistent patterns in the top panel. Specifically, black youth experience gains in achievement with parent-teacher and parent-principal interaction, and the achievement for white youth appears to be negatively associated with parent-principal interaction. Furthermore, some of the estimated effect sizes are substantial. For example, whereas the change in reading for blacks ranges from 13 to 24%, the change in math for whites ranges from 20 to 32%. However, the findings for the older subsample in the bottom panel are quite different. Most of the estimates are negative for both reading and math. There are only two positive estimates for reading (converse with teachers for blacks and converse with principal for Hispanics) and three for math (conference with principal for Hispanics, and converse with principal for whites and blacks). Thus, similar to the previous set of analyses, the benefits of parental involvement appear to be greater for younger children and to become more tempered as they become older.

We present the findings for the final set of parental involvement measures in Figure 8.7, which capture whether parents met with the school counselor and presented in their child's class. The top panel shows that among the younger subsample, Hispanics are the only group who benefit from both measures in both forms of achievement. In contrast, both measures are associated with declines in both forms of achievement for black youth. There is no discernible pattern for whites. The findings for older youth in the bottom panel show that most of the estimates for reading are negative. Regarding math, achievement is higher for youth whose parents

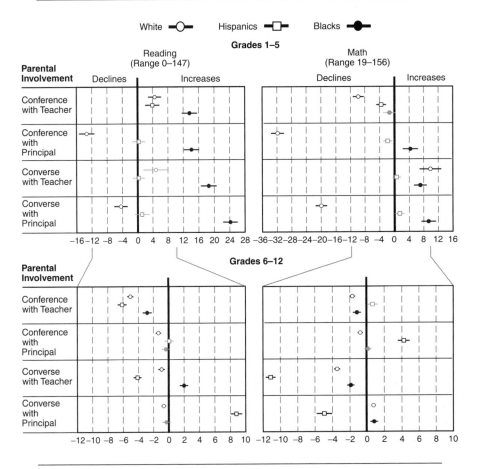

FIGURE 8.6. Gains in achievement associated with parent-teacher interaction by race: CDS. *Note:* Bold estimates are significant at the .05 level. Estimates account for parents' education, household income, family structure, youths' sex, grade in school, and prior achievement. The findings for Hispanics in the younger subsample do not account for prior achievement. Achievement was assessed from CDS-II, and the parenting measures were obtained from CDS-I. Every 1-point change corresponds roughly to a 1% change in reading and math relative to their respective means.

have met with the school counselor than for those whose parents have not for all three groups, and achievement appears to be greater for black youth whose parents have presented in class than their counterparts whose parents have not presented in class.

There is currently no consensus on the relationship between parental involvement at school and children's achievement. The abundance of studies conducted on this topic has produced incredibly mixed results. In a report

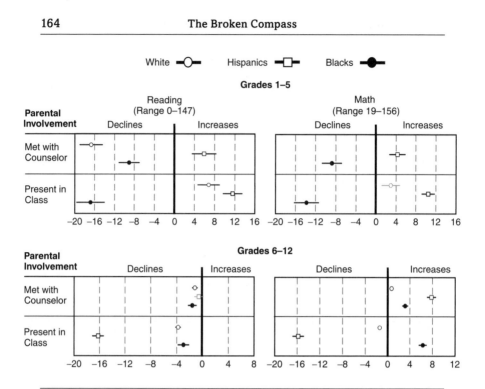

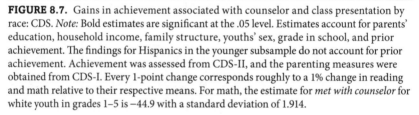

FIGURE 8.7. Gains in achievement associated with counselor and class presentation by race: CDS. *Note:* Bold estimates are significant at the .05 level. Estimates account for parents' education, household income, family structure, youths' sex, grade in school, and prior achievement. The findings for Hispanics in the younger subsample do not account for prior achievement. Achievement was assessed from CDS-II, and the parenting measures were obtained from CDS-I. Every 1-point change corresponds roughly to a 1% change in reading and math relative to their respective means. For math, the estimate for *met with counselor* for white youth in grades 1–5 is −44.9 with a standard deviation of 1.914.

summarizing the involvement-achievement link in prior studies, Epstein (1987) claims that there is clear evidence that parental encouragement, activities, interest, and parental participation in schools and classrooms positively influence achievement, even after the student's ability and family socioeconomic status are taken into account. Several subsequent studies support this claim, illustrating that parents' school participation enhances children's academic performance (Fehrmann, Keith, and Reimers 1987; Useem 1992). For example, attendance at PTA meetings is shown to be positively associated with achievement outcomes (Desimone 1999). Yet, other research studies suggest there is sufficient reason to be guarded about these conclusions. Some reports find no direct link between parents' participation and children's educational outcomes (Baker and Soden 1998; Miedel and Reynolds 1999).

Although our results seem incredibly mixed, our findings provide insight into why such confusion exists about the link between parental involvement and achievement within the literature. Different studies use different measures of parental involvement. It is possible to conduct a study using forms of parental involvement that show minimal or no connection to achievement or vice versa. For example, our finding on the implications of parent-school contact for achievement for whites differs based on whether the contact is initiated by parents (Figure 8.1) or by the school (Figure 8.2). This difference could be the case even if we employed all the measures of parental involvement but used a different measure of achievement. We would report drastically different results if our study were limited to blacks and reading achievement versus grades; according to the findings for blacks in Figure 8.1, parental involvement is consequential to achievement for reading but not grades. Likewise, our findings would be different had we focused exclusively on Hispanics during adolescence (Figures 8.1, 8.2, and 8.3) versus grade school (Figures 8.4 through 8.7).

Our point is that the link between parental involvement and achievement varies widely based on the measures of parental involvement, the racial group, stage of schooling, and the measure of achievement. Thus, there is a major benefit of our extensive examination of parental involvement in which we use many measures of parental involvement for all the major racial groups across the K–12 span; ironically, in producing such varied results, we provide some clarity to the literature about why the findings are so mixed. In the next section, we examine the implication that parental involvement has for academic racial disparities, which has increasingly become the focus of policy discussions.

The Racial Achievement Gap

Perhaps the biggest problem facing educators within the United States is the racial achievement gap. The complexity of the problem becomes apparent when one considers the wide range of theories that have been proposed to explain the gap. Most of the attention, however, has been directed toward the black-white achievement gap. One of the earliest explanations given for this gap was racial differences in genetics (Herrnstein and Murray 1994; Jensen 1969); blacks were posited to be genetically inferior. However, this theory suffers from a lack of convincing empirical evidence (for a review, see Dickens 2005; Fischer et al. 1996; Nisbett 1998).[1]

Explanations for racial differences in achievement that extend beyond blacks and whites are those that draw on socioeconomic factors. Structural transformations of the U.S. economy in areas in which ethnic minorities tend to live has led to concentrated poverty within these segregated contexts. In particular, the out-migration of middle-class residents from urban areas has resulted in the uneven distribution of racial groups across spatial units within large geographic areas (i.e., segregation) (Massey and Denton 1993). Several studies show that academic achievement can be compromised by exposure to poverty (Brooks-Gunn, Klebanov, and Duncan 1996; Duncan, Brooks-Gunn, and Klebanov 1994). Wilson (1987, 1996) and Massey and Denton (1993) note that disadvantaged communities lack the resources to adequately sustain neighborhood institutions and public services and are characterized by persistent joblessness, which contributes to making high-poverty areas breeding places for crime, violence, substance abuse, and sexual promiscuity. These conditions inhibit educational skills, thereby depressing school achievement, which in turn discourages teachers. Wilson (1987, 57) argues that "a vicious cycle is perpetuated through family, through the community, and through the schools." In contrast, neighborhoods where most adults have steady employment foster behaviors and attitudes conducive to success in both school and work (Wilson 1987).

As discussed in Chapter 5, some researchers have posited that the disadvantaged socioeconomic conditions historically experienced by most Hispanics and blacks has led to a culture of poverty (Lewis 1961; Moynihan 1965), characterized by an oppositional culture resistant to academic goals (Ogbu 1978). This theory even extends to parents, who are posited to be important conduits through which oppositional norms are transmitted to youth (Mickelson 1990; Ogbu 1978). The notion that the racial achievement gap persists because Hispanics and blacks undervalue education remains popular among educators and policy makers. However, an extensive body of evidence challenges this explanation (for an extensive review, see Harris 2011).

The very standard by which the racial achievement gap is assessed—standardized tests—has been invoked as a factor that contributes to the gap. Specifically, several scholars note that standardized tests are racially biased (Kozol 2000; Meier 2000; Sacks 1999). Lucas (2008) shows that the procedures involved in the construction of some admission exams actually maintain the existing patterns of inequality. In general, tests administered by the Educational Testing Service (ETS), such as the SAT and

GRE—two of the most widely used admissions tests—are designed to correlate very strongly with one another, and questions selected for inclusion are expected to parallel the outcomes of the test overall. For example, questions for which a greater percentage of low scorers (typically Hispanics and blacks) respond correctly relative to high scorers (typically whites and Asians) are regarded as flawed and excluded from official versions of the test. Although race is not explicitly considered, racially disparate scores drive question selection. Thus, racially disparate test results are maintained by an internally reinforcing cycle (Lucas 2008; Rosner 2003).

Also, as we have discussed throughout this book, even schools have been criticized for perpetuating the achievement gap. Social reproduction theorists argue that existing patterns of inequality persist because schools are structured to reproduce the current social order. This line of reasoning is often attributed to Bowles and Gintis (1976) and Bourdieu and Passeron (1977), who argue that schools socialize children to persist in their social class of origin. Bowles and Gintis (1976, 132) note that whereas disadvantaged minority groups attend schools that "emphasize behavioral control and rule following . . . schools in well-to-do suburbs employ relatively open systems that favor greater student participation, less direct supervision, more electives and in general a value system stressing internalized standards of control."

Several studies reveal that school personnel regard black and Hispanic males as recalcitrant and oppositional and therefore constantly regulate their dress, behavior, and speech (Ferguson 2000; Lopez 2003; Morris 2005). School personnel (often unintentionally) do not enforce standards of behavior uniformly across racial and ethnic groups; positive behaviors by minority youth tend to go unnoticed (and therefore unrewarded), whereas their negative behaviors are often noticed, which is not the case for their white counterparts. Although most studies in this line of research focus on males, Morris's (2007) study of a predominantly black and Latina middle school shows that school personnel are disproportionally concerned with how minority girls enact femininity. He notes that the assertiveness subtly encouraged for white and middle-class children (Lareau 2003) was interpreted as abrasive and aggressive when enacted by black girls. Thus, given the repressive and coercive authority structure in predominantly minority schools, along with constrained advancement opportunities that mirror inferior job situations, minority youth are not trained to feel and appear prepared to occupy jobs beyond the low-wage sector. Tracking is a major mechanism through which group differences in academic experiences and achievement are perpetuated (Bowles and Gintis 1976; Lucas 1999; Tyson 2011).

Although there is not an extensive literature that attributes the racial achievement gap to parental involvement, educators and policy makers tend to view involvement as a potential solution for many of the problems facing the American education system. As we discussed in Chapter 1, increasing parental involvement in children's academic lives has been a consistent part of federal education policy over the past two decades. The Improving America's Schools Act of 1994 proposed to reduce the minority education gap by "affording parents meaningful opportunities to participate in the education of their children at home and at school." The No Child Left Behind Act of 2001 includes increasing parental involvement (see Section 1118) as a major mechanism for achieving its primary goal of closing achievement gaps in reading and math among students from different racial and socioeconomic backgrounds by 2013–14. In Chapter 4, we examined the extent to which parental involvement explains achievement gaps by social class. We now consider the importance of parental involvement for racial achievement gaps.

Can Parental Involvement Explain the Racial Achievement Gap?

Because parent involvement has been positively linked to children's performance across racial groups, increasing involvement has been suggested as a strategy for reducing the racial achievement gap (Lee and Bowen 2006). Yet, few studies have directly tested this proposition. Instead, investigators have generally examined the extent of involvement within racial groups. One exception is a study by Lee and Bowen (2006), which assessed the role of five parental involvement measures for reducing achievement gaps between minority students and whites. These measures included involvement at school, educational discussions, homework help, time management, and educational expectations. They found that after accounting for variation in these factors, the gap between African Americans and whites declined by roughly 44%; however, the Hispanic gap *increased* by 11%, suggesting that the parents from this group were more involved than their white counterparts.

In Figures 8.8 and 8.9, we show the results for analyses that examine the proportion of the achievement gap for each racial group relative to whites

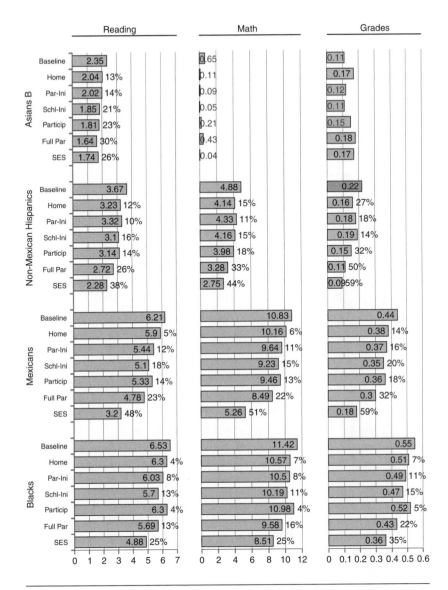

FIGURE 8.8. Achievement gaps (and percent declines) relative to whites: NELS. *Note:* Baseline represents the raw achievement gap relative to whites. Home represents the achievement gaps after accounting for the nine measures of parental involvement at home assessed in Chapter 5. Par-Ini denotes "parent initiated," Schl-Ini denotes "school initiated," and Particip denotes "participation at school." The bars that correspond to these labels represents the achievement gaps after accounting for the measures of parent-initiated contact of schools, school initiated contact of parents, and participation at school contained in Chapter 7, respectively. Full Par denotes "Full Parental involvement" and represents gaps after accounting for all 27 measures of parental involvement in the NELS. The columns labeled *SES* denote "socioeconomic" and represent gaps after accounting for parents' education, family income, family structure, and youths' sex. Achievement was assessed when youth were in grade 12 and the measures of parental involvement and SES were assessed prior to the youth entering high school (grade 8).

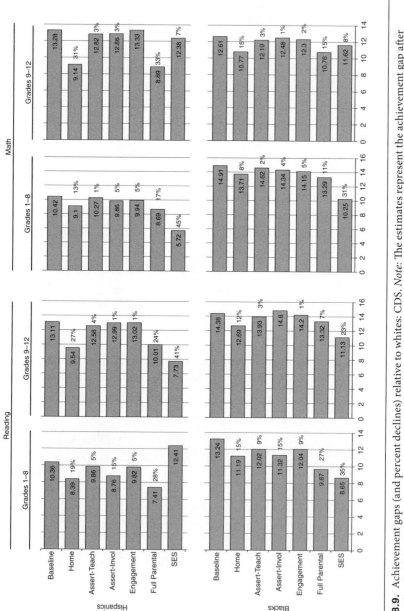

FIGURE 8.9. Achievement gaps (and percent declines) relative to whites: CDS. *Note:* The estimates represent the achievement gap after accounting for all of the parental involvement measures represented by the label. See Figures 6.3 and 6.4 for the measures represented by *home.* See Figures 8.4 through 8.7 for measures represented by *assert-teach* (Figure 8.5), *assert-invol* (Figures 8.6 and 8.7), and *engagement* (Figure 8.4). The estimates represented by the label *full parental* are from a model that accounts for all 18 parental involvement measures in the CDS shown in the aforementioned figures. Social class is a vector that includes parents' education, household income, family structure, and youths' sex. Achievement was assessed from CDS-II, and the measures in both the social class and parental involvement vectors were obtained from CDS-I.

that is accounted for by parental involvement at home and at school. Our aim is to compare the extent to which parent involvement and social class explain racial achievement gaps to provide a sense of scale for understanding the magnitudes of influence from the two sets of variables. Thus, our next set of findings address several questions. Does parental involvement at home explain more of the racial achievement gap than parental involvement at school? Can a greater share of the achievement gap be attributed to either form of involvement (home or school) than to socioeconomic background? Are the patterns similar across racial groups?

In Figure 8.8, we illustrate the achievement gap for each group relative to whites under various scenarios, which are listed along the left side of the graph. The first bar—labeled *baseline*—corresponds to the estimate of the "raw" gap relative to whites, which represents the baseline gap to be explained. The next four bars represent the gap after accounting for parental involvement. Specifically, the second bar represents the gap net of parental involvement at home as measured in Figures 6.1 and 6.2. The third, fourth, and fifth bars show the gap after accounting for parent-initiated school contact (see Figure 8.1), school-initiated school contact (see Figure 8.2), and participation at school (see Figure 8.3), respectively. The sixth bar—labeled *Full Par* for *full parental involvement*—shows the gap after controlling for all measures of parental involvement in the previous scenarios. The estimate for the final bar, labeled *SES* for *socioeconomic status*, is from a model that accounts for parents' education, family income, and family structure, which represents the difference between each racial group and whites who are similarly situated with regard to socioeconomic status. In addition to being labeled with the actual achievement gap, each bar is labeled with the percent change in the gap relative to the baseline and should be interpreted as the percentage of the gap that can be attributed to each set of factors labeled to the left of the bar. Given that our focus is on explaining achievement disadvantages relative to whites and that the bars correspond to the size of the achievement disadvantage for each group, we do not present the results for Asians A, who have higher academic performance than whites.[2]

The findings in the top panel show that Asians B have an achievement disadvantage relative to whites only in reading. The next few bars for reading show that 13% of this gap can be attributed to parental involvement at home, and that parent-initiated school contact, school-initiated school contact, and participation at school each explain 14, 21, and 23% of the gap, respectively. Collectively, the full set of parental involvement measures explain slightly less than a third of the gap, which is more than the portion of the gap that can be attributed to social class (26%). The next three panels contain the results for non-Mexican Hispanics, Mexicans, and blacks. There are two primary similarities in the findings for these groups. First, most of the results for each set of parental involvement factors, depicted by the second through the fifth bars, account for between 10 and 20% of the gap. In some cases, parental involvement at home accounts for less than one-tenth of the gap (i.e., Mexicans and blacks in reading and math).

Second, socioeconomic background explains a greater share of the achievement gap than parental involvement for all three measures of achievement. For non-Mexican Hispanics, the full set of parental involvement measures explain 26 and 33% of the gap in reading and math, respectively, more than 10% less than the portion accounted for by social class. Parental involvement does account for half of their achievement disadvantage in grades, though this figure is still less than the portion explained by social class (59%). This pattern is similar for Mexicans, for whom less than one-fourth of the disadvantage in reading and math can be attributed to parental involvement, substantially less than the roughly 50% explained by social class. Parental involvement explains only a small share of the black-white gap in reading, math, and grades (13, 16, and 22%, respectively). In contrast, social class explains 25% of the black-white gap in reading and math, and 35% of the black disadvantage in grades. Social class appears to have a larger impact on the gap in grades than the gaps in reading and math for all groups; socioeconomic background explains approximately 60% of the disadvantage in grades for Hispanics and Mexicans, and more than a third of the black-white gap in grades.

We display the results for a similar analysis of the achievement gap using the CDS in Figure 8.9. We conducted this analysis for two grade categories: youth in grades 1 through 8 and those in high school. The findings reveal an interesting pattern for Hispanic families. For the younger subsample, parental involvement appears to be more important for gap convergence in reading (28%), and social class seems to explain a greater percentage of the gap in math (45%). In contrast, among students in high school, social class appears to explain more of the Hispanic disadvantage in reading (41%), and parental involvement seems to account for a greater share of their disadvantage in math (33%). Social class accounts for a greater share of the black-white gap in reading for both younger and older youth, and in math for the younger group. In general, the individual groupings of parental involvement measures do not account for much of the black disadvantage in math. Even in instances when parental involvement explains more of the achievement disadvantage than social class (reading for younger Hispanics and math for Hispanics in high school), the proportion of the gaps explained is modest—one-third or less for Hispanics and only 15% for blacks.

Figures 8.8 and 8.9 highlight a troubling aspect of the findings: the presence of substantial racial disparities in achievement after accounting for parental involvement. In most cases socioeconomic background appears to go further in explaining achievement differences than the parental involvement measures we examined. We are not suggesting that because parental involvement appears to have a weaker effect on achievement gaps that it should be considered inconsequential. Parental involvement does hold some relevance for gap convergence, but it is clearly insufficient for narrowing achievement gaps to the extent that many parents and others in the educational community would desire.

As we discussed in previous chapters, parent involvement is widely regarded as a major factor for children's achievement and an important mechanism by which gap convergence can be attained. Yet large differences in achievement still remain when we account for some ways parents can assist with learning at home and at school, particularly for black youth. These findings depict the grim reality facing our education system; greater parental involvement will not bring minorities to achievement parity with white (and Asian) students. It must be only one component of a wider initiative for closing achievement gaps.

Chapter Summary

The purpose of this chapter is to examine the importance of parental involvement at school for the academic lives of youth from various racial groups. As we have done throughout this study, we consider that white, Asian, Hispanic, and black families each have different lived experiences within the United States. We also account for the fact that parental involvement is multifaceted, consisting of parents' involvement with parent-teacher organizations and parents' attempts to contact (and be contacted by) schools. We examine whether parental involvement at school is associated with increases in achievement for each racial group and the proportion of the racial achievement gap that can be attributed to parental involvement at school.

Similar to the findings reported in previous chapters, involvement at school shows some effectiveness for *some* groups, though the preponderance of evidence in this chapter suggests a modest relationship between parents' involvement at school and academic outcomes in general. We provide a summary of the general link between parental involvement and achievement for each racial group in Figure 8.10, which shows the number

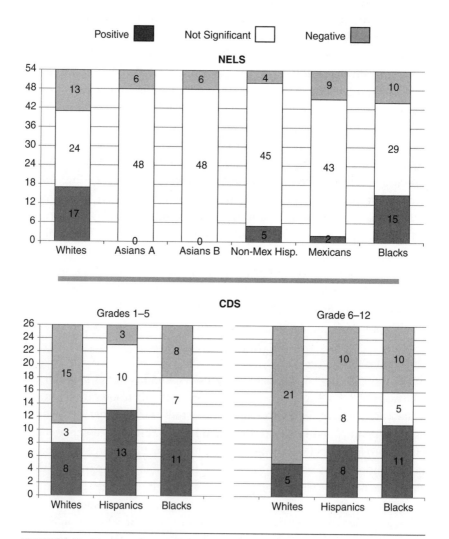

FIGURE 8.10. Number of parental involvement measures associated with changes in achievement by race.

of positive, nonsignificant, and negative estimates for each group in both the NELS (top panel) and CDS (bottom panel). The NELS contains fifty-four possible "effects" for each group—eighteen measures of parental involvement by three academic outcomes (reading, math, and grades). Most of the estimates for each group are not significant. There are only seventeen instances in which parental involvement is associated with increases in achievement for whites (31%). Similarly, only fifteen of the associations are positive for blacks (27%). These numbers far exceed those of the other groups. A total of only seven estimates are positive for non-Mexican Hispanics and Mexicans combined, and there are no measures of parental involvement associated with increases in achievement for either Asian group. There are actually more negative estimates than positive estimates for three of the six racial groups. Overall, the links we examine between parental involvement at school and achievement never yield positive estimates even one-third of the time for any racial group; only 12% of the total estimates across all racial groups are positive, the same exact percentage observed in Chapter 6 for parental involvement at home based on the NELS.

The bottom panel summarizes the results for the analyses based on the CDS. In total, 36% of the estimates in this chapter are positive, nearly the same percentage (35%) observed for parental involvement at home for the CDS in Chapter 6. This result is primarily driven by Hispanics and blacks in grades 1 through 5, for which 50 and 42% of the estimates are positive, respectively. It seems that the forms of parental involvement at school we examined using the CDS are important for the achievement of Hispanics early in the schooling process, as the percentage of positive estimates for them is substantially lower in the older subsample (31%). For whites, there are substantially more negative estimates than positive estimates in both subsamples. Thus, the difference between the two data sets—a total of 12% positive estimates in the NELS compared to 36% for the CDS—might reflect that the CDS contains more measures of parental involvement that require active or assertive participation from parents than the NELS. However, most estimates for both data sets are not positive.

In Figure 8.11, we show the number of positive, nonsignificant, and negative estimates for each measure of parental involvement at school in the NELS examined in this chapter. There are eighteen links between each measure of parental involvement and achievement across all racial groups (3 achievement outcomes by 6 groups). The top panel contains the summary for the measures of parent-initiated contact with school and shows that only

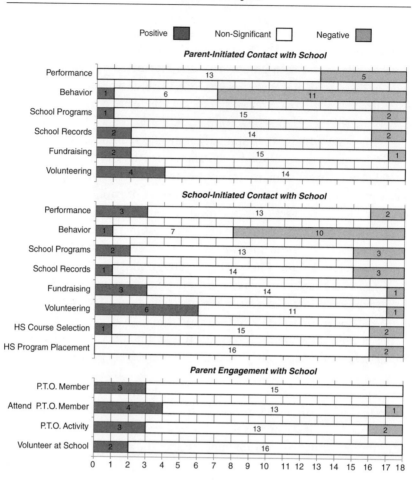

FIGURE 8.11. Number of positive, nonsignificant, and negative estimates for each measure in the NELS.

contacting schools about volunteering produced more than two positive estimates. Similarly, the second panel shows parent-school contact about volunteering is the only school-initiated contact measure that yields more than three positive estimates. The bottom panel shows that there are four positive estimates for attending a PTO meeting and three for being a PTO member and participating in a PTO activity. Overall, only 39 of the 324 total estimates assessed in this chapter using the NELS are positive (12%). In contrast, there are 48 negative estimates (15%). However, nearly three-fourths of the estimates—237 for 73%—are not systematically related to achievement.

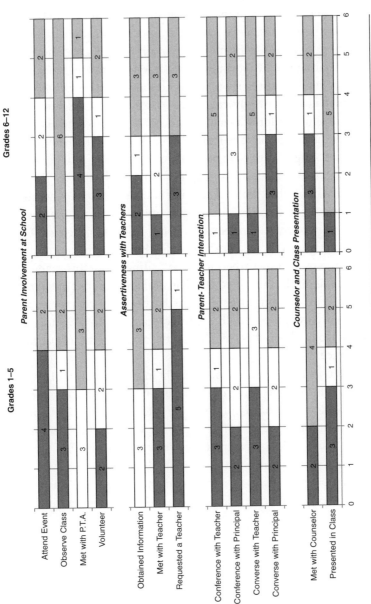

FIGURE 8.12. Number of positive, nonsignificant, and negative estimates for each measure in the CDS.

We show the same information for the findings based on the CDS in Figure 8.12. The findings appear to differ between the two subsamples. For example, whereas youth in the younger subsample appear to benefit most when their parents request a particular teacher and attend school events, PTA meetings appear to be more important for academic success among the older subsample. Also, younger youth seem to benefit more from their parents being more assertive with teachers and from parent-teacher interaction than older youth. Overall, parental involvement at school appears to be more important for academic success of younger youth, as there are a greater number of positive estimates (32 of 78, or 41%) than negative (26, or 33%) and nonsignificant estimates (20, or 26%) for the younger subsample. In contrast, for the older subsample, less than one-third of the estimates are positive (24) and slightly more than half of the estimates are negative (41).

In sum, the patterns in this chapter are similar to those observed in Chapter 6 for parental involvement at home. Parental involvement at school shows some benefit for academic outcomes. However, the connection seems modest in most cases. Furthermore, the findings from this chapter suggest that parental involvement is equally harmful for academic outcomes as it is beneficial. These findings are similar to those observed in previous chapters in which we examined the link between parental involvement and academic outcomes, regardless of whether the assessment was made by social class or race.

Thus far, we have provided some insight into which forms of involvement help and which forms warrant intervention to make them either beneficial for achievement or to minimize the extent to which they compromise achievement (see Appendix D for a summary of this information by race). Like previous studies on parental involvement, our focus has been on how parents are typically involved in their children's academic lives. However, given that parental involvement is commonly regarded as an intervention that could lead to improved achievement, it is important to study how parents are involved when their children perform poorly in school. In the next chapter, we turn our attention to parental involvement in response to poor achievement.

— 9 —

Parenting and Poor Achievement

Despite all the research that has been conducted on parental involvement and achievement, there is virtually no insight into how parents deal with poor academic performance in particular. That is, most research on parenting and achievement examines parental involvement in general; there is a dearth of research on how parents deal specifically with poor achievement and the implications that their approach has for their children's academic outcomes. Asking parents to be involved in their children's schooling is conceptually and empirically distinct from asking them to address inadequate academic performance. Whereas the former condition for involvement is intended to help a child improve or maintain their current level of academic engagement and performance, the latter requires that parents address a problem. The consideration of a "problem" introduces some level of urgency, which could influence a shift in parenting philosophy or style. Parenting under this scenario might trigger responses from parents that they otherwise would not employ absent the need to "fix" a problem.

Thus, an examination of how parents deal with underachievement is especially important as schools around the country seek to inform parents of effective strategies to improve children's achievement and address racial achievement gaps. At the institutional level, schools can enact their own set of strategies to address underachievement, such as recruiting and training high-quality teachers or strengthening instructional quality. However, it is less clear which strategies parents can employ to improve their children's achievement.

An assessment of how parents' philosophy for dealing with underachievement is related to children's academic success is important particularly for black youth, who typically perform inadequately in school. Given

179

the increasing urgency for closing the black-white achievement gap, it is surprising that few empirical studies have focused on racial differences in how parents are oriented toward dealing with their child's inadequate academic performance, and whether achievement differences exist between the various strategies parents are inclined to employ. Examining this link could yield strategies useful for educators and parents of youths from traditionally underperforming groups.

Previous studies provide some reason to suspect that parents may differ in the strategies they employ to address underachievement. For instance, in their study of cultural variation in parenting styles among two-parent families, Julian, McKenry and McKelvey (1994) find that minority parents (e.g., blacks, Asians, and Hispanics) place greater emphasis on academic achievement and use a stricter, more controlling parenting style. Thus, we might expect that black parents feel a disciplinary approach is more effective when dealing with poor achievement. The black achievement disadvantage also means that a greater share of black parents operate in "crisis" mode than in "maintenance" mode when it comes to their children's education. Therefore, it is important to determine parents' preferred strategy for addressing their children's poor achievement.

In this chapter, we approach this issue by answering three questions. First, do black-white differences exist in parenting philosophy for addressing inadequate achievement? Second, given the importance social class can have on both parenting and achievement, what is the relationship between social class and the strategies parents believe to be more effective when dealing with inadequate achievement? Third, is parenting philosophy for dealing with inadequate achievement consequential for children's academic outcomes? Because we are concerned with youth from traditionally underperforming groups, we focus on blacks relative to whites. Also, to assess parents' typical response to their children's poor achievement, we consider parents' penchant for responding in a particular way when their child's achievement does not meet expectations, as well as their actual responses to poor performance. In the following section, we provide a brief discussion of why we expect group differences in parental responses to poor performance. We then proceed to answer each of these questions and conclude with a summary of the findings.

Race and Parenting Philosophy

Historically, the literature on parenting styles by race has attributed drastically different parenting styles to white and black parents. For example, white parents are posited to use inductive reasoning, provide choices, encourage independence, and urge active exploration of the environment (McGroder 2000). By contrast, many twentieth-century scholars have posited that black families operate under a social deficit model of child rearing, that is, expressing low levels of reasoning, intolerance of child self-expression, and high levels of power assertion (Baumrind 1971). In fact, there is a long history of characterizing the black family as consisting of mothers who are harsh and capricious and fathers who are aloof, violent, and uninterested in child affairs (Kardiner and Ovesey 1951).

Although parenting style has primarily been attributed to social class (Lareau 2003; Middlemiss 2003), some studies show that there are racial differences in parenting net of social class. For example, in a study across various social class strata, Hill and Sprague (1999) find that white parents are more likely to emphasize children's happiness and self-esteem and blacks place more emphasis on obedience and school performance. They also find that blacks are more likely to report that being a disciplinarian is a major part of their role as parents. Even among the upper-middle-class subsample, they find that white parents are more likely to use reason and black parents are more likely to withdraw privileges. Some studies suggest that the disciplinary practices of black parents are more severe, punitive, and power assertive than white parents net of socioeconomic background (Allen 1985; Portes, Dunham, Williams 1986).

One explanation for these differences is the family ecology framework, which proposes that black parenting style is a direct result of experiences as a subordinate group within the United States. Specifically, because blacks have been subjected to long-standing discrimination, they have developed "adaptive strategies" particular to their position within larger society (Harrison et al. 1990). Hill (2001) notes that black parents might feel a greater need to adopt forceful parenting styles in response to structural forces that undermine their child-rearing efforts. Similarly, Gonzales, Hiraga, and Cauce (1998) note that black mothers tend to employ a parenting style that sets clear and firm rules and reinforces their role as authority figures. The use of power-assertive discipline is posited to partially stem from parents' attempts to teach functional competences (e.g., self-reliance and mistrust of authority figures) needed to survive in environments marked by marginal conventional economic resources and a robust underground economy (Ogbu 1981). Thus, racial differences in parenting may be partly due to inequality in material resources (e.g., wealth) and environmental support. Blacks' disadvantage on these factors contributes to their higher levels of psychological distress, which is associated with a more punitive parenting style (McLoyd 1990).

It is important to note that black parents have greater educational expectations for their children than white parents (Harris 2011). In fact, a national poll commissioned by the National Center for Public Policy and Higher Education found that black parents place higher value on obtaining an education as a means for advancement than white parents (Public Agenda 2000). Working-class black parents are more likely to discuss their children's school experiences and plans, restrict television on school nights, set rules about grades, and help with homework than their white counterparts (U.S. Department of Education 1992). Furthermore, the similarity between blacks and whites that we observe in parental involvement in the earlier chapters of this book—blacks are substantially lower on only four out of twenty-seven measures of parental involvement from the NELS—contradict the common misconception that black families do not value education. In fact, our findings underestimate the extent to which black parents value schooling as our racial comparisons do not account for socioeconomic background.

In the following section, we examine whether racial differences exist in parents' philosophy for addressing low achievement. Because black parents have greater educational expectations and they are more likely than whites to anticipate that their children will experience discrimination (Harris 2011), we suspect they will differ from white parents in their approach to dealing with poor academic performance. As past studies have shown that high socioeconomic status often fails to protect against racial discrimination (Cose 1993; Feagin and Sikes 1994; Hochschild 1995), we expect a racial difference to exist even after accounting for socioeconomic background.

Racial Differences in Parenting Philosophy

We examine whether differences exist between black and white parents in their preferred approach for dealing with their child's poor school achievement using data from the CDS. To ensure that all children in the sample were in school during both waves of the CDS, we restrict our sample to black ($n = 492$) and white ($n = 549$) children in grades 7–12 in CDS-II. We gauge parenting philosophy from the first wave of the CDS, which asked parents how they would respond "if their child brought home a report card with grades or progress that was lower than expected." We sorted parents into two *mutually exclusive* categories—a punitive response, and a nonpunitive response (see Table C.4 in Appendix C for a detailed description of measures). Within the punitive group, which accounts for 36% of the sample, parents were further sorted into two categories based on their approach: *mild* (those who punish *or* limit their child's activities) or *acute* (those who *both* punish *and* limit activities).

The remaining portion of the sample (64%) consists of parents who generally do not opt for a punitive approach and are therefore considered nonpunitive responders. We sorted this group into four categories: those who (1) contact faculty but do *not* help their child more, (2) help their child more but do *not* contact faculty, (3) *simultaneously* contact faculty and help their child more, and (4) engage in closer monitoring and/or encouragement. These four categories contain 9, 17, 29, and 6% of the sample, respectively; the final 3% did not fall into any of these categories and were labeled as *other*. Although parents in the punitive group could also employ nonpunitive responses, the key distinction between these groups is that punitive approaches are within their parenting repertoire, which was not the case for parents in the nonpunitive groups.

We show how white and black parents sort into these categories in Figure 9.1. The figure shows that black parents express a greater preference for punitive responses to address inadequate academic performance than white parents; less than one-third of whites are in the punitive group (29%) compared to nearly two-thirds for blacks (62%). There is a greater share of blacks in the mild (.39%) and acute (.23%) categories relative to whites (27% and 2, respectively). Alternatively, it seems that white parents' preferred strategy for addressing inadequate performance is to contact school officials in conjunction with providing their child with more help. Whites hold a substantial advantage over blacks in the proportion of parents who fall into the first three nonpunitive categories. These findings support the hypothesis that whites and blacks differ dramatically in their inclinations for dealing with their child's inadequate achievement.

Although the findings in Figure 9.1 suggest substantial racial variation in how parents are inclined to respond to inadequate performance, one

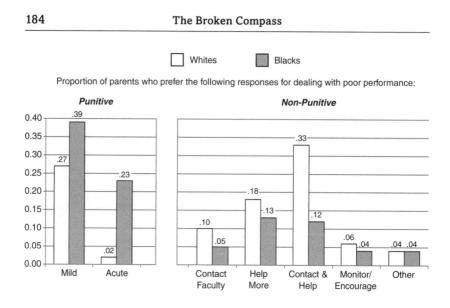

FIGURE 9.1. Parents' preferred strategy for dealing with poor academic performance: CDS. *Note:* Findings are unadjusted. All racial differences are significant at the .05 level with the exception of *Monitor/Encourage* and *Other.* Unweighted *N* is 549 for whites and 492 for blacks. (*Source:* Robinson and Harris 2013, Figure 1.)

could critique that we are capturing a hypothetical rather than what parents actually do. However, we view this as an inclusive measure of parents' behavioral inclination toward academic underperformance. In this case, parents who respond harshly to underperformance might be displaying behavior consistent with how they raise their child(ren) generally. If our question asked, "How *did* you respond when your child brought home . . . lower than expected," we would be capturing a parent's response to a specific instance. This response could be indicative of how parents typically respond, but it could also be reflective of a behavioral "shock" a parent experienced when an unusually stressful moment occurred concomitantly with their child's underperformance, such as marital turmoil or loss of employment. A major strength of the measure we use is that it asks parents about a situation that would elicit a response under normal circumstances. Moreover, we recognize that for some parents inadequate performance can occur if their child scores lower on a test than usual; this circumstance can compel some parents to respond in ways they feel are appropriate. Thus, in addition to capturing students who are not doing well in school, our measure captures those who might be doing well overall but are performing *less* well relative to their usual academic achievement, which might trigger a response from parents.

Despite the strength that we see in our measure, we understand that some readers might approach our findings with some trepidation. Furthermore, it is unclear what the punitive responses actually mean as they are less suggestive than the nonpunitive categories. Therefore, we employ data from the Maryland Adolescent Development in Context Study (MADICS), which contains a unique collection of measures of 1,407 black and white families (66 and 34%, respectively) from a county in Maryland. The sample was selected from approximately 5,000 adolescents in the county that entered middle school during 1991 via a stratified sampling procedure designed to get proportional representations of families from each of the county's twenty-three middle schools. As such, students' socioeconomic backgrounds are varied as the sample includes families from neighborhoods in low-income urban areas, middle-class suburban areas, and rural farm-based areas. We supplement the findings from Figure 9.1 using the MADICS because despite being drawn from a regional sample, it contains a broader set of questions on punitive parenting responses to inadequate achievement than the CDS. Furthermore, parents were asked how they have actually responded in the past when their child performed poorly in school. Thus, the MADICS can provide some insight into whether the patterns observed in Figure 9.1 are robust. We display these findings in Figure 9.2.

The findings in the top panel of Figure 9.2 are consistent with those based on the CDS. Specifically, relative to whites, a greater proportion of black parents respond to their child's inadequate academic performance by threatening to physically punish them, taking away their privileges, grounding them, yelling at them, and physically punishing them. Unlike our analysis from the CDS, these options were not mutually exclusive. However, the bottom panel shows that the ratio of parents in the punitive group to those in the nonpunitive group is similar to the ratio observed in the CDS for both races. The share of white parents who engage in punitive responses is 37%, only 8% more than in the CDS. Similarly, 67% of blacks engage in punitive approaches, only 5% more than recorded using the CDS.

It seems clear that black parents have a penchant for employing punitive strategies when addressing their child's inadequate academic performance. It is important to note that parenting styles are ways of socializing children to accomplish child-rearing goals. Also, the extent to which some parenting approaches are considered to be undesirable varies across families. For example, many black parents who employ physical punishment do not regard it as abuse (Mosby et al. 1999). In fact, Deater-Deckard and

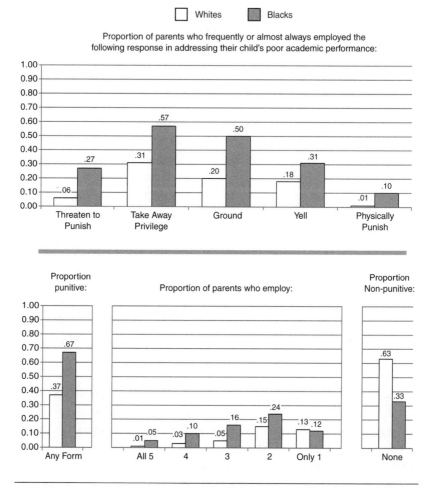

FIGURE 9.2. Parents' response to poor academic performance: MADICS. *Note:* Findings are unadjusted. Findings are for youth in middle school (grade 8). All racial differences in the top panel are significant at the .05 level. In the bottom panel, racial differences are significant at the .05 level for *Any Form, 3,* and *None.* Finally, the racial differences for *All 5, 4,* and *2* in the bottom panel are marginally significant ($p < .10$). Number of observations ranges from 277 to 280. (*Source:* Robinson and Harris 2013, Figure 2.)

colleagues (1996) find that among black parents in their sample, physical punishment is positively associated with warmth and use of reason. Although discipline is more harsh and physical among black families, it is rarely coupled with withdrawal of love, as is often the case among white families (Borkowski, Ramey, and Bristol-Power 2009). In general, researchers agree that there are different parenting styles that can be effective for different racial groups, and that what is the "ideal" response to children depends on cultural beliefs about parenting and child socialization (Luster and Okagaki 2005).

Importantly, however, some scholars caution against a parochial conception of black parents as invariably harsh and suggest prior evidence overstates the claim that black parents are oriented to punitive parenting styles (Bluestone and Tamis-LeMonda 1999). Critics note many examinations of white and black parenting styles fail to account for the confounding effects of socioeconomic status (e.g., Baumrind 1971). This methodological shortcoming obscures the notion that disciplinary forms of parenting may be prominent among blacks for a variety of reasons related to their socioeconomic position in society (e.g., higher incidences of family poverty and lower social status). Furthermore, punitive parenting is likely to be more prevalent among lower socioeconomic parents because of the elevated risk to children in lower-class neighborhoods. These parents attempt to counteract their children's greater susceptibility to deviant activities by employing stricter parenting measures (Kelley, Power, and Wimbush 1992; Ogbu 1981). For these reasons, then, punitive parenting is a product of social class rather than of race.

The Importance of Social Class for Parenting Philosophy

Bronfenbrenner (1979) developed an ecological theory that suggested that family processes (e.g., parental behavior) and contextual factors (e.g., social class or race) interact to affect children's development. There has been a great deal of discussion among sociologists and psychologists on the precise nature of this interaction. Some scholars have argued that social class plays a determinative role that shapes the particular responses parents employ toward their children's academic outcomes. More than four decades ago, Kohn (1963) offered that parents from lower social class positions (particularly those with lower education) were more prone toward child external authority (e.g., punishment). Parents of higher social class pay less attention to raising obedient children, and more attention to children's internal states, relying more on reasoning, explaining, and psychological techniques of discipline (Hughes and Perry-Jenkins 1996). The link in this interpretation is that social class affects which characteristics parents will value for their children, and this variation in values leads to differences in parenting behavior. Though Kohn's theory was developed regarding child rearing more generally, it gives reason to expect parenting strategies for handling inadequate achievement will vary across family contexts as well.

Kohn's theory is certainly not without its critiques. In particular, scholars have criticized Kohn's theory because it suggests that middle- and upper-class parents have better or more worthy values, which can be used evaluatively to blame individuals in lower social class positions for their children's academic difficulties (Hughes and Perry-Jenkins 1996). More recent theories suggest that parents' education affects how they respond to their children's school performance because it impacts their expertise. For example, according to efficacy theory, the extent to which parents directly help their children improve academically will likely depend on how capable they feel in this arena. Lareau and Shumar (1996) report such results in their ethnographic study, in which a working-class parent told her nephew that in order to receive help with fractions he would have to wait until his older brother arrived home. Another parent reported being "embarrassed" that he could not assist his son with third-grade homework. In their view, parents' perceptions of the way they can best help their children is heavily influenced by the social resources (e.g., human capital) they possess. Thus, although the desire to see their child's achievement improve may be nearly uniform among all parents, the approach they use to directly help their child improve is likely to vary widely by their social class position, particularly with respect to level of education.

We examine whether social class—human capital in particular—structures how white and black parents address inadequate academic performance. These findings are displayed in Figure 9.3, which is similar to Figure 9.1. The only difference is Figure 9.3 includes findings for each racial group based on parents' level of education. We stratify social class according to parents' level of education (parents with less than a four-year college degree and those with a four-year degree or greater) because it closely relates to parental expectations and behaviors toward children's schooling, and how effectively they communicate these expectations to their children.

The top panel of Figure 9.3 shows that for whites, parenting philosophy for addressing inadequate academic performance generally varies modestly by level of parental education. The bottom panel shows that a substantially greater share of blacks with lower levels of education prefer acute punitive responses (26%) than those with a four-year degree (6%). By con-

Less than 4-yr Degree   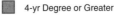 4-yr Degree or Greater

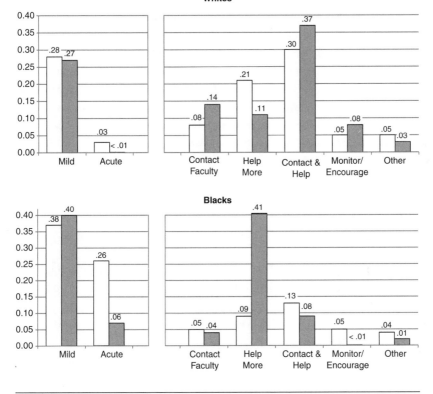

FIGURE 9.3. Parents' preferred response to poor academic performance by social class: CDS. *Note:* Findings are unadjusted. All differences in the top panel are significant at the .05 level with the exception of *Mild.* All differences in the bottom panel are significant at the .05 level with the exception of *Mild* and *Contact faculty.* All racial differences within social class are significant at the .05 level with the exception of *Monitor/encourage* and *Other* for *Less than 4-yr degree.* Unweighted N is 549 for whites and 492 for blacks. (*Source:* Robinson and Harris 2013, Figure 3.)

trast, 41% of blacks with a four-year degree prefer to help their child more compared to only 9% of blacks without a four-year degree. However, social class has minor implications for the racial differences observed in Figure 9.1. Blacks in both the lower and higher social class groups prefer both forms of punitive responses more than their white counterparts. Similarly, both groups of black parents are less inclined to contact faculty and to contact faculty in conjunction with helping their child than both groups of whites. The findings for preferring to provide the child with more help yield a different pattern; whereas whites with a four-year degree have a lower inclination to help than their less educated counterparts (only 11 and 21%, respectively), a much greater proportion of blacks with a four-year degree prefer to help more than less educated blacks (41 and 9%, respectively).

In general, Figure 9.3 shows that blacks prefer punitive responses for dealing with their child's inadequate academic performance more than whites, regardless of parents' level of education. Also, with the exception of providing youth with more help, blacks have a lower preference for nonpunitive responses than whites. Although these findings may be revealing for a number of reasons, the extent to which these patterns have implications for youths' academic outcomes is what we are interested in. We investigate the relationship between parenting philosophy and youths' achievement in the following section.

The Implications of Parenting Philosophy for Achievement

Although most studies on the role of parents in schooling focus on the link between parental involvement and academic outcomes, there is some evidence that suggests parental responses to *inadequate* academic performance might have implications for children's academic outcomes. In a well-conducted study, Dornbusch and colleagues' (1987) utilized self-reports from 7,836 high school students to examine the link between parental behaviors and adolescent performance. Their findings reveal that white and Hispanic adolescents have higher grade-point averages under authoritative parenting styles, whereas parents' use of encouragement after viewing their child's grades lead to increases in effort and academic performance for Asians and Blacks. Although Dornbusch and others' study employed longitudinal data, design issues such as the use of student responses to measure parenting styles prohibited them from establishing a clear link between child performance and parental responses. A related study by Steinberg, Elmen, and Mounts (1989) confirmed Dornbusch and others' (1987) findings using longitudinal data. However, their results are limited by the homogeneity of their sample, which mainly include whites from middle-class and professional backgrounds. Thus, few studies examine achievement *prospectively* to provide a sense of how various parenting philosophies for addressing inadequate achievement are related to academic outcomes.

Developmental theorists have hypothesized that the link between parenting strategies and adolescent achievement operates through (or is explained by) psychological characteristics governing a child's approach toward academics. For example, Gottfried, Fleming, and Gottfried (1998) find that adolescents' intrinsic motivation—characterized by enjoyment and inherent pleasure in school learning—is fostered through environments that provide optimal challenge, competence-promoting feedback, and support for autonomous behavior. Conversely, environments characterized as using higher levels of control, such as those relying on surveillance, often undermine intrinsic motivation (Deci and Ryan 1985). The direction of these findings is consistent with previous research (e.g., Ginsburg and Bronstein 1993). Thus, research generally finds that granting children autonomy by emphasizing independence and reasoning rather than punishment is positively associated with their perceived competence, self-initiated regulation in the classroom, and academic achievement (Grolnick and Ryan 1989; Steinberg, Elmen, and Mounts 1989). For this reason, one should expect that a tendency toward punitive parenting approaches for dealing with inadequate academic performance would be less effective than nonpunitive parenting approaches.

In Figure 9.4, we show the estimated effect of the various approaches within each parenting philosophy for addressing inadequate performance on reading and math achievement. The findings are displayed in estimate graphs similar to those in previous chapters. We show the estimates separately for four subsamples: whites, blacks, youth whose parents do not hold a four-year college degree, and those whose parents have a four-year degree or greater. In general, the findings show that whereas an inclination toward punitive parental responses are associated with declines in achievement, a tendency toward nonpunitive responses to inadequate academic performance are associated with increases in achievement. These patterns are similar for both reading and math. Findings for the punitive philosophy—displayed in the top panel—suggest that both mild and acute punitive responses to inadequate academic performance are associated with declines in achievement for all subsamples (except for the higher social class subsample, for which mild is not associated with declines in reading and neither mild nor acute appear to compromise math).

The bottom panel of Figure 9.4 contains findings for the responses within the nonpunitive philosophy grouping. With the exception of *Help more* for reading (which is not significant), it seems that all nonpunitive responses

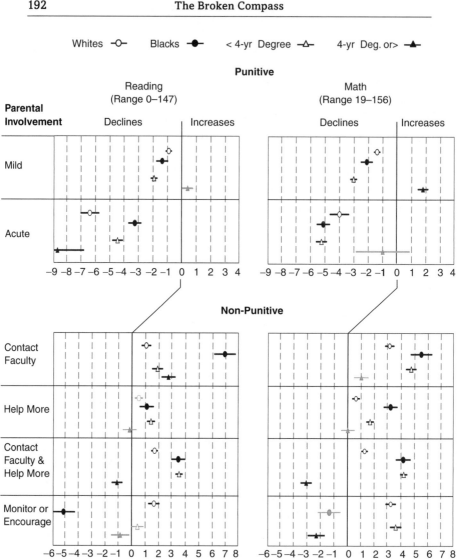

FIGURE 9.4. Implication of parental response to inadequate performance by race and class: CDS. *Note:* Bold estimates are significant at the .05 level. Estimates in the top panel were obtained from an equation in which both forms of punitive responses were included, along with controls for parents' education, household income, family structure, youths' sex, grade in school, prior achievement, and *other* form of response to inadequate performance. Race is included as a control for the analysis by social class. The findings in the bottom panel were obtained from an equation that includes all forms of nonpunitive measures and the aforementioned controls. Whereas the parenting measures are from CDS-I, the measures for youths' academic achievement are from CDS-II. To account for the potential of ceiling and floor effects, these analyses are for the middle 90% of the achievement distribution. Unweighted *N* is 508 for whites, 424 for blacks, 726 for < 4-yr Degree, and 206 for 4-yr Deg. or >.

are associated with increases in achievement for whites. An inclination toward contacting faculty, helping more, and employing both approaches simultaneously is associated with increases in achievement for blacks and youth whose parents do not have a four-year college degree. However, monitoring and/or encouraging youth is associated with a decline in reading for blacks and is not significant for the reading achievement of less advantaged youth. Among youth whose parents hold a four-year degree or greater, only a tendency to contact faculty is associated with increases in reading, and simultaneously contacting faculty and providing more help is associated with a decline in both reading and math.

To determine whether the patterns observed in Figure 9.4 are robust across the achievement distribution, we repeated this analysis for two additional subsamples: students in the 5th to 50th percentile of the achievement distribution and those in the 51st to 95th percentile. Displaying findings for these groups has two advantages. First, this accounts for the potential of ceiling and floor effects—the distortion of estimates resulting from top-performing students having scores with nowhere to go but down (vice versa for inadequately performing youths). Second, the estimates can be displayed separately for students in the top and bottom half of the achievement distribution. Findings for these subgroups are displayed in Figure 9.5.

The findings in the top panel suggest that both mild and acute punitive responses hurt reading and math achievement for students in the lower performing subsample. By contrast, only an acute punitive response is associated with declines in achievement for students in the top half of the achievement distribution. With regard to the findings for the nonpunitive philosophy, the bottom panel suggests that an inclination toward contacting faculty, whether or not it is done in conjunction with providing more help, is associated with an increase in both reading and math achievement for the students in the lower-performing subsample. However, providing more help without consulting teachers and increasing one's level of supervision and encouragement are associated with improvements in achievement only in math for this group. Higher-performing students seem to benefit in both reading and math from parental help, contacting faculty when done simultaneously with parental help, and encouragement.

In addition to examining the link between parenting philosophy and achievement, we examine the implications of parenting philosophy for the black-white achievement gap. Figure 9.6 displays the results from this

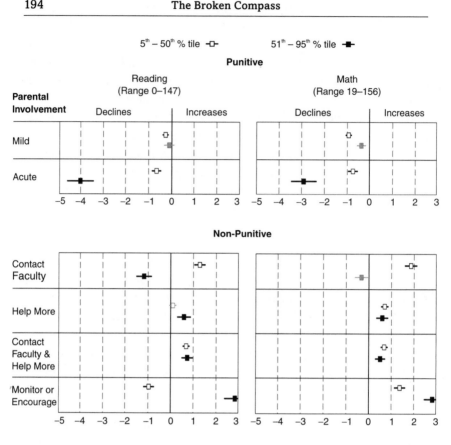

FIGURE 9.5. Implication of parental response to inadequate performance by achievement: CDS. *Note:* Bold estimates are significant at the .05 level. Estimates in the top panel were obtained from an equation in which both forms of punitive responses were included, along with controls for race, parents' education, household income, family structure, youths' sex, grade in school, prior achievement, and *other* form of response to inadequate performance. The findings in the bottom panel were obtained from an equation that includes all forms of nonpunitive measures and the aforementioned controls. The parenting measures are from CDS-I, and the measures for youths' academic achievement are from CDS-II. Unweighted $N=932$.

analysis using data from the CDS. The first bar shows that the baseline gap in reading, which includes the full set of controls, is 7.5 points. After accounting for parents' punitive responses, the gap declines to 7.1 points—approximately a 5% reduction. A similar pattern is observed for math in the right-hand panel, in which the baseline gap declined from 9.3 to 8.8 points after accounting for parents' punitive responses, which is also a 5%

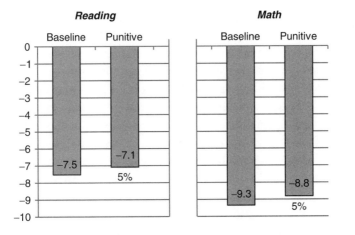

FIGURE 9.6. Achievement for blacks relative to whites and percent declines in the black-white achievement gap based on parenting philosophy: CDS. *Note: Baseline* represents the achievement gap after accounting for parents' education, household income, family structure, youths' sex, grade in school, and prior achievement. The column labeled *Punitive* represents the achievement gap from an equation that includes all factors from the baseline model and the following three variables: mild punitive, acute punitive, and the *other* form of response. All estimates are significant at the .001 level. Unweighted N = 1,041. (*Source:* Robinson and Harris 2013, Figure 4.)

reduction. Overall, it appears that a modest portion of the black-white achievement gap can be attributed to parents' punitive responses to inadequate performance.

Chapter Summary

In this chapter, we examine whether racial and social class differences exist in parenting philosophy for addressing inadequate achievement. We also estimate the extent to which various responses within the nonpunitive and punitive philosophies affect reading and math achievement by race, social class, and achievement level. Lastly, we examine whether punitive parenting has implications for the racial achievement gap. Our investigation reveals several findings relevant for sociological theory and important for educators and policy makers. We offer four main findings.

First, whereas whites appear more inclined to intervene in nonpunitive ways in response to inadequate performance, black parents appear more inclined to respond punitively. Smetana and Gaines' (1999) discussion of their results in a study on conflicts between parents and their adolescent children is useful for interpreting this finding. When parents must decide how to respond to their child's underachievement they are engaging in a form of conflict resolution. Smetana and Gaines (1999) suggest black parents tend to view conflict in terms of respect for parents and obedience to authority. White parents, on the other hand, typically view conflict as a means for establishing personal jurisdiction, which Smetana (1995) labels as a social-cognitive aspect of autonomy development.

Second, whereas a nonpunitive parenting philosophy is associated with improvement in reading and math achievement, a punitive parenting philosophy appears to lead children to perform worse in both subjects. When considered in relation to the aforementioned findings on racial differences, the implication is that white parents are likely to respond in ways that increase future achievement and black parents are drawn toward punitive approaches that are negatively associated with achievement for all adolescents. Although several of the findings are nuanced—for example, that a preference for monitoring and/or encouraging as an intervention is negatively associated with blacks' reading achievement but not associated with their math achievement—the overall patterns are rather consistent. We show that these racial differences do explain a small portion of the black-white achievement gap.

Third, the implication of parenting philosophy for achievement varies by race. Our findings suggest that a greater likelihood for employing nonpunitive responses is associated with greater improvement in reading and math for black youth relative to their white counterparts. Supplemental analyses suggest that blacks would benefit more than whites in both reading and math from parental contact with faculty, greater help from parents, and the employment of both of these strategies simultaneously. Perhaps the most troubling finding reveals that a punitive parenting philosophy (both mild and acute) for dealing with underachievement is *more* negatively associated with math for blacks than whites. This finding is particularly unfortunate because, as previously noted, black parents are much more likely to employ these types of responses.

Fourth, although having a four-year college degree significantly reduced the odds that black parents would likely employ acute punitive responses, the more educated black parents still express a greater preference for punitive responses than their white counterparts. Recall that whites with a four-year degree or greater were more inclined to use nonpunitive strategies such as contacting faculty, both contacting faculty and providing more help to their children, and monitoring/encouraging their child. Returning to the efficacy theory, our findings with regard to blacks without a four-year college degree align with the notion that less educated parents are more likely to use punitive responses, perhaps because they feel incapable of aiding children in nonpunitive ways. Our results support Lareau and Shumar's (1996) claim that more educated parents, equipped with greater amounts of human capital, are more prone to engage with faculty about their child's academic affairs because they feel more comfortable with how schools operate. This support, however, was shown only among whites. Thus, although there is a connection between parents' education and preferred parenting strategies for whites and blacks, the strength and pattern of this link varies across racial groups.

It must be noted that although black parents appear to respond in ways that negatively affect their children's academic performance, one should not assume they are less concerned with improving achievement than whites. Although punitive approaches are typically inversely related to more nurturing parent-child relationships, this relationship is not always a one-to-one correlation. Undoubtedly, some parents will be supportive and encouraging while they employ punitive measures. On the one hand, the use of punishment in general is not surprising because parents may feel an obligation to regulate inadequate achievement based on concerns about their child's future. On the other hand, it is surprising that black parents remain more likely to prefer punishment net of social class, family structure, and family income. This result contrasts with previous findings that attribute punitive parenting styles of blacks to their lower-income status or incidences of single parenting.

The measures we employ in this chapter have both strengths and weaknesses. Survey questions asking parents about their likely response to inadequate achievement precludes us from directly relating their behaviors to child academic outcomes. At the same time, because the question captures expected response, it is likely to be a suitable reflection of parents' normal parenting approach. It represents an implicit control for behavior "shocks" that could arise if a stressor such as job loss or unforeseen financial hardship occurred concomitantly with inadequate academic performance. Additionally, asking parents a hypothetical means the structure of the question reduces the probability of parents falsifying their actual behavior. A stronger sense of stigma may reside over parents' responses if they are asked, "Have you ever punished your child for inadequate performance?" rather than being asked their *likelihood* of engaging in several types of responses to their child's performance.

Nevertheless, we supplement the racial comparisons on parental responses with data from the MADICS, which asked parents about the actual approach they have taken in the past to address their child's inadequate academic performance. The MADICS yields results substantively similar to those based on the CDS: black parents threaten, physically punish, ground, and withhold rewards more than white parents when their children perform inadequately in school. In sum, the findings from this chapter suggest that educators and policy makers should pay particular attention to how parents respond to inadequate achievement. Imploring parents of inadequately performing students to be more involved without providing them with some guidance might exacerbate the problem.

This analysis highlights the importance of understanding parent-child dynamics with regard to education outcomes. The No Child Left Behind initiative calls for schools to increase parental involvement by implementing programs to involve parents in ways that promote academic success. Yet, perhaps NCLB has overlooked strategies parents can employ at home to increase achievement. The present findings suggest that the effects of the NCLB mandate might be different depending on which type of parental involvement is encouraged.

— 10 —

Setting the Stage for Academic Success

The analysis in this book suggests that what is traditionally deemed "parental involvement" is generally inconsequential (or even negatively related) to academic achievement. Yet conventional wisdom tells us that parents play a key role in the educational success of their children. A major question we grappled with conducting this analysis was if our sixty-three involvement measures were failing to capture fundamental ways that parents help their children academically. In reflecting on our own experiences, we recalled that our parents did very few of the activities we discuss in this book, yet they were instrumental to our academic success. Well then, what exactly were they doing? The short answer is that our parents were setting the stage for us to do well in school—that is, they were not involved in the traditional sense, yet created the conditions under which our success could be fostered.

We employ the metaphor of "stage setting" to convey this idea. In theater, stage setters are responsible for creating a context that allows the cast to successfully enact the play. They create a life space—the parameters within which the actor's performance occurs—that corresponds with the intended action. Poor stage setting can compromise an actor's ability to successfully play a role, thereby leading to a poor performance because it does not draw the audience into the world intended by the playwright. The stage setter reinforces the performance at critical transition phases, such as in between acts. Thus, a good performance can be characterized as a partnership between two critical components: (1) the actor embodying the role s/he is portraying, and (2) the stage setter creating and maintaining an environment that reinforces (or at the very least does not compromise) the actor's embodiment of their role. Likewise, many parents construct and manage the social environment around their children in a way that creates the conditions where academic success is possible. In our view, this analogy captures what many parents do to set up their children for academic success. We build on this concept in the following section. We first report on the results of focus groups intended to lay the foundation for understanding how parental involvement actually operates in children's schooling.

How Parents Set the Stage

When we were graduate students at the University of Michigan, one of our Asian American peers (we will call her Tina) informed us during casual conversation that her sibling was enrolled in a prestigious law school. When asked what her parents did to attain such success from their children, she recalled "my parents rarely talked to us about school. They did not help us with homework nor read to us. Their expectations of us were really high though. My sister and I knew from an early age that doing well in school was the only option. Although they had high expectations of us, they were not really involved in our education." Tina identified the important role that her parents played in helping her attain academic success, yet the ways they helped were not through a commitment to a set of home- or school-based practices. This story provided an impetus for us to further explore the types of things parents do that might not be reflected in our analyses.

We conducted two focus groups during the fall of 2009 with students enrolled in two sociology courses at a major public university in the Southwest. Each focus group consisted of thirty students and lasted forty minutes. The participants, most of whom were sociology majors, were asked to reflect on their parents' involvement during their K–12 schooling. Two main questions were asked during these focus groups: (1) "During K–12 schooling, what were the involvement activities your parents employed specifically to help you academically?" and (2) "Thinking back to the ways your parents were involved academically over K–12 schooling, what involvement activities or activity do you feel had the largest contribution to you being where you are now (attending this University)?" An example of ten traditional forms of involvement—including reading books to a child, attending PTA meetings, and discussing school courses with the child—followed the first main interview question. Participants were also asked follow-up questions regarding their family composition, during which specific stage(s) of their K–12 schooling certain involvement activities were conducted, where they lived at various ages of their lives, how often their parent(s) engaged in certain involvement activities, and what extracurricular activities they participated in during their childhood and adolescence. The two main questions were asked the same way in both classes. Both sessions were recorded for analysis.

To be clear, we wish to acknowledge three limitations to this exercise. First, the two samples of students are not representative of the larger population of students between ages 18–22, particularly since they all have performed well enough academically to warrant admission into a flagship university. Second, no serious planning was done before posing questions to the students. Whereas our information is drawn from two forty-minute sessions, rigorous qualitative research is almost always based on *at least* a few hours—if not weeks or months—of interviews and observation. Third, because of time constraints, students were not asked further questions that would help us identify patterns by race or class. For these reasons, we cannot identify the mechanisms by which parental involvement operates from this analysis. However, we can observe patterns in this sample of academically successful students that are helpful when discussing stage setting. This exercise is meant to be illustrative, not conclusive, in conveying some ways in which parental involvement might operate in children's academic lives. In the following subsections, we identify several themes that emerged suggesting the roles parents play in fostering academic success in their children. These themes are not mutually exclusive or cumulative or completely related. Nonetheless, we feel they provide important context for understanding the role of parents in children's schooling.

Theme I: The Supportive Parent

Most students claimed that the main ways their parents were involved in their academic lives was through the support they provided. When pushed to define "support," one student expressed that her parents consistently attended all of the extracurricular activities in which she participated (e.g., soccer and band) while showing equal interest in her schooling. She went on to say that although her parents could not help her much with schoolwork after she finished fifth grade, she took their consistent support in all her activities as an indication that they wanted her to do well in each activity she engaged in—whether it was soccer, school, or band. Many students described their parents' support in nonacademic activities as being equal to their support in school. Importantly, they felt this support was instrumental in helping them do well academically because it was viewed as a general interest in their life overall rather than as "pressure" to do well. These students appreciated feeling that their parents cared about the activities in which they spent their time. Ultimately, we think they were describing a context characterized by a comfortable space where their own academic (or other) motivations could develop.

Similarly, students felt supported by their parents when encouraged to put forth their "best effort." Three students said their parents told them at young ages (in elementary school) that "as long as you put forth your best effort, that is all that matters." When asked why they felt this was such an important contribution, one student expressed that it was because she was given a message to do her best in school that was not replete with an overwhelming pressure to succeed. The other students agreed. Note that this form of support could easily be conceptualized as setting expectations. The supportive parent seems to be effective at communicating to their child that s/he has people who care about their overall success in life while defining a space for their child that is virtually free of parent-imposed pressure to do well academically. This type of support contrasts with support that can be considered micromanagement of students' school affairs—that is, support that could be viewed as intrusive or overbearing.

Theme II: Getting into Good Schools

The second theme emerged from students crediting their parents for steering their school choices as they transitioned through their academic careers. One student felt this guidance was the most important way his parents influenced his academic success. He viewed the quality of instruction he received in the primary and secondary schools he attended as critical for preparing him to attend a top university—which he attributes to his parents' school selection. Three other students cited their parents' skillful navigation of the K–12 school system as the most important contribution their parents made to their academic lives. In some cases, this contribution meant sending them to expensive private schools, which conveyed to the students the importance their parents placed on academic success. Two of the students identified the amounts of money their parents were investing in their private school education as a strong motivation for taking school seriously. The students who did not attend private schools recalled their parents' vigorous efforts to enroll them into high-quality public schools, which they took as indication that academics should be the primary factor in their lives.

Theme III: Conveying the Importance of School

Encouraging best efforts is not the only way parents communicated their academic expectations. One student said his parents drove him to poor and violent areas of town and told him he would end up there if he did not perform well in school. Another student said her parents *repeatedly* told her when she was young that not doing well in school would land her a job at a fast-food restaurant for the rest of her life. It seems these warnings were important in at least two ways. First, at a very early age, they communicated the importance school has for future life opportunities. Second, they provided examples of clear, undesirable outcomes for not taking school seriously. These students talked of being motivated to do well by the time they entered kindergarten and, at the same time, fearful of experiencing an undesirable outcome throughout their K–12 schooling experience. Recall the earlier example of Tina who claimed that she and her sibling *knew* academic success was the only outcome her parents would accept.

Some parents conveyed their expectations in a manner that we thought might lead children to place academic success as central to their purpose in life. Two students mentioned that their parents came to the United States purely in search of better opportunities. Each of these students recalled their parents speaking in direct terms about the educational opportunity the United States provides. One student said her parents told her nearly every day that the sole reason her family had come to this country was so that she could receive a quality education. Another student mentioned that his parents attached school success to self-worth. Not only did he feel that doing well in school was the only option during K–12, but that not attending an elite university and majoring in medicine was considered shameful. In fact, he claimed he is viewed as the "bum" of his family because he is attending a state university and majoring in sociology. Whether expectations were implicitly communicated or plainly stated, they appeared important for motivating academic success and providing these students with a clear focus on schooling that often began in elementary school and continues to present day. Although the expectations for success were high, it bears repeating that parents supported those expectations in ways not considered intrusive or resembling micromanagement.

Theme IV: Adopting an Academic Identity

When asked to name the most important involvement activity or activities that contributed to their academic success, several students recalled being told, "You're the smart one." When asked why this labeling was particularly important for their success, the students described it as motivation to do well in school stemming from a sense of responsibility to their parents and siblings. They each mentioned receiving this message at various points throughout their childhood and adolescence. This labeling defined an academic identity for them that was unique from the identities of their siblings (follow-up questions uncovered that most of the students had siblings). Students described feeling as though their parents were passing the torch to them to bring academic success to the family. One of the students who commented on this theme described her parents' attitudes as "just let her [student] do her thing." In her view, despite their high expectations, her parents were intentionally hands-off because they felt she was smart enough to succeed in school without their assistance. Although some students felt burdened by the "smart one" label, others viewed it as a responsibility they were pleased to embrace.

We would not necessarily suggest instilling motivation in children by defining a child's "smartness" relative to his or her siblings. What seems to be important is the sense of motivation to do well academically that these parents were able to foster through positive labeling and reinforcement. This process of instilling academic motivation was not done on a daily basis; instead it was reinforced at various points in children's lives and maintained its importance over time as children progressed through schooling. Notably, students struggled to provide an answer for the most important involvement activity or activities that contributed to their academic success. This difficulty in responding is a telling point that we will discuss in the next section.

A Return to Stage Setting

So what do we make of all this? Let us first return to the idea of stage setting. Stage setting has more to do with parents' messages about the importance of schooling and the overall quality of life that they create for their children. Although we certainly conceptualize these activities as parental involvement, they are fundamentally distinct from the traditional conception that we examined in Chapters 1–9. Recall that our analysis was on factors that parents employ to *directly* affect their children's achievement, such as reading to the child, helping with homework, and meeting with teachers. With the exception of parents' educational expectations, we examined a conception of involvement that reflects the more mundane day-to-day aspects of children's academic lives and parents' conscious attempts to engage in behaviors or activities that they believe will help their children succeed academically. If parental involvement is conceived of in this manner, then our findings suggest only moderate support for the notion that parental involvement "works." However, stage setting is closer to the intangible type of parenting described by Lareau (2003), which is more about cultivating or enriching the child than affecting a particular academic outcome. For example, activities such as taking a child to museums and involving them in extracurricular endeavors (e.g., ballet or piano lessons) are only tangentially about increasing achievement; the benefits of such activities are related to "broadening horizons" rather than attaining an "A" in math.

Stage setting is a conception of parental involvement that includes two components: (1) conveying the importance of education to a child, and (2) the creation and maintenance of an environment or life space in which learning can be maximized, or at the very least, not compromised. Parents vary in the extent to which they can successfully accomplish these components. For instance, *most* parents express that education is important, yet some parents are able to convey this message in a manner that makes the message more central to children's frame of reference. Parents' level of success in this process can be measured by gauging a student's academic identification, which is the degree to which academic pursuits and outcomes form the basis for overall self-evaluation (i.e., global self-esteem) (Osborne 1997). For a child to sustain school success, s/he must identify school achievement as a part of his/her self-definition (Steele 1997). We found this among parents who conveyed messages about educational opportunity in the United States versus their home country, and parents who inspired motivation through positive labeling like "the smart one."

In terms of creating a life space conducive to academic success, parents who engage in successful stage setting likely consider the impact of both home and school. At home, an ideal learning environment is one where a child's basic and essential needs are met (e.g., food and shelter). As a result, s/he need not worry about the family's ability to survive. Whereas the needs of an economically disadvantaged youth and an affluent youth might be met, the former is likely to be much more aware of the tenuous nature with which their needs are being met than the latter. At the neighborhood level, an environment conducive to learning is one in which children feel safe and residents enjoy a good quality of life. We provide further elaboration on each of these stage-setting components below.

Messages about the Value of Schooling

Although most parents want the best for their children—which in most cases includes some level of academic success—they vary in the degree to which they can *successfully* convey the importance of school to their children. Within the context of stage setting, the difference between conveying the message and *successfully* transmitting the message is that the message "sticks" in the latter case; that is, it becomes a major basis for how children define themselves. Thus, success is entirely measured by how deeply engrained the message is within the child's identity.

Ideally, a student's global self-esteem (i.e., overall view of the self) is entirely determined by his/her academic self-concept; s/he is completely identified with academic success. It is important to note that an individual's self-concept in a particular domain (e.g., academic ability) is both conceptually and empirically distinct from his/her global self-esteem (Marsh 1986; Rosenberg 1979; Rosenberg et al. 1995). On the one hand, a student may evaluate her/himself negatively in terms of academic ability yet still have positive self-esteem, and on the other hand, a student may evaluate her/himself positively in terms of academic ability and have negative self-esteem (Crocker and Major 1989). In both cases, academic ability is not central to that student's identity and thus not crucial for their overall evaluation of self. Osborne (1997, 728) notes that "students who are more identified with academics should be more motivated to succeed because their self-esteem is directly linked to academic performance. For these students, good performance should be rewarding and poor performance should be punishing." By contrast, a low academic identity means that there is no contingency between academic outcomes and self-esteem; good performance is not rewarding, and poor performance is not punishing. As such, a student who does not identify with academics has little incentive to expend effort in academic endeavors and may focus their efforts elsewhere (i.e., whatever is most consequential for their self-esteem).[1]

Some parents experience external challenges linking academic success to their children's global self-esteem. Steele (1997, 613) notes that identification with a particular domain requires that one perceives "good prospects in the domain, that is, that one has the interests, skills, resources, and opportunities to prosper there, as well as that one belongs there, in the sense of being accepted and valued in the domain." He further argues that societal pressures against certain groups "can frustrate this identification; and that in school domains where these groups are negatively stereotyped, those who have become domain identified face the further barrier of stereotype threat, the threat that others' judgments or their own actions will negatively stereotype them in the domain" (1997, 613). Numerous studies demonstrate that school processes such as differential disciplinary enforcement in school, the privileging of white and middle-class norms (Lareau 2003), and tracking (Bowles and Gintis 1976; Lucas 1999; Tyson 2011) perpetuate group differences and make blacks and Hispanics more susceptible to stereotype threat.

We argue that whereas most parents convey the importance of education to their children, socioeconomic status partially determines the extent to which the message becomes a central feature of youths' self-definition. Relative to working class and poor parents, middle-class parents are better able to place their children within contexts that reinforce the connection between youths' academic self-esteem and global self-esteem, or where at the very least the factors that can challenge the centrality of academic success within youths' self-definition are minimal. We discuss this second component of stage-setting further in the next section.

A Life Space Conducive to Learning

The degree to which messages about the importance of education are successfully transmitted also depends on the life space parents create for their children at home and in the neighborhood. The very space itself may transmit messages that have an impact on the way children approach schooling. Additionally, messages from within the home and messages in the neighborhood may conflict with each other. For example, a parent may attempt to link her child's self-esteem with academic success, but if the family is surrounded by a neighborhood context that does not transmit the same messages, these efforts at home could be compromised. Thus, identical academic messages from two different sets of parents could result in different levels of academic identity if they live in different types of neighborhoods (e.g., Beverly Hills versus inner-city Detroit). Not only does the neighborhood context facilitate or hinder parental efforts to convey the importance of academics, it also serves as an important frame of reference in which to identify the connection between school and their future selves in these spaces.

Parents have greater control of their children's life space at home than outside of their homes. They can control the physical space in ways that can reinforce or convey messages about the relative importance of school. For example, the decisions regarding whether to have a television in a child's bedroom, a desk in their bedroom or in a more common area, book shelves in the living room or in a home office each communicate—even if in a nonverbal manner—something about the importance of learning. Outside the home, parental control of the life space is limited. Their control is mainly limited to the "selection" of where to live. Once that decision is made, the neighborhood has its own influence independent of parents. In neighborhoods characterized as unsafe, the most parents can do is limit their children's movement within the neighborhood in hopes of minimizing the effect of factors that may compromise academic success. Thus, parents' ability to secure spaces conducive to learning is not entirely driven by personal choice; social class is a major determinant in the extent to which parents can influence their children's life space.

Stage setting deems the context of children's lived experiences to be just as important as the educational messages they receive from their parents. Consider a fictional middle-class parent named Tom and his child. Tom's home is located in a neighborhood inhabited by professionals and their families. Nearby is a well-funded high school, a thriving business section, coffee shops and restaurants, a major university, and several large parks where youth sporting games are played (e.g., soccer, baseball). On weekends, parents from the neighborhood attend their children's games and often arrange for postgame trips to a local restaurant. Such activities provide opportunities for parents and children to interact about children's current school experiences, academic progress, and college plans.

Tom's child is in a fortuitous position because the pro-academic messages he receives from his father will be reinforced by his interactions with the community. Tom values education and has set the stage for his child to succeed. As a middle class parent, Tom is likely to be quite involved in his child's schooling. His home may contain many books, he attends school functions, he knows his child's teachers, and he is well aware of the literature touting the benefits of involved parents. When we as researchers view Tom in the data set he will be a parent who is high on involvement (home and school) with a child who is high achieving. Others in the data like Tom and his child will lead us toward the connection that highly involved parents tend to produce academically successful children. This conclusion would not recognize the fact that Tom set the stage for his child to do well in school. Once the stage was set, his child was on course to being academically successful. Tom proceeded to be highly involved, which we capture in the data, but his involvement is not what is driving his child's school success. It is the fact that Tom has created a space that sets this child up for success. This stage-setting process is what we do not adequately capture in quantitative data sets.

Effective stage setting becomes easier to conceptualize when one considers the strong connection between the educational attainment of parents and their children. For example, most academicians tend to have children who are academically successful. They also have certain aspects to their lifestyle that reinforce the importance they attribute to education or living a life of the mind, which often includes a home office, regular perusal of national media sources (e.g., *The New York Times* or *Los Angeles Times*, *Washington Post*), occasional dinner parties, effortless (and even oblivious) engagement in (or enactment of) critical thinking in common everyday discussions, and a group of peers with levels of education above the national norm. This lifestyle would describe many academics regardless of whether they have children. In most cases, a child growing up under these conditions cannot help but be academically successful. Whereas for most people a high school diploma is a major marker or transition point, college professors consider K–16 as compulsory; other than occurring at a different location, the difference between grades 13 and 12 is the same as the difference between grades 12 and 11. Thus, for academicians, high educational expectations are built into their lifestyle—and the extent to which they can create such a lifestyle—and not in parental involvement. They are able to (1) convey the importance of education to their children—the very concept of education is woven into the fabric of their identity—and (2) can affect a life space for their children that constantly reinforces the message. Thus, their children are likely to be academically successful regardless of how involved they are in their children's schooling.

Schools are also a component of the life space youth navigate. Schools are not fixed autonomous structures but dynamic social systems comprising teachers and students that have implications for youths' academic experiences. Parents can intervene in this space on behalf of their children in some of the ways that we capture with our measures. Also, a positive life space at home can create a buffer against negative experiences youth might have at school. However, similar to neighborhoods, schools can have an effect on academic achievement independent from the life space parents create in the home.

Stage Setting versus Traditional Parental Involvement

Stage setting is different from the traditional conception of parental involvement that we examined in this study. The difference becomes apparent when one considers how each might be employed by parents. Whereas traditional forms of involvement would require parents to engage in any number of activities similar to those examined in this study, stage setting only requires that parents focus on two factors: messages and life space. Certainly, parents can employ some of the measures that we examined in Chapters 1–9 to accomplish each of these factors. However, stage setting aims can also be achieved without employing any of our measures. Thus, a busy parent with a demanding career could be a successful stage setter with minimal direct involvement in their child's schooling affairs.

The behavior of Tina's parents, discussed at the beginning of this chapter, can be described as stage setting. Her parents created a life space that enables academic success. They might have reinforced the life space by engaging in stage resetting at key transition points, such as from elementary school to junior high, and from junior high to high school. It may also involve reiterating a message at different times in a child's life, such as, "School deserves your best effort." Messages of this kind can be important for placing academics at the center of a child's life among a number of competing activities/interests (e.g., cheerleading, playing video games, leisure time with friends, ballet, sports). Her parents were able to successfully elevate the relevance of success in the academic domain to a more central place in Tina's life than success in other domains.

Survey data reveal that some traditional forms of parental involvement "work" whereas others do not. However, these forms of involvement are not capturing the life space within which children operate, which is independent from activities that parents actually employ. We mentioned that students in our focus groups struggled when asked to name the most important involvement activities that contributed to their academic success. They mentioned things such as, "They were supportive in life"; "They attended my band concerts"; "They left schooling up to me"; or "They did not talk much at all about school." At one point students were asked, "Did any of your parents read books to you when you were a child, join PTA meetings, regularly converse with your teachers, or discuss college plans with you?" Many students shook their heads, and a male student recalled, "My parents didn't do any of those things with me. I have two older siblings that my parents gave attention to, so by the time I came along they were too tired to do anything academically with me."

The struggle students had in answering our questions highlights the challenge of trying to conceptualize how their parents assisted academically. This difficulty in responding is rather revealing. The measures we use in this book are conspicuous. For example, it should be fairly easy to recall your parents being a member of a PTA, reading books to you at younger ages, having rules about homework, or having discussions with you about college or school courses. However, if your parents were in the background, so to speak, affecting your academic performance in abstract ways such as gradually changing your perspective on life, giving you the feeling that they support your efforts in school and extracurricular activities, or instilling an academic motivation in you when you first began formal schooling, it would likely be more difficult to quantify the behavioral contributions they have made to your academic life. After reviewing the discussion with students in both focus groups, we had the impression that most students had never thought about the specific activities their parents' engaged in to enhance their school performance or whether these activities contributed to their academic success.

The themes that emerged from the focus groups describe the importance parents placed on children's academic success in ways that differ from conventional involvement activities schools and policy makers currently advocate. Parents' primary contributions, according to students, stemmed from setting high academic expectations and creating a comfortable space for them to develop their own academic motivations. These are core principles that advocates for parental involvement understand as important. In fact, they are the very same principles that the educational community is attempting to capture in proscribing conventional involvement activities. Yet, the ways in which parents transferred these sentiments to the students we spoke with were different from the sixty-three measures we evaluated in this study.

Stage-Setting Profiles

For further clarity, we provide a cross-tabulation for stage setting in Figure 10.1 that yields four distinct profiles. Whereas children's *quality or conduciveness-to-learning environment* (QCLE) is listed along the *y*-axis, the degree of successful *internalization of the message that schooling is important* is listed along the *x*-axis. Although crosstabs convey that the factors along the *x*- and *y*-axes are dichotomized, they are useful in this case because they highlight four general profiles associated with the concept of stage setting. However, both quality or conduciveness to learning environment and the degree of internalization of messages about education that youth receive fall along a continuum, which we convey with the labels *low, moderate,* and *high* rather than two categories such as low and high.[2]

A general profile of children who fall into each quadrant is contained within each quadrant in Figure 10.1. Children whose values on each factor

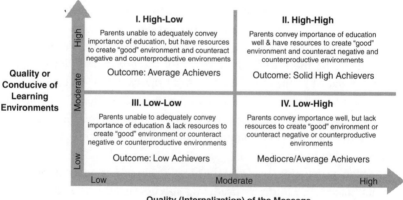

FIGURE 10.1. Learning environment and message about the value of schooling: Stage setting.

would place them in the first quadrant will typically live in environments that can be characterized as very conducive to (and reinforcing of) learning but yet would be low on levels of academic identification (thus the label "high-low"). Despite not feeling strongly defined by academics, these children will perform well enough in school to graduate from high school and even to attend college. This quadrant represents the typical child in a middle-class or affluent community whose academic performance places them within the middle to lower end of the achievement distribution in their schools. Although they are not among the high achievers in their schools, their achievement levels do not raise any flags for serious concern; their likelihood of dropping out of school is low. Children in the second quadrant are those who live in a similar environment (high on QCLE) but have also internalized the positive messages about the value of schooling they receive in a manner that embeds academics within their self-definition. These children would be high achievers, and maybe even overachievers who graduate from high school toward the top of their class and gain admission into selective colleges and universities.

The third quadrant—labeled "low-low"—represents children who live in contexts that are not conducive to learning and are not strongly identified with academics. These children would be low achievers regardless of their parents' level of involvement in their schooling. The message about the importance of schooling is not conveyed in a manner that anchors academics into the core of how children define themselves and the environment children navigate compromise this process. This quadrant captures the typical low achieving child in disadvantaged communities. Finally, children in the "low-high" group described in the fourth quadrant are those who strongly identify with academics but live in contexts that do not reinforce their academic identity. Children in this profile are typically the average to high achievers in disadvantaged communities. Figure 10.1 provides some direction for how the concept of stage setting can be tested. We argue that children's location within the framework depicted in Figure 10.1 strongly determines their achievement independent of their parents' level of *direct* involvement.

This framework is also helpful for understanding why variation in achievement exists between students who appear to be similar in many ways, such as in the school they attend, the community in which they live, and even the family from which they come. For example, although children in the top quadrants could be similar along numerous dimensions, their achievements will be determined by how strongly they identify with academics. At the same time, this framework allows one to identify clear patterns. Students with "high" QCLE levels are virtually ensured that they will never be in any serious risk of becoming high school dropouts. Even when compared to children in the third quadrant, children in the first quadrant will perform better academically; they can ride the wave of their high QCLE in a manner that allows them to overcome their lack of academic identity. In fact, their identity in other domains that can be afforded to them by their middle-class status (e.g., lacrosse, gymnastics, soccer) might enable them to gain admission into good colleges despite their average levels of achievement. Similarly, levels of academic identification vary among children who are situated within "low" QCLE contexts (in the third and fourth quadrants), which might account for the variation in achievement observed among children who appear to be similarly disadvantaged.

Stage Setting, Social Class, and Race

As noted earlier, we did not attach students' family socioeconomic backgrounds to their parental involvement when describing the themes that emerged from our focus groups. We allude to the idea that parents' ease of stage setting is related to socioeconomic resources primarily because the resources commonly found in affluent communities are more reinforcing of parents' attempts at embedding the value of schooling within their children. In fact, spatial concentration of advantage within neighborhoods has an independent effect on youths' academic outcomes. This idea is not new. Ainsworth (2002) finds that as the percentage of adults with a college education and a professional or managerial occupation within a community increases, so do youths' educational aspirations and achievement. Furthermore, Ainsworth shows that the benefit of having high-status residents in a neighborhood overshadows the effects of negative neighborhood characteristics. He finds that more than half of the detrimental effect of living in economically deprived neighborhoods is attributable to a lack of high-status residents in such neighborhoods.

Conversely, living in areas with high concentrations of poverty can compromise the extent to which parents' messages about the value of schooling is ingrained into their children. Classic sociological studies note that disadvantaged communities lack the resources to adequately sustain neighborhood institutions and public services and are characterized by persistent joblessness, which contribute to making high-poverty areas breeding places for factors (e.g., crime, violence, substance abuse) that can dislodge academic self-esteem from global self-esteem (Massey and Denton 1993; Wilson 1987, 1996). These conditions inhibit the development of educational skills, thereby depressing school achievement, which in turn discourages teachers. Wilson (1987, 57) argues that "a vicious cycle is perpetuated through family, through the community, and through the schools"—features we note are part of youths' life space.

Race can also have implications for parents' ability to effectively set the stage for their children. In particular, parents from historically subordinate racial groups—such as black Americans—face challenges within their environments beyond their control that directly affect their children's life space. For example, black parents must raise children to identify with a domain in which evidence suggests they are rejected. Hanushek, Kain, and Rivkin (2004) provide strong evidence that a higher rate of minority enrollment increases the probability that white teachers will exit a school, even more than a lower rate of wages. They find that a 10% increase in black enrollment would require about a 10% increase in salaries to neutralize the elevated probability that white teachers will leave a school. Furthermore, they find that the racial composition of schools is an important determinant of the probability that white teachers—particularly newer teachers—will leave public schools entirely and switch school districts. Freeman, Scafidi, and Sjoquist (2005) also find that white teachers are much more likely to leave schools that serve higher proportions of black students in favor of schools that serve lower proportions of black and low-income students and that have students who scored higher on achievement exams.

The reality that black parents must cultivate an academic identity in children that some educators attempt to avoid is particularly disconcerting given that this avoidance appears to adversely affect the quality of instruction they receive. In a study about the implication of school racial composition for teacher quality, Jackson (2009) found that in schools in which the share of black student enrollment increased following the repeal of a busing program to maintain racial balance across schools within a school district, there was a decrease in the proportion of experienced teachers, in teachers with high licensure exam scores, and in teachers who had previously demonstrated an ability to improve student test scores. Jackson's (2009) study design supports the conclusion that the absence of high-quality teachers in schools with high proportions of black students is caused by the racial composition of the schools rather than by neighborhood characteristics. Jackson further determined that the change in school quality immediately following the repeal of the busing program indicated that teachers exited in anticipation of the arrival of more black students.[3] Thus, given the negative implications of attending a predominantly black school—which is the case for many black youth within the U.S.—black parents have a particularly unique challenge in effectively setting the stage for their children's academic success.

Although stage setting may be easier for families with more socioeconomic resources compared to families with fewer socioeconomic resources, it is important not to conflate stage setting and social class. In theory, socioeconomically disadvantaged parents can effectively set the stage for their child to experience academic success; there are socioeconomically disadvantaged high achievers. However, their exceptionality suggests that disadvantaged parents are less likely to be successful stage setters because they face greater challenges in doing so than more affluent parents. Thus, stage setting is not a proxy for social class but a mechanism that explains the link between social class and achievement. Social class operates through stage setting to affect achievement; social class is highly predictive of stage setting. For example, the reason why scholars have observed a strong negative association between poverty and achievement is that poverty can be disruptive to children's everyday lives (Duncan and Rodgers 1988). Seccombe (2000) highlights several studies that show that over the course of a year a majority of the poorest families experience at least one of the following deprivations: eviction, crowded housing, disconnection of utilities, no stove, no refrigerator, and housing with upkeep problems. All these aspects of the life space have an impact on stage-setting; they are the mechanisms that explain why lower-socioeconomic circumstances are related to poor achievement. In fact, we posit that stage setting explains a greater share of the link between social class and achievement than traditional forms of parental involvement.

We illustrate this link in Figure 10.2, which contains the conceptual and empirical models that we are describing. Specifically, the two models depict the role of parental involvement for children's achievement relative to social class and race. The conceptual model suggests that class/race differences exist in traditional forms of parental involvement (path *b*). However, we portray path *c* in gray to convey that the connection between traditional forms of parental involvement and achievement is tenuous. Instead, it is

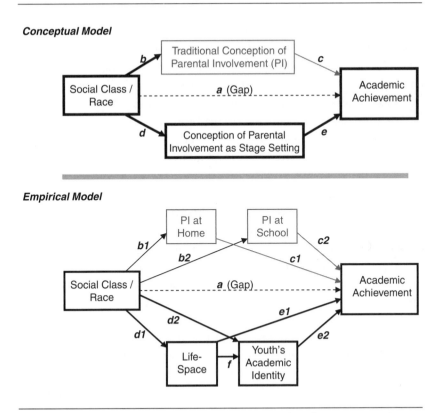

FIGURE 10.2. Conceptual and empirical model for parental involvement as a mechanism for explaining the social class/race-achievement link.

stage setting that accounts for class/race differences in academic achievement; groups vary in their ability to successfully set the stage (path *d*), and stage setting strongly determines academic achievement (path *e*).

Whereas the conceptual model provides the general theoretical framework, the empirical model provides some degree of clarity on the overall process of our perspective. Because the traditional conception of parental involvement contains two components—home and school—we decompose path *b* into paths *b1* and *b2*. Similarly, the "effects" for parental involvement (PI) are decomposed into paths *c1* (home) and *c2* (school). The empirical model depicts that parents vary along class and racial lines in the forms of involvement they employ both at home and at school, but that these forms of involvement are only modestly related to children's achievement, represented by the gray paths. Instead, the factors associated with stage setting illustrated in the bottom portion of the empirical model are the driving forces behind how parents matter in their children's academic lives. Specifically, class and race are major factors in determining the quality or conduciveness to learning of children's life space (path *d1*) and the extent to which children identify with academics (path *d2*), and each of these factors affect academic achievement (paths *e1* and *e2*) independent of traditional forms of parental involvement. Path *f* denotes that the quality of children's life space influences—either reinforces or compromises—youths' academic identity.

The role of stage setting as a mechanism becomes more apparent when one considers that social class strongly predicts achievement, whereas traditional measures of parental involvement do so only moderately at best. Entwisle, Alexander, and Olson (2005, 1460) note, "When children start kindergarten . . . their standardized test scores follow socioeonomic gradient." This claim is consistent with the notion that children's academic prowess is shaped by their social class position even before they begin schooling. Although traditional forms of parental involvement are generally thought to be the reason behind this pattern, the silent part of the story is that the effects of social class operate largely through stage setting. We suspect that affluent parents are being credited with superior parental involvement when in fact it is stage setting—academically identified youth whose basic needs are met, often within "nice" communities—that is driving the academic success of their children.

Recall that our findings in Chapter 2 suggest that affluent parents tend to be more involved and to have high-achieving children. Many educators view the success of these children as resulting in large part to their parents' involvement, which our findings suggest is only moderately the case. These children are likely to attend well-funded schools with excellent teachers, characteristics associated more with life space than parental involvement. We realize that a positive life space alone does not guarantee academic success, as school finance reform has greatly reduced funding disparities between high-performing suburban districts and low-performing urban districts (Odden and Picus 2007). What contributes to the effectiveness of these positive factors within the life space is that the message about the importance of schooling has a more lasting effect on the children of affluent parents because there are fewer threats that can dislodge youths' academic self-esteem from their global self-esteem. To be clear, affluent parents are more involved than their less advantaged counterparts. Educators will find the anecdotally observed relationship between parental involvement and high achievement too appealing to ignore and will promote parental involvement as the answer to most of the problems within K–12. But as we show, an extensive quantitative assessment only lends moderate support for these anecdotal observations. What we propose is that affluent parents have created a space that sets these children up for success.

In sum, effective stage setting is more rooted in lifestyle than in parental involvement activities. Once the stage is set for academic success, children are on course toward being academically successful. A child with an academic profile that places them on course to attend Princeton University will not suddenly "tank" if their parents pull back on their level of involvement. Neither is such a child guaranteed to stay on the Princeton course without further parental involvement. But it would be unlikely that a child with a positive academic profile would drop out of high school—the child would likely gain admission into a top university or other fine institution of higher learning. Our point is that for the child to remain on a positive course—Princeton or elsewhere—the parent might simply need to maintain the positive space conducive to academic success, which may or may not include traditional forms of parental involvement. A key advantage of stage setting over traditional conceptions of parental involvement is that it does not conform to the one-size-fits-all mantra. That is, whereas traditional conceptions advocate for the same activities among all parents, stage setting is contextual and may involve different types of support for different children.

— 11 —

Conclusion

Le mieux est l'ennemi du bien. / The best is the enemy of the good.
—Francois-Marie Aronet, better known as Voltaire,
French philosopher, 1694–1778

The issue of parental involvement is complicated. Research continues to communicate that families provide the child's most important learning environment, yet remains unclear about how exactly parents can contribute to the academic success of their children. A review of the literature on parental involvement provides an informative but limited understanding of this issue. What we are left with is a series of studies that provide snapshots of parental involvement from various angles.

What has been missing from the literature is a study that provides an in-depth quantitative assessment of parental involvement across an extensive set of measures and across the major racial groups in the United States to determine (1) where the differences exist, (2) which forms of involvement are related to increases in achievement for each group, and (3) which forms of involvement can explain racial and class-based disparities in achievement. This book represents our attempt to provide such a study and was designed to address several important questions. Do social class and racial disparities exist in parental involvement at home? Do parents differ by class and by race in the forms of involvement that brings them into contact with schools? What forms of involvement lead to increases in achievement for each major racial group within the United States? What proportion of the achievement gap can parental involvement explain for each racial group relative to whites? Do social class and racial differences exist in how parents respond to their child's poor academic achievement?

To address each of these questions, we conducted copious analyses testing the limits of parental involvement's influence on academic outcomes. We employed nearly every measure of parental involvement that has been

220

used in previous studies—sixty-three in total—and examined their implications on various academic outcomes. We conducted analyses by social class and across six racial groups. Although a critique can be made about each measure of involvement and outcome, we caution critics to consider the epigraph at the opening of this chapter. We concede that our measures cannot elucidate many qualitative aspects of involvement, yet we are satisfied with the contribution our study makes to understanding the role of parental involvement in children's schooling within the United States. If the effects of parental involvement are as strong as purported and these effects are perceptible to quantitative methodology, then the unequivocal benefits for students should surely have been reflected in our findings. The extensiveness of our approach leads us to conclude that policy recommendations for a wholesale increase in parental involvement in children's education are misguided. In the following section, we address several important questions that our findings have raised.

Do Social Class and Racial Differences Exist in Parental Involvement?

In Chapter 2, we examined whether parental involvement at home and at school varies by social class. Our findings are consistent with those from previous studies; parents with higher social class backgrounds are more involved in their children's schooling both at home and at school than those with lower social class backgrounds. This finding suggests that parenting patterns with regard to children's schooling are class driven, which is consistent with the conclusion reached by Lareau (2003) that social class creates distinctive parenting styles. Furthermore, parents with higher social class backgrounds appear to prefer more active or optional forms of involvement than parents from lower social class backgrounds. By contrast, more passive forms of involvement either yield no discernible connection to social class or are adopted by a greater share of parents from lower social class backgrounds.

Our findings by race show that the answer to whether racial differences exist in parental involvement depends upon where the involvement occurs. With regard to parental involvement at home, in Chapter 5 we find that parents across racial groups are relatively similar in their levels of involvement in children's schooling. Our results are not consistent with the cultural deficiency narrative that has been attributed to Hispanics and blacks (Lewis 1961; Moynihan 1965; Ogbu 1978). Similarly, we fail to find support for the Asian cultural superiority narrative implied by the model minority label that is commonly applied to them (Chua 2011; Kao 1995; Osajima 2005). It seems that the minority experience that makes it reasonable for Hispanics and blacks to differ in the importance they attribute to education, and subsequently their levels of involvement in their children's education, does not compromise their involvement at home. The superior value of education attributed to Asian parents and the disregard for the importance of schooling attributed to Hispanic and black parents (Bol and Berry 2005; DeCastro-Ambrosetti and Cho 2005; Souto-Manning and Swick 2006) are overstated, particularly considering that the findings in Chapter 5 did not account for socioeconomic background factors.

Despite the similarity in parental involvement at home across racial groups, the findings in Chapter 7 show that levels of parental involvement with schools differed substantially by race. This finding confirms a pattern that educators have long observed and provides insight into why the popular narrative that Hispanic and black parents are less concerned with their children's education persists. Parents of youth from racial groups with an achievement disadvantage relative to whites were less involved with schools than white parents on twenty-one of the thirty-one measures of parental involvement at school we examined in Chapter 7. Most of these differences were driven by Hispanic parents who had the lowest rates of involvement, particularly in measures of school-initiated contact and assertive forms of involvement. Given the finding that racial groups are relatively similar in their levels of involvement at home, these findings should not be considered as support for the notion that Hispanic parents do not value their children's schooling. Furthermore, our findings did not show large racial variations in parental involvement with schools, and some of the differences partially reflect that schools seem to reach out to minority parents—particularly Hispanics—less than they do to white parents.

Nevertheless, teachers might perceive Hispanic parents' reserved and nonconfrontational demeanor as an indicator that they do not care about their children's education. However, research on Hispanic immigrant families indicates that immigrant parents place a high value on education and being involved in their children's academic lives (Goldenberg and Gallimore 1995; Suarez-Orozco, Suarez-Orozco, Todorova 2008). A recent report from the Pew Hispanic Center finds that Hispanic parents expect more from their children than youth expect for themselves. More than three-quarters

(77%) of Hispanic youths (age 16 to 25) surveyed report that their parents think going to college is the most important thing to do following high school, whereas less than half (48%) say they plan to obtain a bachelor's degree or more (Lopez 2009). It appears that even when parents are new to the United States they continue to have high educational aspirations for their children and value the educational opportunities this country provides for their youth.

We suspect that there are barriers to involvement within schools that perpetuate the types of racial variation we report in Chapter 7. For one, parents' perceptions of teachers and their responses to schools' requests for involvement are highly dependent on social class (Gillies 2008; Lareau 2003). Racial minorities often suffer from a lack of institutional knowledge that determines how to become legitimate participants in schools. Studies have shown that parents from immigrant groups tend to defer to teachers on matters related to their child's classroom activities and behaviors (Suarez-Orozco and Suarez-Orozco 2001). Unfortunately, parents who provide little to no involvement in school activities tend to be viewed as the source of children's academic troubles (Bol and Berry 2005; DeCastro-Ambrosetti and Cho 2005; Souto-Manning and Swick 2006). Educators have been concerned for decades about the low levels of participation of urban, minority parents at formally sanctioned school activities (Chavkin 1993; Dauber and Epstein 1993). At the same time, evidence suggests that low-income, minority parents are eager to be involved in their children's education, but lack the knowledge of how to be involved at home or at school (Chavkin 1993; McKay et al. 2003).

Another important barrier to parental involvement some Hispanic and Asian parents face is limited English proficiency. Communication between parents and teachers can be difficult if school personnel do not speak parents' native language, which can impede discussions concerning students' grades, behavior, progress, and homework. In a study about the factors that impede parental involvement, Smith, Stern, and Shatrova (2008) interviewed Hispanic parents and found that language played a major role in their level of involvement. Hispanic parents placed a high priority on motivating their children to work hard and behave in school, but they were reluctant to talk to the teacher if there was a problem at school. One parent expressed that conversing with a teacher would be awkward because he used his child as an interpreter when he communicated with the school (Smith, Stern, and Shatrova 2008). As the authors point out, schools rarely employ interpreters to help facilitate these discussions. Language difficulties can also compromise involvement at home. Data released by the National Household and Education Survey (NHES) indicated that from 1993 to 1999, Hispanic children (age 3 to 5) were less likely to be read to compared with non-Hispanic children (NHES 2002). Families in which Spanish is the primary language spoken at home tended to have even lower participation in literacy activities. The NHES shows that with respect to reading to children three or more times per week, Hispanic parents who only spoke Spanish at home had participation rates that were roughly 50 percent lower than white families in 1999 (Schneider, Martinez, and Owens 2006).

Does Parental Involvement Improve Achievement?

We examined whether parental involvement at home and at school is related to increases in academic outcomes by social class in Chapters 3 and 4, and by race in Chapters 6 and 8. We summarize the findings for these analyses in Table 11.1. Specifically, we show the frequency (*Freq.*) of relationships we examined between parental involvement and achievement that suggest parental involvement is associated with an increase in achievement (*Positive*), a decline in achievement (*Negative*), or no connection to achievement (not significant, or *Not sig.*). Recall that we employ the CDS to capture parental involvement prior to youth entering the first grade (younger subsample) and from elementary school through early middle school (older subsample). The NELS captures parental involvement during grade 8.

In general, the evidence does not suggest a clear positive connection between parental involvement and academic outcomes. In fact, there are a greater number of negative estimates across both data sets with two exceptions: the younger subsample yields the same number of positive and negative estimates for parental involvement at home by social class (15 in the top panel) and a greater number of positive estimates for parental involvement at school by race (32 in the bottom panel). In all, parental involvement was related to increases in achievement in roughly one-fifth of the 1,556 cases we examined in this book.

It is important to note that the share of positive estimates was higher for analysis based on the CDS. We attribute this finding to two reasons. First, the CDS captures parental involvement earlier in the schooling process than the NELS. Most studies show that parental influence is greatest in earlier stages of education (Jordan et al. 2009; Snow, Burns, and Griffin

TABLE 11.1. Frequency and percent of positive, negative, and nonsignificant estimates for the relationship between parental involvement and achievement: by race and social class

| | CDS | | | | NELS | | Total | |
| | Younger | | Older | | | | | |
	Freq.	%	Freq.	%	Freq.	%	Freq.	%
Social class								
Home								
Positive	15	31	20	33	25	15	60	22
Negative	15	31	27	45	43	27	85	31
Not sig.	18	38	13	22	94	58	125	46
School								
Positive	25	24	33	21	55	17	113	19
Negative	36	35	80	51	62	19	178	30
Not sig.	43	41	43	28	207	64	293	50
Race								
Home								
Positive	10	33	11	37	19	12	40	18
Negative	13	43	14	47	20	12	47	21
Not sig.	7	23	5	17	123	76	135	61
School								
Positive	32	41	24	31	39	12	95	20
Negative	26	33	41	53	48	15	115	24
Not sig.	20	26	13	17	237	73	270	56

Note: Percentages do not equal 100 because figures are rounded off to the nearest tenth.

1998; Whitehurst and Lonigan 1998). Second, relative to the NELS, the CDS contains a greater share of measures of parental involvement that require direct parent-child interaction (reading to child, help with homework, and three measures of parent-child discussions) and that can be characterized as active or assertive involvement at school by parents. However, although the CDS produced a greater share of positive estimates than the NELS, roughly two-thirds of the parental involvement–achievement links we examined using the CDS are not positive and overall, a greater share are negative.

Our results indicate substantial heterogeneity across families regarding which activities benefit children academically. The findings throughout this book suggest that the effects of parental involvement vary with regard to the type of involvement, social class, and race/ethnicity. Whereas our findings show no discernible pattern for the "effects" for parental involvement on achievement by social class in the NELS, the results based on the CDS in Chapter 3 suggest that active forms of involvement at home are beneficial for socioeconomically disadvantaged youth. Similarly, the findings from the CDS in Chapters 6 and 8 show that Hispanics seem to benefit most from active and assertive forms of parental involvement both at home and at school. Blacks also appear to experience gains in achievement from assertive forms of parental involvement at school. However, the findings based on the NELS suggest that the benefits of parental involvement are limited in frequency and impact during adolescence across racial groups, particularly for Asians and Hispanics. Whereas parental involvement at school is related to increases in achievement for whites and blacks in the NELS in less than one-third of the cases we examined, a benefit emerges less than 10% of the time for Hispanics. Shockingly, none of the measures of parental involvement with school are related to increases in reading, math, or grades for Asian youth.

Because conventional wisdom holds that it poses no harm to have an involved parent, why not suggest as many ways as possible for parents to participate in their children's schooling? Our findings show that the conventional wisdom is flawed; we find that there are forms of involvement that are associated with declines in achievement. The counter-intuitiveness of this finding will trouble some readers who believe that any form of parental involvement is always a good thing and that negative associations are reflective of parents' responding to poor achievement. However, the possibility that some forms of involvement as they are currently employed just do not work—or even compromise achievement—for some groups should be considered. Based on our analyses, what we can say is that involvement holds importance in our educational system as one tool for enhancing academic success and should not be cast as a minor player in positively affecting achievement. We can also say that involvement displays uneven importance across racial/ethnic groups and that the educational community needs to do a drastically better job at enhancing involvement's effectiveness for children. This community includes practitioners, parents, and policy makers.

To complicate this discussion even further, we should not be so naïve as to believe that involvement would be highly effective in improving achievement for *all* children—even if its utility were fully maximized. There are inherent limits to the effectiveness of any method designed to affect an outcome. Parental involvement and achievement do not exist in a vacuum. Their relationship exists in a broader context of influences that shape what parents do and how children respond. There is wide variation in the types of schools children attend, their classroom experiences, the neighborhoods children reside in throughout their K–12 years, the events they experience in their lives, and the networks of friends they develop. Additionally, every child is different behaviorally, emotionally, and psychologically. For these reasons, we should not expect uniformity in any achievement benefits that parental involvement confers.

Can Greater Parental Involvement Reduce Racial Achievement Gaps?

One of our major goals for this study was to determine the proportion of the racial achievement gap that can be attributed to parental involvement, particularly in light of the emphasis the No Child Left Behind Act places on parental involvement. Increasing parent involvement has become a critical focus in most school districts throughout the United States. School districts across the country are adopting organized efforts to engage parents in the education of their children. Because parent involvement is thought to be beneficial for all students, policy makers have encouraged increased involvement from low-income and minority parents as a key strategy for narrowing achievement gaps. Even if it were true that parents must become more involved in their children's education to improve achievement levels, would that be sufficient for addressing perhaps the nation's most persistent education problem—unequal achievement?

In general, parental involvement at home explains a modest proportion of the racial achievement gaps. Overall, parental involvement as a mechanism for reducing racial achievement gaps is insufficient. We show that more than 80% of the black-white gap and, in most cases, over two-thirds of the achievement disadvantage for Hispanics remains net of parental involvement (with the exception of the 50% decline in the grades disadvantage for non-Mexican Hispanics). Therefore, it is a mistake to conclude that the level of parental involvement of minority groups is the reason for the racial achievement gap or that greater parental involvement from minority groups will lead to gap convergence. Our findings suggest that socioeconomic resources explain a greater share of the racial achievement disparities than parental involvement. Unfortunately, it is much more difficult for policy to change the distribution of socioeconomic resources than to make parental involvement more efficient at gap convergence. Nevertheless, enthusiasm directed toward parental involvement as *the* answer for racial achievement gaps should be tempered. Suggesting parental involvement as a key strategy for reducing achievement inequality appears to be based more on ideology than empirical evidence.

How Should Parents Respond to Inadequate Achievement?

In Chapter 9, our aim was to test the effectiveness of punitive and nonpunitive parenting philosophies for dealing with poor achievement. We find that a nonpunitive parenting philosophy is associated with improvement in reading and math achievement, whereas a punitive parenting philosophy appears to lead children to perform worse in both subjects. It may be that nonpunitive strategies are particularly effective because they create an optimal setting under which children can devote more attention to schooling. This setting, void of punitive restrictions on activities, might foster the intrinsic motivation necessary for improved performance (Deci and Ryan 1985). It might also be that parents are reorganizing the way children spend their time, for example, suggesting (rather than explicitly demanding) they exchange some time spent on extracurricular activities for time on activities more essential for academic success. An exchange of this sort may involve spending fewer hours watching television or time alone in recreation, to more time studying with friends or attending after-school classes over the same number of hours. In this way, parents are using nonpunitive measures to adjust the way their child spends time, which might be the most effective way to motivate children academically.

Although we feel our results are important, we also recognize that parental intervention for addressing poor achievement is just one factor among many which influence achievement. Factors such as school type, curriculum, school quality, and family socioeconomic status have all been shown to play salient roles in child academic outcomes (Burkam et al. 2004; Card and Krueger 1998; Hanushek 1997; Teitelbaum 2003; White et al. 1996). However, strategies schools enact to improve performance, such as recruiting and training high-quality teachers or strengthening the quality of program instruction, have received more attention than learning which responses parents should employ to improve their children's achievement.

This study could inform policy makers and school personnel of the racial and social class variation in parental approaches for dealing with children's poor achievement and some implications for improvement. It also provides some suggestions on which responses should be encouraged and which should be avoided.

An Alternative Conception of Parental Involvement: Stage Setting

In Chapter 10 we introduced a new conception of parental involvement that we call "stage setting." We draw on the analogy of the theater because it captures our view of how parental involvement operates in children's academic lives. In a theatrical performance, actors must internalize the role they are portraying, and stage setters must ensure that the setting reinforces the performance. Similarly, youth must internalize the role of a student, and parents are responsible for creating a context that allows their children to assume the identity of an academically successful student. Thus, we define stage setting as the process of (1) conveying the importance of education to children in a manner that leads schooling to become central to how they define themselves, and (2) creating and maintaining an environment (or life space) for them in which learning can be maximized or not compromised.

Although stage setting is different from the traditional conception of parental involvement that we examined in this study, parents can employ any of the measures we examined to accomplish successful stage setting. These measures can be employed to make education central to how youth define themselves and to create or manage a life space around youth that reinforces this process. However, we argue that stage setting is a more accurate depiction of how parents affect their children's academic outcomes than the traditional conception of parental involvement. Stage setting is strongly determined by social class because the extent to which parents can control youths' environment outside of their homes is limited. Whereas the context outside the home for parents in socioeconomically advantaged communities reinforces the messages they impart to their children about the importance of schooling, parents living in areas with high concentrations of poverty have the burden of trying to shield their children from factors that can compromise their academic identity. We provide some direction for how the concept of stage setting can be tested in Chapter 10.

Final Thoughts

An obvious question that readers will ask is how should one view the importance of involvement in light of our results? Should our findings be taken as confirming evidence that traditional forms of parental involvement are effective for improving achievement despite having minimal implications for achievement gaps? The answer is ultimately up to the reader. The positive relationships we find could delight many in the educational community because they are seeing the fruits of their labor. Our findings showing that some involvement activities work better than others is a sign that perhaps we are on the right track, and the efforts of parents and teachers are making a difference in children's academic lives. Others could view the same pattern in our results and feel disenchanted that the enormous energy parents, schools, and teachers are putting forth is not more effective for children.

In our view, there are two pressing issues the educational community must address: (1) to find out which involvement activities work best for each racial/ethnic and economic group, and (2) to understand *why* particular activities work for certain groups. These are immense puzzles to solve. At this point, no one can hand parents the right package of activities that will work best for their child. Nonetheless, this package is the direction in which the educational community should be heading. Although this book does not provide all of the answers, it does yield several important lessons that should become part of the national discourse on parental involvement: (1) that families from different socioeconomic and racial/ethnic backgrounds engage in different forms of parental involvement, (2) that schools need to have well-developed programs to assist *and guide* parents with home involvement, and (3) that vast cultural, socioeconomic, and sociodemographic differences in students' backgrounds prevent a one-size-fits-all model of involvement from being widely accepted across families and from generating the type of academic success schools envision.

The ways in which the educational community currently thinks about what it means to be involved are not producing the effect many desire. Of course, the argument can be made that the lack of desired effect stems from low levels of involvement, which is why parents should be encouraged to be more involved in any way that they can. Some readers will point to the numerous instances in which our findings suggest a positive effect for parental involvement. However, we argue that the lack of desired effect for parental involvement currently observed within the United States has more to do with the counterbalancing effect of some forms of involvement that are associated with declines in achievement than with just an implementation problem—that not enough parents are involved. If the focus is on the *effects* rather than *levels* of involvement, our findings could be considered overwhelming as more than two-thirds of the connections we examine between parental involvement and achievement show either no association or a negative association.

At the very least, we need to move away from the idea that everything parents can do will be helpful, and that all that is necessary is to provide parents with a clear pathway to be involved. Perhaps it is helpful to view students (and families) as different from one another and to consider that race and social class matter, so that we can think more creatively about ways to maximize academic benefits for all students with the help of their parents, particularly considering that we do find negative associations operating from parent to child in some of our results. This view could indicate that children are simply different from one another—some children may respond well when their parents are involved on a regular basis; others may have the opposite reaction, developing resentment toward the school or their parents and ultimately struggling academically. As mentioned previously, the negative associations we find could also reflect a parent responding with increased involvement when they have a child who is not performing well in school. Regardless of what accounts for the negative associations we observed, they make clear that there are wide inefficiencies in the ways involvement is currently implemented, particularly when viewed alongside the numerous insignificant results we detected.

We emphasize the overall modesty of the connection between parental involvement and achievement because it reveals missed opportunities; parents are policy levers in the home that are currently not being maximized. Thus, rather than advocate for parental involvement, we propose a guided approach to parental involvement that considers race and social class. The lack of "effects" for Asian and Hispanic parents in our findings might stem from schools, teachers, and policy makers who promote involvement practices that simply do not fit the needs of many parents in these groups (a number of reasons these parents may feel uncomfortable adopting some practices are discussed in Chapters 5–8). The No Child Left Behind initiative calls for schools to increase levels of parental involvement by implementing programs to involve parents in ways that promote academic success. Yet, perhaps NCLB has overlooked strategies parents can employ at home to increase achievement. The present findings suggest the effects of the NCLB mandate might be different depending on a family's social class and racial background and on which type of parental involvement is encouraged.

We believe the examination of the link between parental involvement and achievement warrants further attention. The findings from this study could be greatly enhanced by qualitative analyses aimed at providing greater depth to each parental response measure. Such studies could reveal the underlying sentiment parents have when enacting a given response or could reduce the uncertainty in interpretation of response categories between parents and researchers, a consistent problem of survey research. Nevertheless, this study could inform policy makers and school personnel of racial and social class variations in parental approaches to children's schooling and some of their implications for improving achievement. It also provides some suggestions on which responses should be encouraged and which forms of involvement parents need either to avoid or to adjust so that their children's achievement is not compromised.

Appendixes

Notes

References

Acknowledgments

Index

Sources of Data

This study relied on four data sets: (1) National Education Longitudinal Study of 1988 (NELS), (2) Education Longitudinal Study of 2002 (ELS), (3) the Child Development Supplement (CDS) to the Panel Study of Income Dynamics, and (4) the Maryland Adolescent Development in Context Study (MADICS). See the following for a description of each data set used in this study.

1. National Education Longitudinal Study of 1988 (NELS)

The NELS is a nationally representative longitudinal data set collected by the National Center for Education Statistics (NCES). Sponsored by the U.S. Department of Education (USDOE), it was designed to provide trend data about critical transitions experienced by students as they leave middle or junior high school and progress through high school and into post-secondary institutions or the work force. The sample consists of nearly 25,000 students who were in the eighth grade during the first wave of data collection in 1988. The first and second follow-up surveys were conducted at two-year intervals, when respondents were in grades 10 (1990) and 12 (1992). These waves featured surveys collected from students, parents, and teachers. The NELS also contains two post–high school waves collected in 1994 and 2000, the latter eight years after the scheduled date of high school graduation. The sample was obtained using a two-stage stratified sampling design. In the first stage, NCES selected 1,057 schools from a national sampling frame stratified by region, school type (public or private), urbanicity, and minority concentration. In the second stage, more than 24,000 students in these schools completed base-year surveys.

Our analysis of the NELS is restricted to youth who responded to the 1988, 1990, and 1992 surveys. Attrition across survey waves reduces the sample size to 12,144 respondents. However, the NCES provides a weight that allows for the estimation of parameters that describe the population of eighth graders during the spring of 1988 (USDOE 2002). Thus, all analyses are based on weighted data using the appropriate NELS panel weights to adjust for sampling design (i.e., stratification, disproportionate sampling of certain strata, and clustered, multistage probability sampling), sample attrition, and nonresponse (Ingels et al. 1994), which allows for unbiased population estimates.

The NELS is part of a larger program established by the National Center for Education Statistics, which is the primary federal entity for collecting and analyzing data related to education within the United States. The NELS program was created to study the educational, vocational, and personal development of young people beginning with their elementary or high school years and following them over time as they begin to take on adult roles and responsibilities. Thus far, the NCES longitudinal studies program consists of four major studies: the National Longitudinal Study of the High School Class of 1972 (NLS-72), High School and Beyond (HS&B), the National Education Longitudinal Study of 1988 (NELS), and the Education Longitudinal study of 2002 (ELS). For this study, we used data from the NELS and ELS, which we discuss further in this appendix.

2. Education Longitudinal Study of 2002 (ELS)

The ELS is a nationally representative longitudinal data set that follows a cohort of students from the time they were high school sophomores in 2002 through the rest of their high school careers. It is the fourth in a series of school-based longitudinal studies conducted by the NCES. It contains a freshened sample to represent the high school class of 2004, which allows for trend comparisons against the high school classes of 1972 (NLS-72), 1980 (HS&B), and 1992 (NELS). Therefore, the ELS is an updated version of the NELS and has many of the same qualities of the NELS, with the primary difference being students' grade level at the base year of the study; ELS first sampled students in grade 10 rather than grade 8.

The sample consists of 15,362 students from 752 schools obtained in 2002 using the same two-stage stratified sampling design employed in the NELS. In 2004, the first follow-up year, the sample was augmented to make it representative of seniors as well. Thus, although the ELS began with a representative sample of high school sophomores in 2002, it contains a fully representative sample of high school seniors two years later. The base year cohort was freshened to include seniors who were not sophomores in the United States in 2002 (for example, students who were out of the country or who were in another grade sequence because of skipping or failing a grade). The ELS continued to follow these students into postsecondary education and/or the labor market. Students were surveyed again in 2006, when many sample members were in college for up to their second year of enrollment, while others were employed and may not have ever attended college. All sample members who were respondents in the base year were included in this study.

As part of the NCES longitudinal studies program, the ELS closely reflects the research purposes and designs of its three predecessor studies (NLS-72, HS&B, and NELS-88). For example, the ELS collected data from students and their parents, teachers, and school administrators. Also, it contains measures of student achievement and information about students' attitudes and experiences. It is designed to monitor the transition of young people as they progress from tenth grade through high school and on to postsecondary education and/or the world of work. ELS is conducted on behalf of the NCES by the Research Triangle Institute—a not-for-profit, university-affiliated research organization with headquarters in North Carolina.

3. Child Development Supplement (CDS)

The CDS is a data set collected to provide information about youth from the Panel Study for Income Dynamics (PSID). Since 1968, the PSID has collected data from a nationally representative sample of 5,000 American families on family composition changes, housing and food expenditures, marriage and fertility histories, employment, income, time spent on housework, health, consumption, wealth, pensions and savings, and philanthropic giving. Families were interviewed every year until 1997, after which data collection occurred biannually. Data was collected from members of the original sample families as well as from families formed by children of the initial sample members. In 1997, the PSID added the CDS to address the lack of information on children. Thus, the objective of the CDS is to provide a nationally representative longitudinal database of children and their families to support studies on the dynamic process of early human capital development. It contains a broad array of developmental outcomes including physical health, emotional well-being, and intellectual and academic achievement.

The CDS consists of three waves of data. The first wave (CDS-I) contains 3,563 children between the ages of 0 and 12 sampled from PSID families in 1997. The first follow-up wave (CDS-II) was conducted in 2002–03 among 2,908 children whose families remained active in the PSID panel. The children were then between the ages of 5 and 18. A third wave of data was collected in 2007, when youth were approximately ages 9 to 22. For all analysis based on the CDS, we employ a weighting system devised by the PSID staff to account for the effects of the initial probability of being sampled and attrition over time—which is generally low—and incorporates a post-stratification factor to ensure the data are nationally representative (for a detailed description of the CDS weight construction, see http://psidonline .isr.umich.edu/data/weights/).

4. Maryland Adolescent Development in Context Study (MADICS)

The MADICS contains a unique collection of measures on 1,407 black and white families (66% and 34%, respectively) from a county on the Eastern Seaboard of the United States. The sample was selected from approximately 5,000 adolescents in the county who entered middle school during 1991 via a stratified sampling procedure designed to get proportional representations of families from each of the county's twenty-three middle schools. As such, students' socioeconomic status (SES) is varied, as the sample includes families from neighborhoods in low-income urban areas, middle-class suburban areas, and rural farm-based areas. Although the mean family income in the sample is normally distributed around $45,000–$49,000 (range $5,000–$75,000 or greater), white families report significantly higher incomes ($50,000–$54,999) than black families ($40,000–$44,999).

Data were collected from the time the target youth entered middle school in the fall of 1991 until they were three years removed from high school. Specifically, the MADICS consists of five waves of data collected when youth were in grade 7 ($n = 1,407$), 8 ($n = 1,004$), 11 ($n = 954$), one year post high school ($n = 832$), and three years post high school ($n = 853$). The first three waves of data also include surveys collected from youths' parents (or primary caregiver). In supplemental analyses not shown, blacks were *not* less likely to be retained than whites; the proportion of blacks and whites within the sample remains constant across waves. Also, most attrition occurs between grades 7 and 8; only 3% of the sample is lost between grades 8 and 11. Therefore, it is unlikely that sample attrition results from students dropping out of high school (see Harris 2006 for an assessment of attrition bias).

Despite the limitation that the MADICS was not designed to draw inferences about the national population of students, it is well suited to the goals of this study. The MADICS is primarily used by psychologists for understanding psychological determinants of behavior and developmental trajectories during adolescence. Furthermore, we are unaware of theoretical models positing that the racial or social class differences or underlying causal mechanisms of parental responses to poor achievement vary by geographic area (e.g., east/west, urban/suburban). Therefore, it is not surprising that the MADICS yields results similar to those obtained from national data (e.g., see Harris 2006, 2011).

Methodology

This appendix discusses the technical aspects of the data analysis for this study. The discussion is divided into two sections: general strategy and chapter-specific descriptions. The first section contains information that applies to all analyses throughout the study. Specifically, we discuss (1) what is meant by social class, or socioeconomic status (SES), (2) our coding strategy, and (3) the strategy employed to deal with missing data and sample weights. Because we employ basic mean comparisons of achievement in Chapter 1, we discuss the analytic plan for Chapter 1 in this section. In the second section, we describe aspects of the analyses that are specific to the rest of the chapters in this book.

General Strategy

Nine major points of clarification are central to the interpretation of the findings presented in this study. First, a primary goal of this study is to document social class variation both in achievement among youth and in involvement among parents. Rather than employ a composite measure of social class that combines socioeconomic characteristics, we conduct our class-based analyses separately by parents' education (highest of either parent) and family income, which are perhaps the two most common indicators of social class. Income and education are conceptually and empirically distinct in their connection to parental involvement; each is likely to have separate implications for both the levels and effects of parental involvement. For example, although higher income is generally good for overall child well-being, simply having more material resources does not necessarily mean parents will be more involved or more efficient in their involvement. However, with regard to parents' education, it is plausible to expect that parents who hold college degrees are more knowledgeable about education, which might make them more effective in communicating the importance of education to their children and more efficient in their involvement in their children's schooling than their less educated counterparts.

Our decision to consider two separate dimensions of social class is consistent with a move among some inequality scholars who advocate for independent rather than composite measures of social class. In a critique of the widely embraced Duncan SEI measure, Hauser and Warren (1997) argue that individual measures of social class allow researchers to select the measures most suitable for their research question and guard against erroneous conclusions that might be produced by composite measures. Furthermore, by decomposing two dimensions of social class into the selected categories, we can assess the robustness of the social class–parental involvement link. Thus, for our class-based analyses, we report the values on the outcomes (i.e., achievement or parental involvement) for six groups: three categories of parental education—parents who (1) hold less than a high school diploma, (2) are high school graduates, and (3) have earned a four-year college degree or greater—and three categories of famiy income—those with incomes (1) below the national median, (2) from the median to twice the median, and (3) twice the median or greater. The median household income in 1987 was $26,061. Therefore, for the NELS, the upper limit for the lowest income group is $24,999, the range for families earning from the median to twice the median is from $25,000 to $49,000, and the highest earning group corresponds to families with incomes of $50,000 or greater. For the CDS, the median family income in 1997 was $37,005, and the incomes for families in the low-, middle-, and high-earning categories are less than $37,000, $37,001 to $74,009, and $74,010 or greater, respectively. Table B.1 shows the unweighted sample sizes for all of the models predicting achievement in this study.

Second, our methodological strategy for analysis of race/ethnicity in the NELS is to disaggregate the Asian and Hispanic subsamples. The NELS sample consists of 7,626 whites, 764 Asians, 1,430 Hispanics, and 1,041 blacks. Because subgroups within the Asian category vary considerably in immigration histories (Hirschman and Wong 1986; Zhou 1997), assimilation patterns (Fuligni 1997), language and economic resources (Bankston and Zhou 1995; Zhou and Bankston 1998), and opportunities for social mobility (Chen and Stevenson 1995; Goyette and Xie 1999; Kao 1995; Zhou 1997), we divide them into two groups: *Asians A* (*n* = 537) and *Asians*

TABLE B.1. Unweighted sample size for all regression analyses in Chapters 3, 4, 6, and 8

			Social class				
Data	**Outcome**	**< HS**	**HS grad**	**4-yr. deg. or >**	**< Median**	**1–2 median**	**2x median or >**
NELS	Reading	1,207	4,963	1,761	2,645	3,173	1,832
	Math	1,207	4,964	1,760	2,648	3,171	1,832
	Grades	1,281	5,372	1,917	2,817	3,424	2,025
CDS younger	Reading	260	533	187	602	320	111
	Math	255	531	186	595	319	111
CDS older	Reading	266	714	268	652	411	241
	Math	265	712	267	650	410	239

				Race			
Data	**Outcome**	**Whites**	**Asians A**	**Asians B**	**Non-Mex. Hisp.**	**Mexicans**	**Blacks**
NELS	Reading	5,960	413	182	341	691	765
	Math	5,956	414	182	341	690	767
	Grades	6,461	471	196	362	726	812

		Whites	**Asians**	**Hispanics**	**Blacks**
CDS younger	Reading	489	16	99	429
	Math	485	16	98	426
CDS older	Reading	618	20	91	575
	Math	616	20	91	572

Note: "CDS younger" corresponds to youth in grades 1–5 during CDS-II, and "CDS older" corresponds to youth in grades 6–12 in CDS-II.

B (*n* = 227). The former category comprises groups that have been characterized as "model minority" (Chua 2011; Kao 1995; Osajima 2005): Chinese, Filipino, Japanese, Korean, Middle Eastern, and South Asian respondents. The latter group comprises socioeconomically disadvantaged Asian groups (Cambodians, Laotians, Hmong, Vietnamese, Pacific Islanders, West Asians, and other Asians). Hispanics are disaggregated into two groups: Mexicans (*n* = 945) and non-Mexicans (*n* = 485). Thus, although these groups are far from perfect, we believe it is more appropriate to place both Asians and Hispanics into these groups rather than to treat each as homogeneous. This level of disaggregation is not possible in the CDS. Furthermore, because the sample on Asian families is limited, our use of the CDS is restricted to whites (*n* = 1,240), Hispanics (*n* = 198), and blacks (*n* = 1,087).

Third, we display regression results in estimate graphs rather than traditional regression tables. Estimate graphs allow us to present our findings in a manner that is more accessible to nonspecialists. Also, they visually depict the distance between the estimates of each group for which the analysis was conducted. We provide an example of an estimate graph in Figure B.1. The figure shows estimates for two groups, which are labeled along the *y*-axis. Thus, the *y*-axis does not have meaning in the traditional sense (i.e., the values on the outcome). Instead, we display the values on the outcome along the *x*-axis. The estimates and standard deviations/errors are displayed in shapes and horizontal lines, respectively. The shapes are located above the number along the x-axis that represents the estimated value on the outcome for the groups to which they correspond. The portion of the

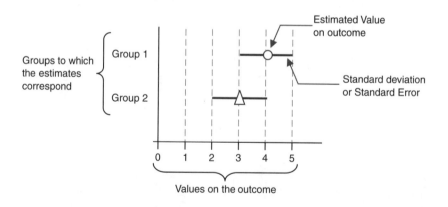

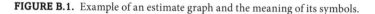

FIGURE B.1. Example of an estimate graph and the meaning of its symbols.

horizontal lines on the right-hand side of the estimates represents the sum of the estimate and its standard deviation/error. The portion of the horizontal lines on the left-hand side of the estimates represents the difference between the estimate and its standard deviation/error. Therefore, in Figure B.1, group 1 has an average of 4 on the outcome with a standard error of 1; the horizontal line goes from 3 to 5 because these values correspond to the numbers obtained when the error is subtracted from and added to the estimate, respectively. Group 2 has a mean of 3 and an error of 1.

In Chapter 1, we show the average achievement for each category of social class in Figures 1.1 and 1.2 using estimate graphs such as the one displayed in Figure B.1. Whereas the group that corresponds to each estimate is listed along the y-axis, the right-hand side of Figures 1.1 and 1.2 list the standardized achievement gap for each group. Those estimates were obtained using the following equation:

$$Ach = \alpha + \beta_1(LowSC) + \beta_2(MiddleSC) + \varepsilon \tag{1}$$

where achievement (Ach) is a function of social class, or having a lower ($LowSC$) or middle ($MiddleSC$) social class background, and the omitted group are youth from the highest social class category. Therefore, α represents the achievement level for youth from the high social class group, β_1 and β_2 represent the achievement levels *relative to* α for youth in the low and middle social class groups, respectively, and e represents an error term (all other factors that contribute to achievement besides the measures in the equation).

Equation 1 represents the baseline model for the achievement gap by social class, which we return to in the chapter-specific portion of this appendix. Although we will refer to Equation 1 when we discuss our class-based analyses, given that we conduct analysis for two dimensions of social class, Equation 1 actually represents the following two models:

$$Ach = \alpha + \beta_1(<HSgrad) + \beta_2(HSgrad) + e \tag{1a}$$

$$Ach = \alpha + \beta_1(<1Median) + \beta_2(1\text{-}2Median) + e \tag{1b}$$

where (Ach) represents youths' achievement, $<HSgrad$ is for youth whose parents hold less than a high school diploma, $HSgrad$ is for youth whose parents are high school graduates, $<1Median$ is for youth whose families earn below the national median, and $1\text{-}2Median$ is for youth whose families earn between the national median to twice the median. The omitted category for Equation 1a, which corresponds to the model for analyses conducted by parents' education, are youth whose parents have earned a four-year college degree or greater. For Equation 1b, which is the model used for analysis by family income, the omitted category is youths in families with household incomes twice the national median or greater.

Fourth, we present the racial comparisons on the parental involvement measures in Chapters 5 and 7 without accounting for socioeconomic background. Teachers, other school personnel, and the general public typically do not cognitively adjust for social class when they develop perceptions about race and parental involvement based on their observations within their schools. Therefore, we believe it is important to display the raw averages for each racial group during racial comparisons on parental involvement because the findings might lend credibility to educators' real-time assessments of the level of involvement for parents from the various racial groups. Accounting for social class background would explain away some of the racial differences in parental involvement, which is not our intention in Chapters 5 and 7.

Fifth, we are interested in isolating the estimated effect that parental involvement has on achievement. As such, we lag achievement and account for socioeconomic status in assessments of the link between parental involvement and academic outcomes. Therefore, for analysis based on the NELS, we estimate the increase in achievement from middle school to high school that can be attributed to parental practices *net* of social class. For the CDS, the change in achievement is estimated from wave 1 to wave 2. Within the context of methodological discussions *throughout* this appendix (and book), the use of the term *social class* (or SES) is in reference to a vector comprised of family income, parental education, family structure (single or two-parent household), and youth's sex. Although these measures are far from perfect, they are a reasonable set of factors that characterize the socioeconomic standing of youths' families.

Sixth, sixty of the sixty-three measures of parental involvement in this study are coded as dichotomous variables. Ten indicators of parental involvement are yes/no questions. The other fifty indicators that we dichotomized gave parents the option to select from a series of response categories such as the following: (1) not at all, (2) rarely, (3) occasionally, or (4) regularly. However, for these types of indicators, we decided to sort parents into two categories (0 = not regularly; 1 = regularly) for four reasons:

- The distinction between "rarely" and "occasionally" can be ambiguous. We argue that a separation between parents who engage in a particular form of involvement regularly and those who do not is a more meaningful distinction.

- We are interested in the pervasiveness of involvement for parents across social class and racial groups rather than the average magnitude of involvement on particular measures of parental involvement. Coding variables as 0-1 (such as no/yes or "not regularly"/"regularly") converts the means for the variables into proportions, which allows us to determine the share of parents from each social class and racial group that engage in a particular form of parental involvement. Although assessing the average level of involvement along a 4- or 5-point scale allows one to determine the magnitude of involvement, parental involvement is often discussed in dichotomous terms (e.g., whether parents are involved or not).
- For many parental measures, the top response option is selected as often as the other response categories combined.
- When examining the association between variables, dichotomous predictors provide a greater ease of interpretation; the estimated "effect" represents the difference on the outcome (e.g., achievement) between those who affirm (response = 1) and those who do not affirm (response = 0) the predictor (i.e., the particular form of parental involvement being examined).

Seventh, returning to our major methodological points, we use test scores as an academic outcome. Despite the fact that test scores are viewed by many as problematic, using test scores as a measure of academic progress has three advantages: (1) they reflect mastery of academic concepts and therefore are the primary measure by which students and schools are evaluated; (2) unlike grades, test scores are a more stable measure of students' academic preparation and less vulnerable to variations that can result from teachers' own perceptions and expectations of students within the classroom; and (3) we feel the use of achievement scores makes a contribution to the literature because most prior studies have focused on other child outcomes, including grades, substance abuse, mental health, social competence, and self-concepts (Gunnoe, Hetherington, and Reiss 1999; Jackson, Henriksen, and Foshee 1998).

Eighth, regarding missing data, we include missing values as dummy categories within each predictor variable because an analysis using listwise deletion rapidly reduces sample size, particularly with an increase in covariates. Thus, missing cases for the predictors were bottom coded (0), and each predictor was entered into the models along with a corresponding flag or "missing information" measure—coded as 0 if not missing and 1 if missing. This coding has certain advantages because it (1) prevents the loss of explanatory power that would come from listwise deletion; (2) allows for the direct modeling of missing data rather than imputing values, for example by mean substitution, which has its own interpretative problems; (3) ensures a consistent base in terms of the sample size across a range of regression models that include an increasing number of explanatory variables; (4) yields estimates identical to those attained via listwise deletion for the variable with the substituted values; and (5) allows all cases with values on the outcome to remain in the analysis. Therefore, the number of cases (n) in all analyses totals the n that responded to the outcome being assessed.

Ninth, to obtain unbiased population estimates, we employ sample weights for analyses based on the NELS and ELS, which employ two-stage stratified sampling design. Specifically, the weights account for sampling design (i.e., stratification, disproportionate sampling of certain strata, and clustered, multistage probability sampling), sample attrition, and nonresponse (Ingels et al. 1994). Furthermore, the sum of the sample weights were adjusted to equal the size of the unweighted sample, which accounts for the extremely small standard errors and inflated likelihood of finding significance because of panel weights' adjustment of the sample size to the national population of high school youths (Hanson 1994; Moser and Kalton 1972; Muller, Stage, and Kinzie 2001). For analyses based on the CDS, we also employ a weighting system devised by the PSID staff to account for the effects of the initial probability of being sampled and attrition over time—which is generally low—and incorporates a post-stratification factor to ensure the data are nationally representative. (See Appendix C for detailed information on all measures used in this study.)

Chapter-Specific Analytic Descriptions

Chapters 2–4

The purpose of Chapter 2 is to assess the proportion of parents from each social class category that engage in various forms of parental involvement both at home and school. We use data from the NELS and CDS. We obtained the findings using Equation 1 after replacing achievement with each measure of parental involvement and display the results in Figures 2.2 through 2.5. We summarize the results from this chapter in Table 2.1.

In the next two chapters, we examine whether the measures of parental involvement at home (Chapter 3) and school (Chapter 4) assessed in Chapter 2 are associated with achievement. For analysis based on the NELS, the effects of parental involvement are estimated in the following manner:

$$Ach_{HS} = \alpha + \beta_1(PI_{MS}) + \beta_2(Ach_{MS}) + X\beta_3 + e \tag{2a}$$

where achievement (*Ach*) in high school ($_{HS}$), which was measured when youth were in grade 12, is a function of parental involvement (PI) assessed during middle school ($_{MS}$), youths' prior achievement (Ach$_{MS}$), the matrix of the aforementioned SES variables and observations specified in the model (*X*), and its associated vector of coefficients (β_3). Unlike the NELS, youth in the CDS are distributed across grade levels. Thus, the following equation illustrates the modeling strategy used for analysis based on the CDS:

$$Ach_{W2} = \alpha + \beta_1(PI_{W1}) + \beta_2(Ach_{W1}) + X\beta_3 + e \tag{2b}$$

where achievement (*Ach*) is assessed in wave 2 of the CDS ($_{W2}$), during which time all youth were of school age, and the predictors are from the first wave ($_{W1}$) of the CDS, which were collected five years prior to wave 2. Analyses were conducted separately for youth in grades 1–5 and 6–12 during wave 2.

There are several important points with regard to Equations 2a and 2b. First, all predictors are from the baseline waves of both data sets. As such, parental involvement in the NELS was measured when youth were in grade 8. For the younger subsample in the CDS, parental involvement was assessed during early childcare or preschool, which is prior to youth entering elementary school when achievement was assessed. For the older subsample in the CDS, parental involvement was assessed when youth were in elementary school and early middle school (grade 7). Therefore, between the NELS and CDS, we capture parental involvement from early child care through middle school. Most studies suggest that parents are most consequential for their children's schooling during earlier stages of education (Jordan et al. 2009; Snow, Burns, and Griffin 1998; Whitehurst and Lonigan 1998). Parents tend to decrease their involvement as children enter middle school and high school (Catsambis 1998; Epstein and Dauber 1991).

Second, Equation 2 was estimated separately for each category of social class discussed earlier. Third, to avoid multicolinearity, Equation 2 was estimated for *each* measure of parental involvement *separately*. Therefore, Equation 2 shows the estimated change in achievement—denoted by β_1—from middle school to high school (EQ 2a) and from wave 1 to wave 2 (EQ 2b) that can be attributed to the indicator of parental involvement (PI in EQ 2) for youth whose parents engage in the particular type of parental involvement measure being assessed relative to those whose parents do not.

We report the estimated effects for measures of parental involvement at home in Chapter 3. For analysis based on the NELS, we estimate the effects of nine measures of parental involvement for reading, math, and grades, so that Equation 2a was estimated twenty-seven times for each social class group (9 measures of parental involvement by 3 measures of achievement). For analysis based on the CDS, we examined the implication of five measures of parental involvement for reading and math. Thus, Equation 2b was estimated ten times for each social class group in both the younger and older subsamples. We follow the same strategy in Chapter 4 for parental involvement at school. Therefore, we estimate Equation 2a fifty-four times (18 measures of parental involvement by 3 measures of achievement) and Equation 2b twenty-six times (13 measures of parental involvement by 2 measures of achievement) for each social class category.

Fourth, we display the findings from Equation 2 in estimate graphs. Figure B.2 contains an example of the estimate graphs we employ throughout the book to show the estimated effects of parental involvement. The findings in the figure are not real and are solely intended for the purposes of illustrating how these figures should be interpreted. The key above the figure shows which symbol corresponds to each group. The estimates for groups 1, 2, and 3 are represented by circles, triangles, and squares, respectively. There are three panels, one for each measure of parental involvement, and three estimates in each panel—one for each group. The top panel suggests that reading to children is beneficial for youth in all three groups. The values along the *x*-axis represent the estimated effect for reading to children on achievement. The estimated effects actually represent the achievement gap between youth whose parents read to them and those whose parents do not. Thus, among youth in group 1, youth whose parents read to them score 4 points higher on achievement than those whose parents do not read to them.

Because parental involvement is posited to be effective for increasing academic achievement, the estimates should be on the positive side of the graphs. In the second panel of Figure B.2, we illustrate how we display

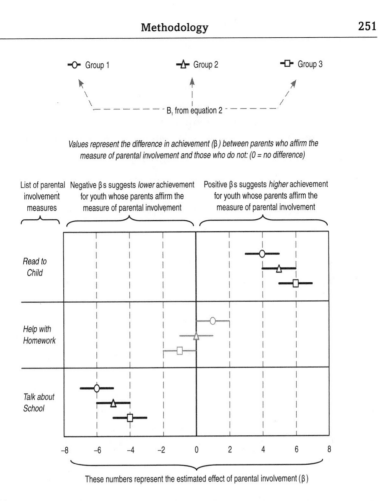

FIGURE B.2. Example of how estimated effects on achievement are displayed throughout this study.

results when there is no significant difference in achievement between youth whose parents affirm the parental involvement measure and those whose parents do not. Specifically, we show nonsignificant estimates in gray. Estimates are nonsignificant at the .05 level if their standard errors do not remain positive (or negative in the case of negative effects) when subtracted from the estimate twice. In the bottom panel, we show that for all three groups youth whose parents talk to them about school have lower achievement than those whose parents do not. The location of the estimates relative to one another is helpful in gauging the relative influence of each parental involvement measure.

In the final set of analyses in Chapter 4, we examine the extent to which the measures of parental involvement assessed in Chapter 2 account for the achievement gaps by social class reported in Figures 1.1 and 1.2. We establish the baseline gap using Equation 1. Next, we examine the share of the achievement gaps that can be attributed to parental involvement at home, at school, and both using the following equations:

$$Ach = \alpha + \beta_1(\text{LowSC}) + \beta_2(\text{MiddleSC}) + \beta_3(\text{PI}_{\text{HOME}}) + e \qquad (3)$$

$$Ach = \alpha + \beta_1(\text{LowSC}) + \beta_2(\text{MiddleSC}) + \beta_3(\text{PI}_{\text{SCHOOL}}) + e \qquad (4)$$

$$Ach = \alpha + \beta_1(\text{LowSC}) + \beta_2(\text{MiddleSC}) + \beta_3(\text{PI}_{\text{HOME}})$$
$$+ \beta_4(\text{PI}_{\text{SCHOOL}}) + e \qquad (5)$$

where PI represents the matrix of the parental involvement variables denoted by the subscripts (home and school) and β_3 (and β_4) represents the vector of coefficients associated with their corresponding subscripts. Thus, to determine the extent to which parental involvement explains the achievement gaps by social class, β_1 and β_2 from Equations 3, 4, and 5 are compared to β_1 and β_2 from Equation 1. Similar to the previous analysis, the measures of parental involvement are from the baseline wave of the data sets, and achievement is from grade 12 in the NELS and from the second wave of the CDS. We then examine the share of the achievement gaps that can be attributed to socioeconomic background as follow:

$$Ach = \alpha + \beta_1(\text{LowSC}) + \beta_2(\text{MiddleSC}) + X\beta_3 + e \qquad (6)$$

where X represents the matrix of variables consisting of family income (when achievement gaps are assessed by parents' education), parental education (when achievement gaps are assessed by family income), family structure (single- or two-parent household), and youth's sex, and β_3 represents its associated vector of coefficients. We report β_1 and β_2 from Equations 1, 3, 4, 5, and 6 in Figure 4.8 for the NELS, Figure 4.9 for the younger CDS subsample, and Figure 4.10 for the older CDS subsample.

Chapters 5 and 7

The purpose of chapters 5 and 7 is to assess the proportion of parents from each racial group that engage in various forms of parental involvement at home and at school, respectively. We use data from the NELS, ELS, and CDS and display the results in basic bar graphs.

Chapters 6 and 8

The purpose of these chapters is to examine how consequential the measures of parental involvement are for achievement for each racial group. We use the same analytic plan that was used for Chapters 3 and 4 and simply replace social class with race. Specifically, we estimate Equation 2 for each measure of parental involvement at home (Chapter 6) and school (Chapter 8) for each of the aforementioned racial groups and display the findings in the manner described in Figure B.2.

After reporting on these analyses in Chapter 8, we examine the extent to which parental involvement can explain racial differences in achievement. We establish the baseline achievement gap in the NELS as follows:

$$Ach_{HS} = \alpha + \beta_1(AsianA) + \beta_2(AsianB) + \beta_3(NM\text{-}Hisp)$$
$$+ \beta_4(Mexican) + \beta_5(black) + e \qquad (7)$$

where Ach_{HS} is achievement in grade 12, α represents the constant (which in this case is achievement for whites), β_1 through β_5 represent the estimated achievement relative to whites for Asians A, Asians B, non-Mexican Hispanics, Mexicans, and blacks, respectively, and e represents the error term. Therefore, the βs represent the achievement gap for the racial groups relative to whites. For analysis based on the CDS, only two racial groups are in the equation: Hispanics and blacks.

We examine the share of racial differences in achievement that can be attributed to various groupings of parental involvement measures from the NELS in the following set of equations:

$$Ach_{HS} = \alpha + \beta_1(RACE) + \beta_2(HOME) + e \qquad (8)$$

$$Ach_{HS} = \alpha + \beta_1(RACE) + \beta_2(PAR\text{-}INI) + e \qquad (9)$$

$$Ach_{HS} = \alpha + \beta_1(RACE) + \beta_2(SCHL\text{-}INI) + e \qquad (10)$$

$$Ach_{HS} = \alpha + \beta_1(RACE) + \beta_2(PARTICIP) + e \qquad (11)$$

$$Ach_{HS} = \alpha + \beta_1(RACE) + \beta_2(FULLPAR) + e \qquad (12)$$

$$Ach_{HS} = \alpha + \beta_1(RACE) + \beta_2(SES) + e \qquad (13)$$

where *RACE* represents a vector consisting of the racial groups in Equation 7 and β_1 the racial achievement gaps, *HOME* is a vector of 9 measures of parental involvement at home, *PAR-INI* is a vector of 6 measures for parent-initiated school contact, *SCHL-INI* is a vector of 8 measures for school-initiated school contact, *PARTICIP* is a vector of 4 measures for parents' participation at school, *FULLPAR* is a vector that consists of all 27 measures of parental involvement, and *SES* is a vector consisting of parents' education, family income, family structure, and youth's sex. The results for this analysis are displayed in Figure 8.8.

For analysis of the racial achievement gaps based on the CDS, we employ the following set of equations:

$$Ach_{HS} = \alpha + \beta_1(\text{RACE}) + \beta_2(\text{HOME}) + e \tag{14}$$

$$Ach_{HS} = \alpha + \beta_1(\text{RACE}) + \beta_2(\text{ASSERT-TEACH}) + e \tag{15}$$

$$Ach_{HS} = \alpha + \beta_1(\text{RACE}) + \beta_2(\text{ASSERT-INVOLV}) + e \tag{16}$$

$$Ach_{HS} = \alpha + \beta_1(\text{RACE}) + \beta_2(\text{ENGAGEMENT}) + e \tag{17}$$

$$Ach_{HS} = \alpha + \beta_1(\text{RACE}) + \beta_2(\text{FULLPAR}) + e \tag{18}$$

$$Ach_{HS} = \alpha + \beta_1(\text{RACE}) + \beta_2(\text{SES}) + e \tag{19}$$

where *RACE* represents a vector consisting of Hispanics and blacks, *HOME* is a vector of five measures of parental involvement at home, *ASSERT-TEACH* is a vector of the three measures for parents' assertiveness with teachers (i.e., obtaining information about, meeting, or requesting a particular teacher), *ASSERT-INVOLV* is a vector of six measures for parents' assertive involvement with teachers and principals (e.g., formal conference or casual conversation), *ENGAGEMENT* is a vector of four measures for parents' general involvement at school (e.g., observe class, attend school event), *FULLPAR* is a vector that consists of all eighteen measures of parental involvement, and *SES* is a vector consisting of parents' education, family income, family structure, and youth's sex. The results for this analysis are displayed in Figure 8.9.

Chapter 9

The purpose of Chapter 9 is to examine whether racial differences exist in how parents address poor academic performance, and the implication that these strategies have for achievement. We employ the CDS and supplement portions of the analysis with the MADICS. In Figures 9.1 through 9.3, we simply show the proportion of whites and blacks who fall into each of the designated categories. These proportions are unadjusted. We then examine the implication that parental preferences for dealing with children's poor academic performance have for achievement. This analysis is conducted separately for whites, blacks, youth whose parents hold less than a four-year college degree, and those whose parents hold a four-year degree or greater. These findings are displayed in Figure 9.4 in the manner described for Figure B.2. We repeat the analysis for youth in the bottom and top halves of the achievement distribution and display those findings in Figure 9.5. We obtained the findings for the top panel of Figures 9.4 and 9.5 as follows:

$$Ach_{W2} = \alpha + \beta_1(Mild_{W1}) + \beta_2(Acute_{W1}) + \delta \, (Other) + X\lambda$$
$$+ \xi \, (Ach_{W1}) + \xi \, (Grade_{W2}) + e \qquad (20)$$

where achievement measured during the second wave of the CDS ($_{w2}$) is a function of *mild* and *acute* punitive parental response (β_1 and β_2, respectively). Parents who reported a preference for nonpunitive approaches served as the reference group. These parents were grouped separately from those that did not affirm any of the preferences we examined, which is reflected by δ—the estimate for "other." The next estimate (λ) is for a vector of social class (X), which includes race when the analysis is conducted by parents' level of education in Figure 9.4 and for all analyses in Figure 9.5. The final two estimates are for youths' prior achievement and grade level in school during CDS-II. To obtain the findings in the bottom panel of Figures 9.4 and 9.5, we employed the following equation:

$$Ach_{W2} = \alpha + \beta_1(Contact_{W1}) + \beta_2(Help_{W1}) + \beta_3(Contact\&Help_{W1})$$
$$+ \beta_4(Monitor/Encourage_{W1}) + \delta \, (Other) + X\lambda + \xi \, (Ach_{W1})$$
$$+ \xi \, (Grade_{W2}) + e \qquad (21)$$

For these analyses, parents who reported a preference for punitive responses served as the reference group.

Descriptive Tables

TABLE C.1. Means, standard deviations, and descriptions for academic outcomes used in this study

Variable name	Description	Metric	Means (SD)	N	Data
Academic outcomes in high school (grade 12)					
Reading	Item Response Theta (IRT) estimated number right	Min = 10.55 Max = 51.16	33.41 (10.00)	8,352	NELS
Math	IRT estimated number right	Min = 16.97 Max = 78.10	48.53 (14.39)	8,350	NELS
Grades	Combined grades in reading, math, science, and social studies	0 to 4.0	1.99 (.85)	9,028	NELS
Academic outcomes for the younger subsample (grades 1–5)					
Reading	Scores on the Woodcock-Johnson reading achievement standardized test, which is a summation of the letter-word and passage comprehension scores	Min = 0 Max = 147	107.06 (19.71)	1,033	CDS
Math	Scores on the Woodcock-Johnson math achievement standardized test, which is based on a summation of the calculation and applied problems tests	Min = 19 Max = 156	106.70 (17.75)	1,025	CDS
Academic outcomes among adolescents (grades 6–12)					
Reading	Scores on the Woodcock-Johnson reading achievement standardized test, which is a summation of the letter-word and passage comprehension scores	Min = 00 Max = 194	104.22 (19.62)	1,304	CDS
Math	Scores on the Woodcock-Johnson math achievement standardized test, which is a summation of the calculation and applied problems tests	Min = 49 Max = 171	104.84 (16.45)	1,299	CDS

Notes: SD = standard deviation; N = sample size; Max = maximum; Min = minimum.

258

TABLE C.2. Means, standard deviations, and descriptions for parental involvement at home

Variable name	Description	Metric	Means (SD)	N	Data
Parents' academic discussions					
School experiences	How often do you or your spouse/partner talk with your eighth grader about his or her experiences in school?	0 = ~ Regularly 1 = Regularly	.80	10,073	NELS
HS plans	How often do you or your spouse/partner talk with your eighth grader about his or her plans for high school?	0 = ~ Regularly 1 = Regularly	.47	10,257	NELS
Post-HS plans	How often do you or your spouse/partner talk with your eighth grader about his or her educational plans after high school?	0 = ~ Regularly 1 = Regularly	.38	10,259	NELS
Parents' rules/expectations					
Are there family rules that are enforced for your eighth grader about any of the following activities:					
GPA	Maintaining a certain grade average.	0 = No 1 = Yes	.71	9,884	NELS
HW	Doing homework.	0 = No 1 = Yes	.92	10,044	NELS
Expect post-HS	Do you expect that your eighth grader will go on to additional education beyond high school?	0 = No 1 = Yes	.91	10,217	NELS

(continued)

TABLE C.2 (continued)

Variable name	Description	Metric	Means (SD)	N	Data
Parents' value of schooling					
Parent decide	Whether parents think that they will be the most influential person in deciding what courses their child will take in high school.	0 = Other decides 1 = Parents decide	.22	9,839	NELS
HW worth	Whether parents strongly agree that the homework assigned is worthwhile.	0 = ~ Strongly agree 1 = Strongly agree	.23	10,002	NELS
HW help	How often do you or your spouse/partner help your eighth grader with his or her homework?	1 = Seldom or never 4 = Almost every day	2.23 (.99)	10,032	NELS
Parents' academic practices					
How often have you and/or your spouse/partner provided advice or information about the following to your tenth grader?					
Courses/programs	Selecting courses or programs at school.	0 = ~ Often 1 = Often	.50	11,716	ELS
Entrance exams	Plans and preparation for college entrance exams such as ACT, SAT, or ASVAB.	0 = ~ Often 1 = Often	.34	11,667	ELS
Post-HS plans	Applying to college or other schools after high school.	0 = ~ Often 1 = Often	.35	11,619	ELS
General info	Community, national, and world events.	0 = ~ Often 1 = Often	.43	11,634	ELS

				N	
Advise	Things that are troubling your tenth grader.	0 = ~ Often 1 = Often	.67	11,682	ELS
Report card	How often do you discuss your tenth grader's report card with him/her?	0 = ~ Always 1 = Always	.87	11,710	ELS

Parental involvement at home

Read to youth	How often do you read to (child)?	1 = Never 6 = Every day	4.37 (1.69)	2,556	CDS
Help HW	Frequency with which parent has worked on homework with (child).	1 = Not in the past mo. 5 = Every day	3.31 (1.54)	2,008	CDS

Parent-child discussion
Since the beginning of the school year, please tell me how often you discussed the following with (child):

School activities	School activities or events of particular interest to (child).	0 = ~ Regularly 1 = Regularly	.69	1,542	CDS
Studies	Things he/she has studied in class.	0 = ~ Regularly 1 = Regularly	.79	1,542	CDS
Experiences	Experiences at school.	0 = ~ Regularly 1 = Regularly	.81	1,542	CDS

Notes: SD = standard deviation; N = sample size.

261

TABLE C.3. Means, standard deviations, and descriptions for parental involvement at school

Variable name	Description	Metric	Means	N	Data
Parent-school contact: parent initiated					
Since your eighth grader's school opened last fall, how many times HAVE YOU OR YOUR SPOUSE/PARTNER CONTACTED the school about the following?					
Youth performance	Your eighth grader's academic performance.	0 = None	.52	9,783	NELS
		1 = Once or more			
Behavior	Your eighth grader's behavior in school.	0 = None	.27	9,736	NELS
		1 = Once or more			
Program	Your eighth grader's academic program for this year.	0 = None	.35	9,729	NELS
		1 = Once or more			
Records	Providing information for school records such as your address or work telephone number.	0 = None	.40	9,745	NELS
		1 = Once or more			
Fund-raise	Participating in school fund-raising activities.	0 = None	.21	9,732	NELS
		1 = Once or more			
Volunteer	Doing volunteer work such as supervising lunch or chaperoning a field trip.	0 = None	.20	9,743	NELS
		1 = Once or more			
Parent-school contact: school initiated					
Since your eighth grader's school opened last fall, how many times HAVE YOU BEEN CONTACTED BY THE SCHOOL about the following?					
Youth performance	Your eighth grader's academic performance.	0 = None	.56	10,016	NELS
		1 = Once or more			
Behavior	Your eighth grader's behavior in school.	0 = None	.28	9,993	NELS
		1 = Once or more			
Program	Your eighth grader's academic program for this year.	0 = None	.36	9,950	NELS
		1 = Once or more			

Variable	Description	Coding		Value	N	Source
Records	Obtaining information for school records such as your address or work telephone number.	0 = None	1 = Once or more	.48	9,975	NELS
Fund-raise	Participating in school fund-raising activities.	0 = None	1 = Once or more	.42	9,989	NELS
Volunteer	Doing volunteer work such as supervising lunch or chaperoning a field trip.	0 = None	1 = Once or more	.32	10,000	NELS
Courses	Your eighth grader's course selection for high school.	0 = None	1 = Once or more	.41	9,977	NELS
Placement	Placement decisions regarding your eighth grader's high school program.	0 = None	1 = Once or more	.31	9,952	NELS

Parents' involvement with school
Do you and your spouse/partner do any of the following at your eighth grader's school?

Variable	Description	Coding		Value	N	Source
PTO	Belong to a parent-teacher organization (PTO)?	0 = No / 1 = Yes		.34	9,948	NELS
Attend PTO	Attend meeting of a PTO?	0 = No / 1 = Yes		.37	9,948	NELS
PTO activities	Take part in the activities of a PTO?	0 = No / 1 = Yes		.27	9,899	NELS
Volunteer	Act as a volunteer at the school?	0 = No / 1 = Yes		.20	9,853	NELS

Parental involvement at school
During the current school year, how often have you participated in any of the following activities at (child's) school?

Variable	Description	Coding		Value	N	Source
Volunteer	Volunteered in the classroom, school office, or library?	0 = Not in current year	1 = Once or more	.35	1,539	CDS
Observe	Observed (child's) classroom?	0 = Not in current year	1 = Once or more	.52	1,535	CDS

(continued)

TABLE C.3 (*continued*)

Variable name	Description	Metric	Means (SD)	N	Data
Attend event	Attended a school event such as a play, sporting event, or concert (whether for youth or not)?	0 = Not in current year 1 = Once or more	.67	1,537	CDS
PTA meeting	Attended a meeting of the PTA or other such organization?	0 = Not in current year 1 = Once or more	.40	1,539	CDS
Parents' assertiveness regarding teachers					
Before the start of the school year, did you:					
Teacher info	Obtain information about who would be (child's) teacher?	0 = No 1 = Yes	.74	1,540	CDS
Meet teacher	Meet with (child's) teacher?	0 = No 1 = Yes	.60	1,539	CDS
Request teacher	Request a particular teacher for (child)?	0 = No 1 = Yes	.16	1,531	CDS
Parental involvement at school: assertive					
During the current school year, how often have you participated in any of the following activities at (child's) school?					
Conference with teacher	Had a conference with (child's) teacher?	0 = Not in current year 1 = Once or more	.80	1,539	CDS

Variable	Question	Coding	Mean (SD)	N	Source
Conference with principal	Had a conference with (child's) school principal?	0 = Not in current year 1 = Once or more	.23	1,532	CDS
Converse with teacher	Had an informal conversation with (child's) teacher?	0 = Not in current year 1 = Once or more	.78	1,536	CDS
Converse with principal	Had an informal conversation with (child's) principal?	0 = Not in current year 1 = Once or more	.42	1,534	CDS
Met school counselor	Met with a school counselor?	0 = Not in current year 1 = Once or more	.15	1,527	CDS
Presentation	Made a presentation to (child's) class?	0 = Not in current year 1 = Once or more	.13	1,538	CDS
Parents' perceptions of youths' school					
Learning	The school places a high priority on learning.	1 = Strongly disagree 4 = Strongly agree	3.26 (.62)	10,003	NELS
HS prep	The school is preparing students well for high school.	1 = Strongly disagree 4 = Strongly agree	3.04 (.66)	9,970	NELS
College prep	The school is preparing students well for college.	1 = Strongly disagree 4 = Strongly agree	2.85 (.71)	9,785	NELS
Parents in policy	Parents have an adequate say in setting school policy.	1 = Strongly disagree 4 = Strongly agree	2.64 (.73)	9,717	NELS

Notes: SD = standard deviation; N = sample size.

265

TABLE C.4. Means, standard deviations, and descriptions for variables used in Chapter 9

Variable name	Description	Metric	Means	N	Data
Parents' philosophy toward poor performance					
If (child) brought home a report card with grades or progress lower than expected, would you be likely to:					
1. Punitive					
Mild	Punish or limit or reduce (child's) nonschool activities.	0 = Not very likely 1 = Very likely	.30	1,017	CDS-I
Acute	Both punish *and* limit (child's) nonschool activities.	0 = Not very likely 1 = Very likely	.06	1,017	CDS-I
2. Nonpunitive					
Contact	Contact (child's) teacher or principal.	0 = Not very likely 1 = Very likely	.09	1,017	CDS-I
Help	Spend more time helping (child) with homework.	0 = Not very likely 1 = Very likely	.17	1,017	CDS-I
Contact and help	Both contact and help.	0 = Not very likely 1 = Very likely	.29	1,017	CDS-I

Monitor/encourage	Keep a close eye on (child's) activities and/or tell child to spend more time on schoolwork.	0 = Not very likely 1 = Very likely	.06	1,017	CDS-I
Other	None of the above responses.	0 = Not very likely 1 = Very likely	.03	1,017	CDS-I

Parents' response to poor performance
When (child) did poorly in school, how often did you do the following things?

Threat	Threaten to physically punish or spank child?	0 = ~Frequently or always 1 = Frequently or always	.20	279	MADICS
Take privilege	Take privileges away from child?	0 = ~Frequently or always 1 = Frequently or always	.49	280	MADICS
Ground	Ground child?	0 = ~Frequently or always 1 = Frequently or always	.41	277	MADICS
Yell	Yell at child?	0 = ~Frequently or always 1 = Frequently or always	.28	280	MADICS
Physically punish	Physically punish or spank child?	0 = ~Frequently or always 1 = Frequently or always	.07	280	MADICS

Notes: N = sample size.

267

TABLE C.5. Means, standard deviations, and descriptions for control variables used throughout this study

Variable name	Description	Metric	Means (SD)	N	Data
Socioeconomic status					
Parents' education	Highest level of education by either parent	1 = < 8th grade 13 = PhD/JD/MD	6.64 (3.42)	10,251	NELS
Household income	Total household income	1 = None 15 = $200,000 or more	9.73 (2.53)	9,874	NELS
Family structure	Two-parent household	0 = Not two-parent 1 = Two-parent	.81	10,033	NELS
Sex	Youth's sex	0 = Male 1 = Female	.50	10,771	NELS
Parents' education	Highest level of education by either parent, measured in years of education	0-17 (17 => 4-yr degree)	12.81 (3.23)	2,443	CDS
Household income	Total household income in dollars (× 10,000)	$0-$57.70	5.54 (5.06)	2,337	CDS

			Mean (SD)	N	Source
Family structure	Two-parent household	0 = Not two-parent 1 = Two-parent	.80	2,561	CDS
Sex	Youth's sex	0 = Male 1 = Female	.50	2,561	CDS
Prior achievement					
Academic outcomes in middle school (grade 8)					
Reading	Item Response Theta (IRT) estimated number right	Min = 10.61 Max = 43.83	27.18 (8.65)	10,448	NELS
Math	IRT estimated number right	Min = 16.03 Max = 66.81	36.22 (11.90)	10,448	NELS
GPA	Cumulative grade point average	.50 to 4.0	2.93 (.76)	10,772	NELS
Academic outcomes in Wave 1					
Reading	Scores on the Woodcock-Johnson reading achievement standardized test, which is a summation of the letter-word and passage comprehension scores	Min = 42 Max = 186	107.08 (17.60)	1,037	CDS
Math	Scores on the Woodcock-Johnson math achievement standardized test, which is a summation of the calculation and applied problems tests	Min = 33 Max = 184	108.24 (18.59)	1,028	CDS

Notes: SD = standard deviation; N = sample size.

Guide of "Effects" by Race

Positive Estimate ●   Negative Estimate ⊗

Parental Involvement		Involvement at Home									Contact School						Contacted by School								PTO				TOTALS		
		Regularly talk / school exp.	Regularly talk / HS plans	Regularly talk / post-H.S.	Have a rule about HW	Have a rule about GPA	Parent decide HS Courses	Help youth with Homework	Agree HW is worthwhile	Expect post-HS education	Academic Performance	Behavior	Academic Program	Info on School Records	School Fundraising Activity	Volunteering	Academic Performance	Behavior	Academic Program	Info on School Records	School Fundraising Activity	Volunteering	Course Selection for H.S.	Program Placement for H.S.	P.T.O. Member	Attend P.T.O. Meeting	Participate in P.T.O. Activity	Volunteer at School	Positive Estimates	Negative Estimates	Non-Significant Estimates
Reading	Whites	●						⊗	●	●	⊗	⊗						⊗					●	●		●	●		7	4	16
	Asians A		⊗	⊗	⊗		●					⊗						⊗								⊗			1	6	20
	Asians B											⊗			⊗														0	2	25
	NonMexicans															●		⊗				●							2	1	24
	Mexicans								●		●						●											●	3	0	24
	Blacks	⊗	●		⊗						●	●	●	●			●	●	●	●		●			●	●		●	12	2	13
Math	Whites						●	⊗	●	●	⊗	⊗	⊗				●	●	⊗	⊗	⊗	●	●	●		●	●	●	11	7	9
	Asians A				⊗						⊗	⊗						⊗									⊗		0	4	23
	Asians B	⊗	⊗	⊗								⊗						⊗									⊗		0	6	21
	NonMexicans																	⊗											0	1	26
	Mexicans				●	●			●				⊗	⊗		⊗		⊗											3	4	20
	Blacks	⊗	●	●							⊗	⊗		●			●			⊗					●	●			6	4	17
Grades	Whites		⊗	⊗	⊗	⊗		⊗		●	⊗	⊗			●	●	⊗	⊗				●						●	5	9	13
	Asians A							●																					1	0	26
	Asians B											⊗																	0	1	26
	NonMexicans			⊗				⊗							●	●	⊗									●		⊗	3	4	20
	Mexicans	●									⊗						⊗	⊗	⊗								⊗		1	5	21
	Blacks			●				●	⊗		⊗	⊗				●	⊗	⊗	⊗	⊗						⊗			3	8	16
TOTALS	Positive	2	2	4	0	0	1	1	3	6	0	1	1	2	2	4	3	1	2	1	3	6	1	0	3	4	3	2	58		
	Negative	3	2	3	4	3	0	5	0	0	5	11	2	2	1	0	2	10	3	3	1	1	2	2	0	1	2	0		68	
	Non-Significant	13	14	11	14	15	17	12	15	12	13	6	15	14	15	14	13	7	13	14	14	11	15	16	15	13	13	16			360

FIGURE D.1. Positive and negative associations for parental involvement and achievement by race: NELS.

Positive Estimate ●   Negative Estimate ⊗

Grades 1 - 5

Parental Involvement		Read to Child	Help with Homework	Discuss School Activities	Discuss School Studies	Discuss School Experiences	Attend Events at School	Observe Class	Met with P.T.A	Volunteer at School	Obtained Info on Teacher	Met with Teacher	Requested a Teacher	Conference with Teacher	Conference with Principal	Converse with Teacher	Converse with Principal	Met with Counselor	Presented in Class	Positive Estimates	Negative Estimates	Non-Significant Estimates
		Involve at Home					*PTO*				*Teachers*			*School*						*Totals*		
Reading	Whites	●	⊗	●	⊗	⊗	●	●		⊗	⊗	⊗	●	●	●	⊗		⊗	●	7	9	2
	Hispanics	●	⊗	●	●	●	●	●				●	●	●				●	●	11	1	6
	Blacks	⊗				⊗	⊗		⊗	●		●	●	●	●	●	●	⊗	⊗	7	6	5
Math	Whites	●	⊗		⊗	⊗	●	⊗	⊗	⊗	⊗	⊗		⊗	⊗	●	⊗	⊗		4	12	2
	Hispanics	⊗	⊗	●	●	●	●	●	⊗		⊗	●	●	⊗				●	●	9	5	4
	Blacks	⊗		⊗			⊗	⊗		●					●	●	●	⊗	⊗	4	6	8
TOTALS	**Positive**	3	0	3	2	2	4	3	0	2	0	3	5	3	2	3	2	2	3	42		
	Negative	3	4	1	2	3	2	2	3	2	3	2	0	2	2	0	2	4	2		39	
	Not Significant	0	2	2	2	1	0	1	3	2	3	1	1	1	2	3	2	0	1			27

Grades 6 - 12

		Read to Child	Help with Homework	Discuss School Activities	Discuss School Studies	Discuss School Experiences	Attend Events at School	Observe Class	Met with P.T.A	Volunteer at School	Obtained Info on Teacher	Met with Teacher	Requested a Teacher	Conference with Teacher	Conference with Principal	Converse with Teacher	Converse with Principal	Met with Counselor	Presented in Class	Positive Estimates	Negative Estimates	Non-Significant Estimates
Reading	Whites	⊗	⊗	●	⊗		⊗	⊗	●	⊗	●	⊗	⊗	⊗	⊗	⊗	⊗	⊗	⊗	3	14	1
	Hispanics	⊗	⊗	●	●	●		⊗		●		⊗	⊗		⊗	●			⊗	5	7	6
	Blacks	⊗	⊗	●		⊗	●	⊗	●	●	⊗	⊗	●	⊗		●		⊗	⊗	6	9	3
Math	Whites	⊗	⊗	●	●	●	⊗	⊗	●	⊗	⊗	⊗	⊗	⊗	⊗	⊗	●	●	⊗	6	12	0
	Hispanics	⊗	⊗	●	●	●	●	⊗	●		⊗	●	●		●	⊗	⊗	●	⊗	9	7	2
	Blacks	⊗	⊗				⊗	⊗	●	●		●	⊗		⊗	●	●	●	●	6	6	6
TOTALS	**Positive**	0	0	5	3	3	2	0	4	3	2	1	3	0	1	1	3	3	1	35		
	Negative	6	6	0	1	1	2	6	1	2	3	3	3	5	2	5	2	2	5		55	
	Not Significant	0	0	1	2	2	2	0	1	1	1	2	0	1	3	0	1	1	0			18

FIGURE D.2. Positive and negative associations for parental involvement and achievement by race: CDS.

Notes

1. The Role of Parental Involvement in Children's Schooling

1. We do not employ a composite measure of social class that combines income and education for several reasons. First, our indicators are consistent with a move among some inequality scholars who advocate for independent rather than composite measures of social class. In Hauser and Warren's (1997) critique of the widely embraced Duncan Socioeconomic Index (SEI) measure, they argue that a social class composite divided into single measures not only allows researchers to select the measures most suitable for their research question, but that composite measures may produce erroneous conclusions. We avoid this pitfall by decomposing our measures of social class. Second, conducting an assessment along two dimensions of social class allows us to determine whether the social class–parental involvement link is robust. Third, we believe that income and education are conceptually and empirically distinct in their connection to parental involvement; each measure of social class is likely to have separate implications for both the levels and effects of parental involvement. For example, simply giving more material resources to parents does not necessarily mean they will be more involved (or even more knowledgeable about how to be involved) in their children's schooling in a manner that is beneficial for achievement. To be sure, higher income is generally good for overall child well-being, but it does not necessarily follow that parents with greater economic resources are more likely to take a hands-on approach toward their children's education. However, there may be clear and meaningful differences in the approach to (and the importance placed on) education between parents who hold college degrees and those who do not, which may bear on parents' involvement in their children's schooling.

2. It is important to note that the pervasiveness of achievement gaps means that it appears in just about every source of data. This is important because in order to study the extent to which group differences in parenting contribute to these gaps, studies must draw on data sets that contain systematically collected information on both achievement and the factors posited to contribute to these gaps. Articles in the mainstream media that report group differences in scores by relying on entrance exams (e.g., SAT, LSAT) or state-wide assessment tests are unable to provide systematic explanations of these gaps because the test scores are often the only information collected from test-takers (other than the necessary identification information to know which exam corresponds to each youth). Researchers circumvent this problem by relying on data sets intended for scientific research, which contain information for each sample member on many factors including family life, health, peers, beliefs, and various other factors. These data sets are the source of most of the empirical information generated by the social scientific community. The NELS is perhaps the most popular data set for scholars interested in education research over the past two decades (see Appendix A for further information about the NELS).

3. "Standard deviation" is a statistical term that represents the average distance of each unit—in this case individual students—from the mean for the entire sample. Standard deviation is useful because it illustrates the width of a distribution of scores around an average score. Most students will score below or above the group average, and the standard deviation formula calculates the *average distance* between each student's score and the group average. If the standard deviation for a particular test with an average of 100 is 10, then a score of 115 is 1.5 standard deviations from the mean. Likewise, a score of 66 on an exam with an average of 60 and a standard deviation of 4 is 1.5 standard deviations above the mean. Thus, standard deviations are useful because they are "scale free"; expressing scores in standard deviations allows for comparisons to be made across exams that measure achievement along different metrics, samples, and time.

4. Although the black population is not homogeneous, black immigrants account for less than 2% of the U.S. population and 8% of the black population (Kent 2007). Furthermore, in supplemental analysis, the differences in most of the measures used in this study between native and nonnative (i.e., either parent or youth is foreign born) blacks are negligible. Thus, we do not disaggregate the black population.

5. Baumrind's (1971) typology identified three distinct parental styles—authoritarian, authoritative, and permissive. Authoritarian parents expect a high level of obedience from their children, are prone to punitive actions for compliance, and discourage two-way communication. Parents who are authoritative enforce rules through nonpunitive methods of discipline, encourage mature and responsible behavior, recognize their child's autonomy, and are warm

and supportive. Permissive parents typically avoid punishing their child when rules are violated, make few demands for mature behavior, and allow substantial self-regulation by the child. We are not focusing on parenting within this context; rather, we are concerned with individual activities parents engage in that may promote achievement.

3. Implications of Parental Involvement at Home by Social Class

1. The standard error is useful in illustrating the size of uncertainty in the estimate. Because the statistics are based on a sample drawn from the full population of students, they are estimates of the "true" value that would be observed if the entire population were surveyed. Therefore, estimates have a margin of error, which in statistics is referred to as the "standard error" because it represents the average discrepancy of the means that would be obtained among all possible samples (of a given size) drawn from the population and the real population mean. Given the assumption of normality (that the values in the population are distributed in a manner that can be described by a bell-shaped curve), an estimate is significant only if it is twice the size of the standard error. That is, in the case of a positive estimate (say, 0.3), the standard error (say, 0.1) could be subtracted from the estimate twice, and the estimate would still remain above zero, which would suggest that we could be 95% confident that the true value in the population is greater than zero—or simply "significant." However, because subtracting a standard error of 0.2 from an estimate of 0.3 twice would equal -0.1, we could not be 95% certain that the population value we are estimating is greater than zero. In this case, the estimate would be described as "not significant."
2. See Table B.1 in Appendix B for the unweighted sample sizes for all analyses predicting achievement in this study.
3. There are trade-offs in both unscaled and scaled analytic approaches. Individual measures allow us to determine the precise estimated effect of any particular form of involvement, but are isolated measures that may not capture real-life patterns of involvement. Scales mask the effect of individual activities but may be more accurate representations of the ways parents are actually involved in schooling. Therefore, we chose to display findings for analyses that account for both.

5. Academic Orientation among Parents at Home by Race

1. Another minority group within the resistance model that is rarely discussed is autonomous minorities. Despite experiencing some discrimination, autonomous minorities (e.g., Amish, Jews, and Mormons)—which may be small in number and/or different in race/ethnicity, religion, or language from the dominant group

(i.e., white Americans)—are not dominated or oppressed, and their achievement is similar to the dominant group (Ogbu 1978; Ogbu and Simons 1998). We do not provide further discussion of this group because they are not central to the framework (or the current discussion).

2. Portes and Rumbaut (2001) assert that immigrants arrive in their destination countries with a strong disposition for achievement—the "immigrant drive"—which parents attempt to instill in their youths by emphasizing educational attainment. This emphasis is driven by immigrant parents' belief that their children will encounter barriers in future employment opportunities (Sue and Okazaki 1990; Xie and Goyette 2003). Preferences among parents for their youths to maximize schooling reflect cultural values often learned in their home countries, which can become reinforced in the United States via dense social networks comprising co-ethnics (Hao and Bonstead-Bruns 1998; Portes and Rumbaut 2001; Zhou and Bankston 1994). However, Portes and Rumbaut (2001) stress that the resources of immigrants' co-ethnic communities in the United States may have pronounced effects on the occupational attainment of the first generation, thereby affecting the resources available to enhance educational opportunities and disposition toward education for their youths. We discuss some of these resources later in this chapter.

3. Although many Asians and Hispanics might not identify themselves as immigrants, the topic of assimilation is applicable to nearly any discussion on people of Asian descent and Hispanics within the United States. With regard to Asians, since Congress's repeal of the Chinese Exclusion Act in 1943 and the relaxation of immigration laws under the McCarran Act of 1952, there has been a dramatic increase in immigration from Asian countries. The population of Asian origin within the United States has tripled over the past three decades (Xie and Goyette 2004), which makes the designation of Asians as an immigrant group rather accurate. With regard to Hispanics, Latinos alone currently constitute more than half of the nation's 40 million foreign-born individuals (Grieco and Trevelyan 2010). Furthermore, most Mexican Americans—who comprise roughly two-thirds of the nearly 50 million Hispanics living in the United States (U.S. Census 2006; 2008)—are immigrants or descendants of immigrants who arrived after the Mexican Revolution of 1910 (see Jaffe, Cullen, and Boswell 1980).

8. Implications of Parental Involvement at School by Race

1. Although the genetic argument can be critiqued on the basis of the evidence presented by its proponents—for example, most of the evidence that undergirds the arguments in *The Bell Curve* (Herrnstein and Murray 1994) are based on minuscule R^2 reported in the book's fourth appendix—it is more intuitive (and less technical) to present evidence that counters the genetic deficiency thesis.

Studies show that test scores are strongly conditioned by social class, particularly among young children. In a study of racial differences in intelligence tests among children in preschool, Brooks-Gunn, Klebanov, and Duncan (1996) find that 52% of the black disadvantage in intelligence quotient (IQ) scores can be attributed to family and neighborhood economic characteristics, and that there is no substantial black-white difference when quality of the home learning environment is taken into account. Although the study was conducted using data from the Infant Health and Development Program, a study on low birth-weight children in eight sites across the United States, the findings are consistent with studies that use nationally representative samples. For example, using data from the Early Childhood Longitudinal Study-Kindergarten (ECLS-K), Fryer and Levitt (2006) show that after accounting for social class, black children actually enter school with an advantage in reading achievement relative to whites and that social class accounts for 85% of the black-white gap in math. They show that blacks lose ground relative to whites as they matriculate through the first three years of schooling. Furthermore, over the past forty years, blacks have gained on their white counterparts on standardized tests, both on achievement-based tests and intelligence tests (Dickens and Flynn 2006). Using data from nine standardization samples for four major IQ tests, Dickens and Flynn (2006) show that the black-white gap in IQ declined from 4 to 7 points between 1972 and 2002, and these reductions were fairly uniform across the entire range of cognitive ability. These findings suggest that either the genetic deficiency thesis is flawed or that blacks have experienced a genetic boost over the past forty years that has eluded whites.

2. The estimates for parental involvement represent the achievement gap after accounting for all of the parenting measures represented by the label. See Figure 6.1 and 6.2 for the measures represented by *parenting at home*. See Figures 8.1, 8.2, and 8.3 for measures represented by *parent-initiated contact, school-initiated contact,* and *participation at school,* respectively. The estimates represented by the label *Full Par (parenting)* are from a model that accounts for all 27 parenting measures shown in the aforementioned figures. Social class is a vector that includes parents' education, household income, family structure, and youths' sex. Achievement was assessed when youth were in grade 12, and the measures in both the social class and parenting vectors were assessed when youth were in grade 8.

10. Setting the Stage for Academic Success

1. Academic disidentification is not synonymous with a resistance to schooling. Although students who resist academic success as described by the oppositional culture theory may not identify with schooling, some students may disidentify

from academics simply to avoid further feelings of inadequacy or to protect their global self-esteem (Crocker and Major 1989). However, one can disidentify from a particular domain without engaging in active or purposeful resistance within the domain. Furthermore, one can disidentify from a domain while understanding the value associated with success in the domain. For example, an inability to regularly exercise and maintain a healthy diet can lead one to disidentify from both despite having a strong understanding of the value associated with each of these endeavors. The disidentification would simply mean that the results from one's performance in both have no bearing on how one feels about oneself in general.

2. It is more accurate to imagine the figure superimposed on a scatterplot of the relationship between measures that capture conduciveness to learning of children's environments and the degree to which they identify with success in academic domains.

3. Jackson's research investigated the impact of a policy change that ended a busing program in 2002 in the Charlotte-Mecklenburg school district in North Carolina. The busing program entailed busing students across neighborhoods to maintain racial balance of the student bodies across schools within the district. The repeal of the program led to a sudden convergence between the demographic makeup of schools and their surrounding neighborhoods, whereas other school and neighborhood characteristics remained largely unchanged. Jackson's findings revealed that schools with an inflow of black students experienced an exodus of high-quality teachers. He contends that the avoidance of black students by high-quality teachers may substantially contribute to the black-white achievement gap, as black students consequently receive lower-quality instruction.

References

Addi-Raccah, Audrey, and Ronit Ainhoren. 2009. "School Governance and Teachers' Attitudes to Parents' Involvement in Schools." *Teaching and Teacher Education* 25:805–813.

Ainsworth, James W. 2002. "Why Does It Take a Village? The Mediation of Neighborhood Effects on Educational Achievement." *Social Forces* 81:117–152.

Ainsworth-Darnell, James W., and Douglas B. Downey. 1998. "Assessing the Oppositional Culture Explanation for Racial/Ethnic Differences in School Performance." *American Sociological Review* 63:536–553.

Akom, A. A. 2003. "Reexamining Resistance as Oppositional Behavior: The Nation of Islam and the Creation of a Black Achievement Ideology." *Sociology of Education* 76:305–325.

Allen, Walter Recharde. 1985. "Race, Income and Family Dynamics: A Study of Adolescent Male Socialization Processes and Outcomes." In *Beginnings: The Social And Affective Development of Black Children,* ed. M. Spencer, G. Brookins, and W. Allen, 273–292. Hillsdale, NJ: Erlbaum.

Alliance for Excellent Education. 2008. "Understanding High School Graduation Rates in the United States." http://www.all4ed.org/publication_material /understanding_HSgradrates.

Amato, Paul R., and Frieda Fowler. 2002. "Parenting Practices, Child Adjustment, and Family Diversity." *Journal of Marriage and Family* 64:703–716.

Anderson, James D. 1988. *The Education of Blacks in the South, 1860–1935.* Chapel Hill: University of North Carolina Press.

Armor, David J., Patricia Conry-Oseguera, Millicent Cox, Nicelma King, Lorraine McDonnell, Anthony Pascal, Edward Pauly, and Gail Zellman. 1976. *Analysis of the School Preferred Reading Program in Selected Los Angeles Minority Schools.* Santa Monica, CA: Rand.

Baker, Amy J., and Laura M. Soden. 1998. "The Challenges of Parent Involvement Research." *ERIC/CUE Digest*, no. 134. http://www.ericdigests.org/1998-3/parent.html.

Baldi, Stephane, Ying Jin, Melanie Skemer, Patricia J. Green, and Deborah D. Herget. 2007. *Highlights from PISA 2006: Performance of U.S. 15-Year-Old Students in Science and Mathematics Literacy in an International Context.* NCES 2008-016. Washington, DC: National Center for Education Statistics, U.S. Department of Education.

Baldi, Stephane, and Debra Branch McBrier. 1997. "Do the Determinants of Promotion Differ for Blacks and Whites?" *Work and Occupations* 24:478–497.

Ballenger, Julia. 2009. "Parental Involvement: Low-Socioeconomic Status and Ethnic Minority Parents' Struggle for Recognition and Identity." In *The Struggle for Identity in Today's Schools,* ed. P. M. Jenlink and F. H. Townes, 156–168. New York: Rowman & Littlefield.

Bankston, Carl L., and Min Zhou. 1995. "Effects of Minority-Language Literacy on the Academic Achievement of Vietnamese Youths in New Orleans." *Sociology of Education* 68:1–17.

Barnard, Wendy Miedel. 2004. "Parent Involvement in Elementary School and Educational Attainment." *Children and Youth Services Review* 26:39–62.

Baumrind, Diana. 1971. "Current Patterns of Parental Authority." *Developmental Psychology Monographs* 41:1–103.

Bee, Helen L., Kathryn E. Barnard, Sandra J. Eyres, Carol A. Gray, Mary A. Hammond, Anita L. Spietz, Charlene Snyder, and Barbara Clark. 1982. "Prediction of IQ and Language Skill from Perinatal Status, Child Performance, Family Characteristics, and Mother-Infant Interaction." *Child Development* 53:1134–1156.

Behrman, Jere R., Lori G. Kletzer, Michael S. McPherson, and Morton Owen Schapiro. 1998. "The Microeconomics of College Choice, Careers, and Wages: Measuring the Impact of Higher Education." *Annals of the American Academy of Political and Social Science* 559:12–23.

Bempechat, Janine, Suzanne E. Graham, and Norma V. Jimenez. 1996. "The Socialization of Achievement in Poor and Minority Students." *Journal of Cross-Cultural Psychology* 30:139–158.

Berger, Eugenia H. 1983. *Beyond the Classroom: Parents as Partners in Education.* St. Louis: C.V. Mosby.

Bertrand, Marianne, and Sendhil Mullainathan. 2004. Are Emily and Brendan More Employable than Lakisha and Jamal? A Field Experiment on Labor Market Discrimination. *American Economic Review* 94:991–1013.

Bluestone, Cheryl, and Catherine S. Tamis-LeMonda. 1999. "Correlates of Parenting Styles in Predominantly Working- and Middle-Class African American Mothers." *Journal of Marriage and the Family* 61:881–893.

Bol, Linda, and Robert Q. Berry III. 2005. "Secondary Mathematics Teachers' Perceptions of the Achievement Gap." *High School Journal* 88:32–45.

Borkowski, John G., Sharon L. Ramey, and Marie Bristol-Power. 2009. *Parenting and the Child's World: Influences on Academic, Intellectual, and Socio-Emotional Development.* Mahwah, NJ: Erlbaum.

Bourdieu, Pierre. 1984. *Distinction: A Social Critique of the Judgement of Taste.* Cambridge, MA: Harvard University Press.

———. 2008. "The Forms of Capital." In *Readings in Economic Sociology,* ed. N. W. Biggart, 280–291. Oxford, UK: Blackwell.

Bourdieu, Pierre, and Jean Claude Passeron. 1977. *Reproduction in Education, Society, and Culture.* London: Sage.

Bowles, Samuel, and Herbert Gintis. 1976. *Schooling in Capitalist America: Educational Reform and the Contradictions of Economic Life.* New York: Basic Books.

Bowman, Phillip J., and Cleopatra Howard. 1985. "Race-related Socialization, Motivation, and Academic Achievement: A Study of Black Youths in Three-generation Families." *Journal of the American Academy of Child Psychiatry* 24:134–141.

Bradley, Robert H., and Robert F. Corwyn. 2002. "Socioeconomic Status and Child Development." *Annual Review of Psychology* 53:371–399.

Bradley, Robert H., Robert F. Corwyn, Harriette Pipes McAdoo, and Cynthia Garcia-Coll. 2001. "The Home Environments of Children in the United States, Part I: Variations by Age, Ethnicity, and Poverty Status." *Child Development* 72:1844–1867.

Bradley, Robert H., and L. Whiteside-Mansell. 1997. "Children in Poverty." In *Handbook of Prevention and Treatment with Children and Adolescents,* ed. R. T. Ammerman and M. Hersen, 13–58. New York: Wiley.

Bronfenbrenner, Urie. 1979. "Contexts of Child-Rearing: Problems and Prospects." *American Psychologist* 34:844–850.

Brooks-Gunn, Jeanne, Pamela K. Klebanov, and Greg J. Duncan. 1996. "Ethnic Differences in Children's Intelligence Test Scores: Role of Economic Deprivation, Home Environment, and Maternal Characteristics." *Child Development* 67:396–408.

Brooks-Gunn, Jeanne, Pamela Kato Klebanov, and Fong-Ruey Liaw. 1995. "The Learning, Physical, and Emotional Environment of the Home in the Context of Poverty: The Infant Health and Development Program." *Children and Youth Services Review* 17:251–276.

Brubaker, Rogers. 2005. "Rethinking Classical Theory: The Sociological Vision of Pierre Bourdieu." In *After Bourdieu: Influence, Critique, Elaboration,* ed. D. L. Swartz and V. L. Zolberg, 25–64. Boston, MA: Kluwer Academic.

Burkam, David T., Douglas D. Ready, Valerie E. Lee, Laura F. LoGerfo. 2004. "Social-Class Differences in Summer Learning between Kindergarten and

First Grade: Model Specification and Estimation." *Sociology of Education* 77:1–31.

Card, David, and Alan B. Krueger. 1998. "School Resources and Student Outcomes." *Annals of the American Academy of Political and Social Science* 559:39–53.

Carger, Chris Liska. 1996. *Of Borders and Dreams: A Mexican-American Experience of Urban Education.* New York: Teachers College Press.

Carter, Prudence. 2005. *Keepin' it Real.* New York: Oxford University Press.

Catsambis, Sohpia. 1998. *Expanding Knowledge of Parental Involvement in Secondary Education: Effects on High School Academic Success.* CRESPAR Policy Report R-117-D4005. Washington, DC: Center for Research on the Education of Students Placed at Risk, U.S. Department of Education.

Center on Education Policy. 2009. "State High School Exit Exams: Trends in Test Programs, Alternate Pathways, and Pass Rates." Washington, DC: Center on Education Policy.

Chao, Ruth K. 2000a. "Cultural Expectations for the Role of Parenting in the School Success of Asian-American Children." In *Resilience Across Contexts: Family, Work, Culture, and Community,* ed. M. C. Wang and R. Taylor, 333–363. Mahwah, NJ: Erlbaum.

———. 2000b. "The Parenting of Immigrant Chinese and European American Mothers: Relations between Parenting Styles, Socialization Goals, and Parental Practices." *Journal of Applied Developmental Psychology* 21:233–248.

Chavkin, Nancy Feyl. 1993. "School Social Workers Helping Multiethnic Families, Schools, and Communities Join Forces." In *Families and Schools in a Pluralistic Society,* ed. N. F. Chavkin, 217–227. Albany: State University of New York Press.

Chavkin, Nancy F., and David L. Williams. 1993. "Minority Parents and the Elementary Schools: Attitudes and Practices." In *Families and Schools in a Pluralistic Society,* ed. N. F. Chavkin, 73–83. Albany: State University of New York Press.

Cheadle, Jacob E. 2008. "Educational Investment, Family Context, and Children's Math and Reading Growth from Kindergarten through Third Grade." *Sociology of Education* 81:1–31.

Chen, Chuanshen, and Harold Stevenson. 1995. "Motivation and Mathematics Achievement: A Comparative Study of Asian-American, Caucasian-American, and East Asian High School Students." *Child Development* 66:1215–1234.

Chua, Amy. 2011. *Battle Hymn of the Tiger Mother.* New York: Penguin.

Coleman, James S. 1988. "Social Capital in the Creation of Human Capital." Supplement, *American Journal of Sociology* 94:S95–S120.

Collins, Andrew W., Eleanor E. Maccoby, Laurence Steinberg, Mavis E. Hetherington, and Marc H. Bornstein. 2000. "Contemporary Research on Parenting: The Case for Nature and Nurture." *American Psychologist* 55:218–232.

Comer, James P. 1988. "Educating Poor Minority Children." *Scientific American* 259:42–48.

——. 1992. "Educational Accountability: A Shared Responsibility between Parents and Schools." *Stanford Law and Policy Review* 4:113–122.

Connors, Lori J., and Joyce L. Epstein. 1995. "Parent and School Partnerships." In *The Handbook of Parenting,* ed. M. H. Bornstein, 437–445. Mahwah, NJ: Erlbaum.

Cook, Philip J., and Jens Ludwig. 1997. "Weighing the 'Burden of Acting White': Are There Race Differences in Attitudes toward Education?" *Journal of Policy Analysis and Management* 16:256–278.

——. 1998. "The Burden of 'Acting White': Do Black Adolescents Disparage Academic Achievement?" In *The Black-White Test Score Gap,* ed. C. Jencks and M. Phillips, 375–400. Washington, DC: Brookings Institution.

Cooper, Carey E., and Robert Crosnoe. 2007. "The Engagement in Schooling of Economically Disadvantaged Parents in Children." *Youth Society* 38:372–393.

Cose, Ellis. 1993. *The Rage of a Privileged Class.* New York: HarperCollins.

Crocker, Jennifer, and Brenda Major. 1989. "Social Stigma and Self-Esteem: The Self-Protective Properties of Stigma." *Psychological Review* 96:608–630.

Crosnoe, Robert. 2001. "Academic Orientation and Parental Involvement in Education during High School." *Sociology of Education* 74:210–230.

Cross, William E., Thomas A. Parham, and Janet E. Helms. 1991. "The Stages of Black Identity Development: Nigrescence Models." In *Black Psychology,* ed. R. Jones, 319–338. Berkeley, CA: Cobb and Henry.

Cucchiara, Maia Bloomfield, and Erin McNamara Horvat. 2009. "Perils and Promises: Middle-Class Parental Involvement in Urban Schools." *American Educational Research Journal* 46:972–1004.

Cutler, David M., and Adriana Lleras-Muney. 2008. "Education and Health: Evaluating Theories and Evidence." In *Making Americans Healthier: Social and Economic Policy as Health Policy,* ed. R. Schoeni, J. House, G. Kaplan, and H. Pollack, 29–60. New York: Russell Sage Foundation.

d'Ailly, Hsiao. 2003. "Children's Autonomy and Perceived Control in Learning: A Model of Motivation and Achievement in Taiwan." *Journal of Educational Psychology* 98:653–664.

Daniel-White, Kimberly. 2002. "Reassessing Parent Involvement: Involving Language Minority Parents in School Work at Home." *Working Papers in Educational Linguistics* 18:1–24.

Dauber, Susan L., and Joyce L. Epstein. 1993. "Parents' Attitudes and Practices of Involvement in Inner-City Elementary and Middle Schools." In *Families and*

Schools in a Pluralistic Society, ed. N. F. Chavkin, 53–71. Albany: State University of New York Press.

Davies, Don. 1993. "A More Distant Mirror: Progress Reports on a Cross-National Project to Study Family-School Partnerships." *Equity and Choice* 10:41–46.

Dearing, Eric, Holly Kreider, Sandra Simpkins, and Heather B. Weiss. 2006. "Family Involvement in School and Low-Income Children's Literacy: Longitudinal Associations between and within Families." *Journal of Educational Psychology* 98:653–664.

Dearing, Eric, and Beck A. Taylor. 2007. "Home Improvements: Within-Family Associations between Income and the Quality of Children's Home Environments." *Journal of Applied Developmental Psychology* 28:427–444.

Deater-Deckard, Kirby, Kenneth A. Dodge, John E. Bates, and Gregory S. Pettit. 1996. "Physical Discipline among African American and European American Mothers: Links to Children's Externalizing Behaviors." *Developmental Psychology* 32:1065–1072.

De Carvalho, Maria Eulina P. 2001. *Rethinking Family-School Relationships: A Critique of Parental Involvement in Schooling.* Mahwah, NJ: Erlbaum.

DeCastro-Ambrosetti, Debra, and Grace Cho. 2005. "Do Parents Value Education?: Teachers' Perceptions of Minority Parents." *Multicultural Education* 13:44–46.

Deci, Edward L., and Richard M. Ryan. 1985. *Intrinsic Motivation and Self-Determination in Human Behavior.* New York: Plenum.

Dee, Thomas S. 2004. "Are There Civic Returns to Education?" *Journal of Public Economics* 88:1697–1720.

Delgado-Gaitan, Concha. 1990. *Literacy for Empowerment: The Role of Parents in Children's Education.* New York: Routledge/Falmer Press.

———. 1991. "Involving Parents in the Schools: A Process of Empowerment." *American Journal of Education* 100:20–46.

Delpit, Lisa. 1995. *Other People's Children: Cultural Conflict in the Classroom.* New York: Free Press.

Desimone, Laura. 1999. "Linking Parent Involvement with Student Achievement: Do Race and Income Matter?" *Journal of Educational Research* 93:11–31.

Deutsch, Martin. 1967. "The Disadvantaged Child and the Learning Process." In *The Disadvantaged Child,* ed. M. Deutsch, 39–58. New York: Basic Books.

Diamond, John B., Antonia Randolph, and James P. Spillane. 2004. "Teachers' Expectations and Sense of Responsibility for Student Learning: The Importance of Race, Class, and Organizational Habitus." *Anthropology & Education Quarterly* 35:75–98.

Diamond, Karen E., Amy J. Reagan, and Jennifer E. Bandyk. 2000. "Parents' Conceptions of Kindergarten Readiness: Relationships with Race, Ethnicity, and Development." *Journal of Educational Research* 94:93–100.

Dickens, William T. 2005. "Genetic Differences in School Readiness." *Future of Children* 15:55–69.

Dickens, William T., and James R. Flynn. 2006. "Black Americans Reduce the Racial IQ Gap: Evidence from Standardization Samples." *Psychological Science* 17:913–920.

Domina, Thurston. 2005. "Leveling the Home Advantage: Assessing the Effectiveness of Parental Involvement in Elementary School." *Sociology of Education* 78:233–249.

Dornbusch, Sanford M., Philip L. Ritter, P. Herbert Leiderman, Donald F. Roberts, and Michael J. Fraleigh. 1987. "The Relation of Parenting Style to Adolescent School Performance." *Child Development* 58:1244–1257.

Downey, Carolyn J., Betty E. Steffy, William K. Poston, and Fenwick W. English. 2009. *50 Ways to Close the Achievement Gap.* Thousand Oaks, CA: Corwin Press.

Downey, Douglas B., and Shana Pribesh. 2004. "When Race Matters: Teachers' Evaluations of Students' Classroom Behavior." *Sociology of Education* 77:267–282.

Duncan, Greg J., Jeanne Brooks-Gunn, and Pamela Kato Klebanov. 1994. "Economic Deprivation and Early Childhood Development." *Child Development* 65:296–318.

Duncan, Greg J., and Willard L. Rodgers. 1988. "Longitudinal Aspects of Childhood Poverty." *Journal of Marriage and the Family* 50:1007–1021.

Eccles, Jacquelynne S., and Rena D. Harold. 1993. "Parent-School Involvement during the Early Adolescent Years." *Teachers College Record* 94:568–587.

Elliott, James R., and Ryan A. Smith. 2004. "Race, Gender, and Workplace Power." *American Sociological Review* 69:365–386.

Englund, Michelle M., Amy E. Luckner, Gloria J. L. Whaley, and Byron Egeland. 2004. "Children's Achievement in Early Elementary School: Longitudinal Effects of Parental Involvement, Expectations, and Quality of Assistance." *Journal of Educational Psychology* 96:723–730.

Entwisle, Doris R., Karl L. Alexander, and Linda S. Olson. 2005. First Grade and Educational Attainment by Age 22: A New Story. *American Journal of Sociology* 110:1458–1502.

Epstein, Joyce L. 1983. "Effect on Parents of Teacher Practices of Parent Involvement." Report No. 346. Baltimore: Center for the Social Organization of Schools, Johns Hopkins University.

———. 1985. "Home and School Connections in Schools on the Future: Implications of Research on Parental Involvement. *Peabody Journal of Education* 62:18–41.

———. 1987. "Parental Involvement: What Research Says to Administrators." *Education and Urban Society* 19:119–136.

———. 1996. "Perspectives and Previews on Research and Policy for School, Family, and Community Partnerships." In *Family-School Links: How Do They Affect Educational Outcomes?*, ed. A. Booth and J. Dunn, 209–246. Mahwah, NJ: Erlbaum.

———. 2001. *School, Family, and Community Partnerships: Preparing Educators and Improving Schools.* Boulder, CO: Westview Press.

———. 2005. "Attainable Goals? The Spirit and Letter of the No Child Left Behind Act on Parental Involvement." *Sociology of Education* 78:179–182.

———. 2010. "School/Family/Community Partnerships: Caring for the Children We Share." *Phi Delta Kappan* 92:81–96.

Epstein, Joyce L., and Susan L. Dauber. 1991. "School Programs and Teacher Practices of Parent Involvement in Inner-City Elementary and Middle Schools." *Elementary School Journal* 91:289–305.

Esparza, Patricia, and Bernadette Sanchez. 2008. "The Role of Attitudinal Familism in Academic Outcomes: A Study of Urban, Latino High School Seniors." *Cultural Diversity and Ethnic Minority Psychology* 14:193–200.

Fan, Xitao. 2001. "Parental Involvement and Students' Academic Achievement: A Growth Model Analysis." *Journal of Experimental Education* 70:27–61.

Fan, Xitao, and Michael Chen. 2001. "Parental Involvement and Students' Academic Achievement: A Meta-Analysis." *Educational Psychology Review* 13:1–22.

Fantuzzo, John, Erin Tighe, and Stephanie Childs. 2000. Family Involvement Questionnaire: A Multivariate Assessment of Family Participation in Early Childhood Education. *Journal of Educational Psychology* 92:367–376.

Farkas, George, Christy Lleras, and Steve Maczuga. 2002. "Does Oppositional Culture Exist in Minority and Poverty Peer Groups?" *American Sociological Review* 67:148–155.

Farkas, George, and Keven Vicknair. 1996. "Appropriate Tests of Racial Wage Discrimination Require Controls for Cognitive Skills." *American Sociological Review* 61:557–560.

Feagin, Joe R., and Melvin P. Sikes. 1994. *Living with Racism: The Black Middle-Class.* Boston: Beacon Press.

Federman, Maya, Thesia I. Garner, Kathleen Short, W. Boman Cutter, John Kiely, David Levine, Duane McGough, and Marilyn McMillen. 1996. "What Does It Mean to be Poor in America?" *Monthly Labor Review* 119:3–17.

Fehrmann, Paul G., Timothy Z. Keith, and Thomas Reimers. 1987. "Home Influence on School Learning: Direct and Indirect Effects of Parental Involvement on High School Grades." *Journal of Educational Research* 80:330–337.

Ferguson, Ann Arnett. 2000. *Bad Boys: Public Schools in the Making of Black Masculinity.* Ann Arbor: University of Michigan Press.

Finders, Margaret, and Cynthia Lewis. 1994. "Why Some Parents Don't Come to School." *Educational Leadership* 51:50–54.

Fine, Michelle. 1993. "[Ap]parent Involvement: Reflections on Parents, Power, and Urban Public Schools." *Teachers College Record* 94:682–710.

Fischer, Claude S., Michael Hout, Martin Sanchez Jankowski, Samuel R. Lucas, Ann Swidler, and Kim Voss. 1996. *Inequality by Design: Cracking the Bell Curve Myth.* Princeton, NJ: Princeton University Press.

Fordham, Signithia. 1988. "Racelessness as a Factor in Black Students' School Success: Pragmatic Strategy or Pyrrhic Victory?" *Harvard Educational Review* 58:54–84.

———. 1996. *Blacked Out: Dilemmas of Race, Identity, and Success as Capital High.* Chicago: University of Chicago Press.

Fordham, Signithia, and John U. Ogbu. 1986. "Black Students' School Success: Coping with the Burden of 'Acting White.'" *Urban Review* 18:176–206.

Freeman, Catherine, Benjamin Scafidi, and David L. Sjoquist. 2005. "Racial Segregation in Georgia Public Schools, 1994–2001: Trends, Causes, and Impact on Teacher Quality." In *School Segregation: Must the South Turn Back?,* ed. J. C. Boger and G. Orfield, 148–163. Chapel Hill: University of North Carolina Press.

Fryer, Ronald G., and Steven D. Levitt. 2006. "The Black-White Test Score Gap through Third Grade." *American Law and Economics Review* 8:249–281.

Fryer, Roland, and Paul Torelli. 2010. "An Empirical Analysis of 'Acting White.'" *Journal of Public Economics* 94:380–396.

Fuligni, Andrew J. 1997. "The Academic Achievement of Adolescents from Immigrant Families: The Roles of Family Background, Attitudes, and Behavior." *Child Development* 68:351–363.

Furstenberg, Frank, Thomas Cook, Jacquelynne Eccles, Glen H. Elder, and Arnold A. Sameroff. 1999. *Managing to Make It: Urban Families and Adolescent Success.* Chicago: University of Chicago Press.

Furstenberg, Frank F., and Mary Elizabeth Hughes. 1995. "Social Capital and Successful Development among At-Risk Youth." *Journal of Marriage and the Family* 57:580–592.

Gans, Herbert J. 1968. "Culture and Class in the Study of Poverty: An Approach to Antipoverty Research." In *On Understanding Poverty: Perspectives from the Social Sciences,* ed. D. P. Moynihan, 201–228. New York: Basic Books.

Gillies, Val. 2008. "Perspectives on Parenting Responsibility: Contextualizing Values and Practices." *Journal of Law and Society* 35:95–112.

Ginsburg, Golda S., and Phyllis Bronstein. 1993. "Family Factors Related to Children's Intrinsic/Extrinsic Motivational Orientation and Academic Performance." *Child Development* 64:1461–1475.

Goldenberg, Claude, and Ronald Gallimore. 1995. "Immigrant Latino Parents' Values and Beliefs about their Children's Education: Continuities and Discontinuities across Cultures and Generations." In *Advances in Motivation and Achievement: Culture, Ethnicity, and Motivation,* ed. P. R. Pintrich & M. Maehr, 183–228. Greenwich, CT: JAI Press.

Goldenberg, Claude, Leslie Reese, and Ronald Gallimore. 1992. "Effects of Literacy Materials from School on Latino Children's Home Experiences and Early Reading Achievement." *American Journal of Education* 100:497–536.

Goldsmith, Arthur H., Darrick Hamilton, and William Darity Jr. 2006. "Shades of Discrimination: Skin Tone and Wages." *American Economic Review* 96:242–245.

Gonzales, Nancy A., Yumi Hiraga, and Ana Mari Cauce. 1998. "Observing Mother-Daughter Interaction in African-American and Asian American Families." In *Resiliency in African-American Families,* ed. H. I. McCubbin, E. A. Thompson, A. I. Thompson, and J. A. Futrell, 259–286. Thousand Oaks, CA: Sage.

Gottfried, Adele Eskeles, James S. Fleming, and Allen W. Gottfried. 1998. "Role of Cognitively Stimulating Home Environment in Children's Academic Intrinsic Motivation: A Longitudinal Study." *Child Development* 69:1448–1460.

Goyette, Kimberly, and Yu Xie. 1999. "Educational Expectations of Asian American Youths: Determinants and Ethnic Differences." *Sociology of Education* 72:22–36.

Green, Christa L., Joan M. T. Walker, Kathleen V. Hoover-Dempsey, and Howard M. Sandler. 2007. "Parents' Motivation for Involvement in Children's Education: An Empirical Test of a Theoretical Model of Parental Involvement." *Journal of Educational Psychology* 99:532–544.

Grenfell Michael, and David James. 1998. *Bourdieu and Education: Acts of Practical Theory.* London: Routledge/Falmer Press.

Grieco, Elizabeth M., and Edward N. Trevelyan. 2010. "Place of Birth of the Foreign-Born Population: 2009." *American Community Survey Briefs.* Washington, DC: Economics and Statistics Administration, U.S. Department of Commerce.

Grissmer, David, Ann Flanagan, and Stephanie Williamson. 1998. "Why Did the Black-White Test Score Gap Converge in the 1970s and 1980s?" In *The Black-White Test Score Gap,* ed. C. Jencks and M. Phillips, 182–226. Washington, DC: Brookings Institution.

Grolnick, Wendy S., Corina Benjet, Carolyn Kurowski, and Nicholas H. Apostoleris. 1997. "Predictors of Parent Involvement in Children's Schooling." *Journal of Educational Psychology* 89: 538–548.

Grolnick, Wendy S., and Richard M. Ryan. 1989. "Parent Styles Associated with Children's Self-Regulation and Competence in School." *Journal of Educational Psychology* 81:143–154.

Grolnick, Wendy S., and Maria L. Slowiaczek. 1994. "Parents' Involvement in Children's Schooling: A Multidimensional Conceptualization and Motivational Model." *Child Development* 64:237–252.

Gunnoe, Marjorie Lindner, E. Mavis Hetherington, and David Reiss. 1999. "Parental Religiosity, Parenting Style, and Adolescent Social Responsibility." *Journal of Early Adolescence* 19:199–225.

Gutman, Leslie Morrison, and Jacquelynne S. Eccles. 1999. "Financial Strain, Parenting Behaviors, and Adolescents' Achievement: Testing Model Equivalence between African American and European American Single- and Two-Parent Families." *Child Development* 70:1464–1476.

Gutman, Leslie Morrison, and Vonnie M. McLoyd 2000. "An Examination of African-American Families Living in Poverty." *Urban Review* 32:1–24.

Hango, Darcy. 2007. "Parental Investment in Childhood and Educational Qualifications: Can Greater Parental Involvement Mediate the Effects of Socioeconomic Disadvantage?" *Social Science Research* 36:1371–1390.

Hanson, Sandra L. 1994. "Lost Talent: Unrealizing Educational Aspirations and Expectations among U.S. Youths. *Sociology of Education* 67:159–183.

Hanushek, Eric A. 1997. "Assessing the Effects of School Resources on Student Performance: An Update." *Educational Evaluation and Policy Analysis* 19:141–164.

Hanushek, Eric A., John F. Kain, and Steven G. Rivkin. 2004. "Why Public Schools Lose Teachers." *Journal of Human Resources* 39:326–354.

Hanushek, Eric A., and Richard R. Pace. 1995. "Who Chooses to Teach (and Why)?" *Economics of Education Review* 14:101–117.

Hao, Lingxin, and Melissa Bonstead-Bruns. 1998. "Parent-Child Differences in Educational Expectations and the Academic Achievement of Immigrant and Native Students." *Sociology of Education* 71:175–198.

Harris, Angel L. 2006. "I (Don't) Hate School: Revisiting 'Oppositional Culture' Theory of Blacks' Resistance to Schooling." *Social Forces* 85:797–834.

———. 2008. "Optimism in the Face of Despair: Black-White Differences in Beliefs about School as a Means for Upward Social Mobility." *Social Science Quarterly* 89:629–651.

———. 2011. *Kids Don't Want to Fail: Oppositional Culture and the Black-White Achievement Gap.* Cambridge, MA: Harvard University Press.

Harris, Angel L., and Kris Marsh. 2010. "Is a Raceless Identity an Effective Strategy for Academic Success among Blacks?" *Social Science Quarterly* 91: 1242–1263.

Harris, Angel L., and Keith Robinson. 2007. "Schooling Behaviors or Prior Skills?: A Cautionary Tale of Omitted Variable Bias within the Oppositional Culture Theory." *Sociology of Education* 80:139–157.

Harrison, Algea O., Melvin N. Wilson, Charles J. Pine, Samuel J. Chan, and Raymond Buriel. 1990. "Family Ecologies of Ethnic Minority Children." *Child Development* 61:347–362.

Hart, Betty, and Todd R. Risley. 1995. *Meaningful Differences in the Everyday Experience of Young American Children.* Baltimore: Paul H. Brookes.

Haskins, Ron, and Isabel Sawhill. 2003. *Work and Marriage: The Way to End Poverty and Welfare.* Policy Brief, no. 28. Washington, DC: Brookings Institution.

Hauser, Robert, and John Warren. 1997. "Socioeconomic Indexes for Occupations: A Review, Update, and Critique." *Sociological Methodology* 27:177–298.

Hauser-Cram, Penny, Selcuk R. Sirin, and Deborah Stipek. 2003. "When Teachers' and Parents' Values Differ: Teachers' Ratings of Academic Competence in Children from Low-Income Families." *Journal of Educational Psychology* 95:813–820.

Hayward, Mark D., Eileen M. Crimmins, Toni P. Miles, and Yu Yang. 2000. "The Significance of Socioeconomic Status in Explaining the Racial Gap in Chronic Health Conditions." *American Sociological Review* 65:910–930.

Heckman, Paul E., and Francine Peterman. 1996. "Indigenous Invention: New Promises for School Reform." *Teachers College Record* 98:307–327.

Hedges, Larry V., and Amy Nowell. 1998. "Black-White Test Score Convergence since 1965." In *The Black-White Test Score Gap,* ed. C. Jencks and M. Phillips, 149–181. Washington, DC: Brookings Institution.

———. 1999. "Changes in the Black-White Gap in Achievement Test Scores." *Sociology of Education* 72:111–135.

Heineman, Dave. 2010. "2010 Leaders in Parental Involvement." November 19. http://www.governor.nebraska.gov/columns/2010/11/19_parental_involvement.html.

Herrnstein, Richard, and Charles Murray. 1994. *The Bell Curve: Intelligence and Class Structure in American Life.* New York: Free Press.

Hickman, Catherine Wehlburg. 1996. "The Future of High School Success: The Importance of Parent Involvement Programs." *The Future of Secondary Education.* http://horizon.unc.edu/projects/HSJ/Hickman.html.

Hill, Nancy E., and Stracie A. Craft. 2003. "Parent-School Involvement and School Performance: Mediated Pathways among Socioeconomically Comparable African American and Euro-American Families." *Journal of Educational Psychology* 95:74–83.

Hill, Shirley A. 2001. "Class, Race, and Gender Dimensions of Child Rearing in African American Families." *Journal of Black Studies* 31:494–508.

Hill, Shirley A., and Joey Sprague. 1999. Parenting in Black and White Families: The Interaction of Gender with Race and Class. *Gender and Society* 13:480–502.

Hirschman, Charles, and Morrison G. Wong. 1986. "The Extraordinary Educational Attainment of Asian Americans: A Search for Historical Evidence and Explanations." *Social Forces* 65:1–27.

Ho, David Y. F. 1994. "Cognitive Socialization in Confucian Heritage Cultures." In *Cross-Cultural Roots of Minority Child Development*, ed. P. M. Greenfield and R. R. Cocking, 285–313. Hillsdale, NJ: Erlbaum.

Hochschild, Jennifer L. 1995. *Facing Up to the American Dream: Race, Class, and the Soul of the Nation*. Princeton, NJ: Princeton University Press.

Hoge, Dean R., Edna K. Smit, and John T. Crist. 1997. "Four Family Process Factors Predicting Academic Achievement in Sixth and Seventh Grade." *Educational Research Quarterly* 21:27–42.

Hoover-Dempsey, Kathleen, and Howard M. Sandler. 1997. "Why Do Parents Become Involved in Their Children's Education?" *Review of Educational Research* 67:3–42.

Horvat, Erin McNamara, and Kristine S. Lewis. 2003. "Reassessing the 'Burden of "Acting White'": The Importance of Peer Groups in Managing Academic Success." *Sociology of Education* 76:265–280.

Hughes, Robert J., and Maureen Perry-Jenkins. 1996. "Social Class Issues in Family Life Education." *Family Relations* 45:175–182.

Hyslop, Nancy. 2000. *Hispanic Parental Involvement in Home Literacy*. ERIC ED446340. Washington, DC: Education Resources Information Center Clearinghouse on Reading English and Communication, U.S. Department of Education.

Ingels, Steven J., Kathryn L. Dowd, James L. Stipe, John D. Baldridge, Virginia H. Bartot, Martin R. Frankel. 1994. *National Education Longitudinal Study of 1988, Second Follow-Up: Dropout Component Data File User's Manual*. Washington, DC: U.S. Department of Education.

Izzo, Charles V., Roger P. Weissberg, Wesley J. Kasprow, and Michael Fendrich. 1999. "A Longitudinal Assessment of Teacher Perceptions of Parent Involvement in Children's Education and School Performance." *American Journal of Community Psychology* 27:817–839.

Jackson, C. Kirabo. 2009. "Student Demographics, Teacher Sorting, and Teacher Quality: Evidence from the End of School Desegregation." *Journal of Labor Economics* 27:213–256.

Jackson, Christine, Lisa Henriksen, and Vangie A. Foshee. 1998. "The Authoritative Parenting Index: Predicting Health Risk Behaviors among Children and Adolescents." *Health Education and Behavior* 25:319–337.

Jaffe, Abram J., Ruth M. Cullen, and Thomas D. Boswell. 1980. *The Changing Demography of Spanish Americans*. New York: Academic Press.

Jarrett, Robin L. 1995. "Growing up Poor: The Family Experiences of Socially Mobile Youth in Low-Income African-American Neighborhoods." *Journal of Adolescent Research* 10:111–135.

Jensen, Arthur. 1969. "How Much Can We Boost IQ and Scholastic Achievement?" *Harvard Educational Review* 39:1–123.

Jeynes, William. 2003. "A Meta-Analysis: The Effects of Parental Involvement on Minority Children's Achievement." *Education and Urban Society* 35:202–223.

Jordan, Nancy C., David Kaplan, Chaitanya Ramineni, and Maria N. Locuniak. 2009. "Early Math Matters: Kindergarten Number Competence and Later Mathematics Outcomes." *Developmental Psychology* 45:850–867.

Julian, Teresa W., Patrick C. McKenry, and Mary W. McKelvey. 1994. "Cultural Variations in Parenting; Perceptions of Caucasion, African-American, Hispanic, and Asian-American Parents." *Family Relations* 43:30–37.

Kao, Grace. 1995. "Asian-Americans as Model Minorities? A Look at Their Academic Performance." *American Journal of Education* 103:121–159.

Kao, Grace, and Marta Tienda. 1995. "Optimism and Achievement: The Educational Performance of Immigrant Youth." *American Journal of Education* 106:349–384.

Kardiner, Abram, and Lionel Ovesey. 1951. *The Mark of Oppression.* New York: World.

Karen, David. 2005. "No Child Left Behind? Sociology Ignored!" *Sociology of Education* 78:165–182.

Keith, Timothy Z., Patricia B. Keith, Kimberly J. Quirk, Jodi Sperduto, Stephanie Santillo, and Stacy Killings. 1998. "Longitudinal Effects of Parent Involvement on High School Grades: Similarities and Differences across Gender and Ethnic Groups." *Journal of School Psychology* 36:335–363.

Keith, Timothy Z., Thomas M. Reimers, Paul G. Fehrmann, Sheila M. Pottebaum, and Linda W. Aubey. 1986. "Parental Involvement, Homework, and TV time: Direct and Indirect Effects on High School Achievement." *Journal of Educational Psychology* 78:373–380.

Kelley, Michelle L., Thomas G. Power, and Dawn D. Wimbush. 1992. "Determinants of Disciplinary Practices in Low-Income Black Mothers." *Child Development* 63:573–582.

Kelly, Sean. 2004. "Do Increased Levels of Parental Involvement Account for Social Class Differences in Track Placement?" *Social Science Research* 33:626–659.

Kent, Mary Mederios. 2007. "Immigration and America's Black Population." *Population Bulletin* 62:1–16.

Kim, Uichol, and Maria B. J. Chun. 1994. "Educational Success of Asian Americans: An Indigenous Perspective." *Journal of Applied Developmental Psychology* 15:329–339.

Kim, Yanghee. 2009. "Minority Parental Involvement and School Barriers: Moving the Focus Away from Deficiencies of Parents." *Educational Research Review* 4:80–102.

Kohn, Melvin L. 1963. "Social Class and Parent-Child Relationships: An Interpretation." *American Journal of Sociology* 68:471–480.

Kozol, Jonathan. 2000. Forward to *Will Standards Save Public Education?*, ed. D. Meier, vii–xiii. Boston: Beacon Press.

Lareau, Annette. 1987. "Social Class Differences in Family-School Relationships: The Importance of Cultural Capital." *Sociology of Education* 60:73–85.

———. 2000. *Home Advantage: Social Class and Parental Intervention in Elementary Education.* 2nd ed. Lanham, MD: Rowman & Littlefield.

———. 2002. "Invisible Inequality: Social Class and Childrearing in Black Families and White Families." *American Sociological Review* 67:747–776.

———. 2003. *Unequal Childhoods: Class, Race, and Family Life.* Berkeley: University of California Press.

Lareau, Annette, and Erin McNamara Horvat. 1999. "Moments of Social Inclusion and Exclusion Race, Class, and Cultural Capital in Family-School Relationships." *Sociology of Education* 72:37–53.

Lareau, Annette, and Wesley Shumar. 1996. "The Problem of Individualism in Family-School Policies." *Sociology of Education* 69:24–39.

Lee, Guang-Lea, and M. Lee Manning. 2001. "Working with Asian Parents and Families." *Multicultural Education* 9:23–26.

Lee, Jung-Sook, and Natasha K. Bowen. 2006. "Parent Involvement, Cultural Capital, and the Achievement Gap among Elementary School Children." *American Educational Research Journal* 43:193–218.

Lewis, Amanda, and Tyrone A. Foreman. 2002. "Contestation or Collaboration? A Comparative Study of Home-School Relations." *Anthropology & Education Quarterly* 33:1–30.

Lewis, Oscar. 1961. *The Children of Sanchez.* New York: Random House.

———. 1968. "The Culture of Poverty." In *On Understanding Poverty: Perspectives from the Social Sciences,* ed. D. P. Moynihan, 187–220. New York: Basic Books.

Lieberman, Ann, and Lynne Miller. 1999. *Teachers: Transforming Their World and Their Work.* New York: Teachers College Press.

Litwack, Leon F. 1998. *Trouble in the Mind: Black Southerners in the Age of Jim Crow.* New York: Vintage Books.

Lochner, Lance, and Enrico Moretti. 2004. "The Effect of Education on Crime: Evidence from Prison Inmates, Arrests, and Self-Reports." *American Economic Review* 94 1:155–189.

Lopez, Mark Hugo. 2009. *Latinos and Education: Explaining the Attainment Gap.* Washington, DC: Pew Hispanic Center.

Lopez, Nancy. 2003. *Hopeful Girls, Troubled Boys.* New York: Routledge.

Lott, Bernice. 2001. "Low-Income Parents and the Public Schools." *Journal of Social Issues* 57:247–259.

———. 2002. "Cognitive and Behavioral Distancing from the Poor." *American Psychologist* 57: 100–110.

Louie, Vivian. 2001. "Parents' Aspirations and Investment: The Role of Social Class in the Educational Experiences of 1.5-and Second-Generation Chinese Americans." *Harvard Educational Review* 71:438–476.

Lucas, Samuel Roundfield. 1999. *Tracking Inequality: Stratification and Mobility in American High Schools.* New York: Teachers College Press.

———. 2008. *Theorizing Discrimination in an Era of Contested Prejudice.* Philadelphia: Temple University Press.

Luster, Tom, and Lynn Okagaki. 2005. *Parenting: An Ecological Perspective.* Mahwah, NJ: Erlbaum.

Lynch, Scott M. 2003. "Cohort and Life-Course Patterns in the Relationship between Education and Health: A Hierarchical Approach." *Demography* 40:309–331.

MacLeod, Jay. 2009. *Ain't No Making It: Aspirations and Attainment in a Low-Income Neighborhood.* Philadelphia: Westview Press.

Marjoribanks, Kevin. 1979. *Families and Their Learning Environments: An Empirical Analysis.* London: Routledge & Kegan Paul.

Markell, Jack. 2010."Our Children—Our Schools—Our Future." Delaware Governor's Weekly Message, October 1. http://www.youtube.com/watch?v=3nVHjhla5GQ.

Marsh, Herbert W. 1986. "Global Self-Esteem: Its Relation to Specific Facets of Self-Concept and their Importance." *Journal of Personality and Social Psychology* 51:1224–1236.

Marzano, Robert J. 2003. *What Works in Schools: Translating Research into Action.* Alexandria, VA: Association for Supervision and Curriculum Development.

Massey, Douglas, and Nancy Denton. 1993. *American Apartheid.* Cambridge, MA: Harvard University Press.

Matthews, Julie. 2002. "Racialised Schooling, 'Ethnic Success' and Asian-Australian Students." *British Journal of Sociology of Education* 23:193–207.

Mau, Wei-Cheng. 1997. "Parental Influences on the High School Students' Academic Achievement: A Comparison of Asian Immigrants, Asian Americans, and White Americans." *Psychology in the Schools* 34:267–277.

McCaleb, Sudia Paloma. 1997. *Building Communities of Learners: A Collaboration among Teachers, Students, Families, and Community.* Mahwah, NJ: Erlbaum.

McCartney, Kathleen, Eric Dearing, Beck A. Taylor, and Kristen L. Bub. 2007. "Quality Child Care Supports the Achievement of Low-Income Children: Direct and Indirect Effects through Caregiving and the Home Environment." *Journal of Applied Developmental Psychology* 28:411–426.

McGroder, Sharon M. 2000. "Parenting among Low-Income, African American Single Mothers with Preschool-Age Children: Patterns, Predictors, and Developmental Correlates." *Child Development* 71:752–771.

McKay, Mary McKernan, Marc S. Atkins, Tracie Hawkins, Catherine Brown, and Cynthia J. Lynn. 2003. "Inner-City African American Parental Involvement in Children's Schooling: Racial Socialization and Social Support from the Parent Community." *American Journal of Community Psychology* 32:107–115.

McKown, Clark, and Rhona S. Weinstein. 2008. "Teacher Expectations, Classroom Context, and the Achievement Gap." *Journal of School Psychology* 46:235–261.

McLoyd, Vonnie C. 1990. "The Impact of Economic Hardship on Black Families and Children: Psychological Distress, Parenting, and Socioemotional Development." *Child Development* 61:311–346.

McNeal, Ralph B., Jr. 1999. "Parental Involvement as Social Capital: Differential Effectiveness on Science Achievement, Truancy, and Dropping Out." *Social Forces* 78:117–144.

McNeil, Linda M. 2000. *Contradictions of School Reform: Educational Costs of Standardized Testing.* New York: Routledge.

McWhorter, John. 2000. *Losing the Race.* New York: Free Press.

Meier, Deborah. 2000. *Will Standards Save Public Education?* Boston: Beacon Press.

Mickelson, Roslyn Arlin. 1990. "The Attitude-Achievement Paradox among Black Adolescents." *Sociology of Education* 63:44–61.

Middlemiss, Wendy. 2003. Brief Report: Poverty, Stress, and Support: Patterns of Parenting Behavior among Lower-Income Black and Lower-Income White Mothers. *Infant and Child Development* 12:293–300.

Miedel, Wendy T., and Arthur J. Reynolds. 1999. "Parent Involvement in Early Intervention for Disadvantaged Children: Does It Matter?" *Journal of School Psychology* 37:379–402.

Miller, Jane E., and Diane Davis. 1997. "Poverty History, Marital History, and Quality of Children's Home Environments." *Journal of Marriage and the Family* 59:996–1007.

Milligan, Kevin, Enrico Moretti, and Philip Oreopoulos. 2004. "Does Education Improve Citizenship?: Evidence from the United States and the United Kingdom." *Journal of Public Economics* 88:1667–1695.

Milne, Ann M., David E. Myers, Alvin S. Rosenthal, and Alan Ginsburg. 1986. "Single Parents, Working Mothers, and the Educational Achievement of School Children." *Sociology of Education* 59:125–139.

Morris, Edward. 2007. "'Ladies' or 'Loudies'?: Perceptions and Experiences of Black Girls in Classrooms." *Youth & Society* 38:490–515.

Morris, Edward W. 2005. "'Tuck in that Shirt!': Race, Class, Gender, and Discipline in an Urban School." *Sociological Perspectives* 48:25–48.

Morrison, Frederick J., Heather J. Bachman, and Carol McDonald Connor. 2005. *Improving Literacy in America: Guidelines from Research.* New Haven, CT: Yale University Press.

Mosby, Lynetta, Anne Warfield Rawls, Albert J. Meehan, Edward Pettinari Mays, and Catherine Johnson. 1999. "Troubles in Interracial Talk about Discipline: An Examination of African American Childrearing Narratives." *Journal of Comparative Family Studies* 30:489–521.

Moser, Claus A., and Graham Kalton. 1972. *Survey Methods in Social Investigation.* 2nd ed. New York: Basic Books.

Moynihan, Daniel Patrick. 1965. *The Negro Family: The Case for National Action.* Washington, DC: Office of Planning and Research, U.S. Department of Labor.

Muller, Chandra. 1995. "Maternal Employment, Parental Involvement, and Mathematics Achievement among Adolescents." *Journal of Marriage and the Family* 57:85–100.

——. 1998. "Gender Differences in Parental Involvement and Adolescents' Mathematics Achievement." *Sociology of Education* 71:336–356.

Muller, Patricia A., Frances K. Stage, and Jillian Kinzie. 2001. "Science Achievement Growth Trajectories: Understanding Factors Related to Gender and Racial-Ethnic Differences in Precollege Science Achievement." *American Educational Research Journal* 38:981–1012.

Murnane, Richard J., John B. Willett, and Frank Levy. 1995. "The Growing Importance of Cognitive Skills in Wage Determination." *Review of Economics and Statistics* 77:251–266.

National Education Association. 1985. "Teacher-Parent Partnership Program, 1984–1985 Status Report." Unpublished paper. Washington, DC: National Education Association.

Neal, Derek A., and William R. Johnson. 1996. "The Role of Premarket Factors in Black-White Wage Differences." *Journal of Political Economy* 104:869–895.

Neal, La Vonne I., Audrey Davis McCray, Gwendolyn Webb-Johnson, and Scott T. Bridgest. 2003. "The Effects of African American Movement Styles on Teachers' Perceptions and Reactions." *Journal of Special Education* 37:49–57.

Newsroom and Media Center. 2009. "Governor Bredesen Promotes National Parent Involvement Day." November 19. http://news.tn.gov/node/4039.

Nisbett, Richard E. 1998. "Race, Genetics, and IQ." *The Black-White Test Score Gap,* ed. C. Jencks and M. Phillips, 86–102. Washington, DC: Brookings Institution.

Novas, Himilce. 2008. *Everything You Need to Know about Latino History.* New York: Penguin.

O'Connor, Carla. 1997. "Dispositions toward (Collective) Struggle and Educational Resilience in the Inner City." *American Educational Research Journal* 34:593–629.

Odden, Allen R., and Lawrence O. Picus. 2007. *School Finance: A Policy Perspective.* New York: McGraw-Hill.

Ogbu, John U. 1978. *Minority Education and Caste: The American System in Cross-Cultural Perspective.* New York: Academic Press.

———. 1981. "Origins of Human Competence: A Cultural-Ecological Perspective." *Child Development* 52:413–429.

———. 2003. *Black American Students in an Affluent Suburb: A Study of Academic Disengagement.* Mahwah, NJ: Erlbaum.

Ogbu, John U., and Maria Eugenia Matute-Bianchi. 1986. "Understanding Sociocultural Factors: Knowledge, Identity and School Adjustment." In *Beyond Language: Social and Cultural Factors in Schooling Language Minority Students,* 73–142. Los Angeles: Evaluation, Dissemination, and Assessment Center, University of California.

Ogbu, John U., and Herbert D. Simons. 1998. "Voluntary and Involuntary Minorities: A Cultural-Ecological Theory of School Performance with Some Implications for Education." *Anthropology & Education Quarterly* 29:155–188.

Okpala, Comfort O., and Amon Okpala. 2001. "Parental Involvement, Instructional Expenditures, Family Socioeconomic Attributes, and Student Achievement." *Journal of Educational Research* 95:110–115.

O'Neill, June. 1990. "The Role of Human Capital in Earnings Differences between Black and White Men." *Journal of Economic Perspectives* 4:25–45.

Osajima, Keith. 2005. "Asian Americans as the Model Minority: An Analysis of the Popular Press Image in the 1960s and 1980s." In *A Companion to Asian American Studies,* ed. K. A. Ono, 215–225. Malden, MA: Blackwell.

Osborne, Jason W. 1997. "Race and Academic Disidentification." *Journal of Educational Psychology* 89:728–735.

Pager, Devah. 2007. *MARKED: Race, Crime, and Finding Work in an Era of Mass Incarceration.* Chicago: University of Chicago Press.

Pena, Delores C. 2000. "Parent Involvement: Influencing Factors and Implications." *Journal of Educational Research* 94:42–54.

Planty, Michael, William Hussar, Thomas Snyder, Grace Kena, Angelina KewalRamani, Jana Kemp, K. Bianco, and Rachel Dinkes. 2009. *The Condition of Education 2009.* NCES 2009-081. Washington, DC: National Center for Education Statistics, U.S. Department of Education.

Planty, Michael, William Hussar, Thomas Snyder, Stephen Provasnik, Grace Kena, Rachel Dinkes, Angelina KewalRamani, and Jana Kemp. 2008. *The Condition of Education 2008.* NCES 2008-031. Washington, DC: National Center for Education Statistics, U.S. Department of Education.

Pomerantz, Eva, Elizabeth Moorman, and Scott D. Litwack. 2007. "The How, Whom, and Why of Parents' Involvement in Children's Academic Lives: More Is Not Always Better." *Review of Educational Research* 77:373–410.

Portes, Alejandro, and Dag MacLeod. 1996. "Educational Progress of Children of Immigrants: The Roles of Class, Ethnicity, and School Context." *Sociology of Education* 69:255–275.

Portes, Alejandro, and Ruben G. Rumbaut. 2001. *Legacies: The Story of the Immigrant Second Generation.* Berkeley: University of California Press.

———. 2006. *Immigrant American: A Portrait.* Berkeley: University of California Press.

Portes, Alejandro, and Min Zhou. 1993. "The New Second Generation: Segmented Assimilation and Its Variants." *Annals of the American Academy of Political and Social Science* 503:74–96.

Portes, Pedro R., Richard M. Dunham, Shavon Williams. 1986. "Assessing Child-Rearing Style in Ecological Settings: Its Relation to Culture, Social Class, Early Age Intervention and Scholastic Achievement." *Adolescence* 21:723–735.

Public Agenda. 2000. *Great Expectations: How the Public and Parents—White, African American and Hispanic—View Higher Education.* Report #00-2. Washington, DC: National Center for Public Policy and Higher Education.

Reay, Diane. 1998. *Class Work: Mothers' Involvement in Their Children's Primary Schooling.* London: UCL Press.

Reese, Leslie, Silvia Balzano, Ronald Gallimore, and Claude Goldenberg. 1995. "The Concept of *Educación:* Latino Family Values and American Schooling." *International Journal of Educational Research* 23:57–81.

Rivera, Ralph, and Sonia Nieto. 1993. *The Education of Latino Students in Massachusetts: Issues, Research, and Policy Implications.* Amherst: University of Massachusetts Press.

Rivkin, Steven G. 1995. "Black/white Differences in Schooling and Employment." *Journal of Human Resources* 30:826–852.

Robinson, Keith, and Angel L. Harris. 2013. "Racial and Social Class Differences in How Parents Respond to Inadequate Achievement: Consequences for Children's Future Achievement." *Social Science Quarterly* 94:1346–1371.

Roscigno, Vincent J., and James W. Ainsworth-Darnell. 1999. "Race, Cultural Capital, and Educational Resources: Persistent Inequalities and Achievement Returns." *Sociology of Education* 72:158–178.

Rosenberg, Morris. 1979. *Conceiving the Self.* New York: Basic Books.

Rosenberg, Morris, Carmi Schooler, Carrie Shoenbach, and Florence Rosenberg. 1995. "Global Self-Esteem and Specific Self-Esteem: Different Concepts, Different Outcomes." *American Sociological Review* 60:141–156.

Rosner, Jay. 2003. "On White Preferences." *Nation,* April 14, 24.

Ross, Catherine E., and Chia-Ling Wu. 1996. "Education, Age, and the Cumulative Advantage in Health." *Journal of Health and Social Behavior* 37:104–120.

Rumberger, Russell W., and Katherine A. Larson. 1998. "Student Mobility and the Increased Risk of High School Dropout." *American Journal of Education* 107:1–35.

Sacks, Peter. 1999. *Standardized Minds: The High Price of America's Testing Culture and What We Can Do about It.* New York: Perseus Books.

Schneider, Barbara, Sylvia Martinez, and Ann Owens. 2006. "Barriers to Educational Opportunities for Hispanics in the U.S." In *Hispanics and the Future of America,* ed. M. Tienda and F. Mitchell, 179–227. Washington, DC: National Academies Press.

Schulting, Amy B., Patrick S. Malone, and Kenneth A. Dodge. 2005. "The Effect of School-Based Kindergarten Transition Policies and Practices on Child Academic Outcomes." *Developmental Psychology* 41:860–871.

Scribner, Jay D., Michelle D. Young, and Anna Pedroza. 1999. "Building Collaborative Relationships with Parents." In *Lessons from High Performing Hispanic Schools: Creating Learning Communities,* ed. P. Reyes, J. D. Scribner, and A. Paredes Scribner, 36–60. New York: Teachers College Press.

Seccombe, Karen. 2000. "Families in Poverty in the 1990s: Trends, Causes, Consequences, and Lessons Learned." *Journal of Marriage and the Family* 62:1094–1113.

Seeley, David. 1984. "Home-School Partnership." *Phi Delta Kappan* 65:383–393.

Shannon, Sheila. 1996. "Minority Parental Involvement: A Mexican Mother's Experience and a Teacher's Interpretation." *Education & Urban Society* 29:71–84.

Shaver, Ann V., and Richard T. Walls. 1998. "Effect of Title I Parent Involvement on Student Reading and Mathematics Achievement." *Journal of Research and Development in Education* 31:90–97.

Shore News Today. 2011. "Pleasantville parent liaison selected for national PTA conference." May 27. http://www.shorenewstoday.com/snt/news/index.php /pleasantville/pleasantville-general-news/11798-pleasantville-news-in-brief -edition-of-may-27-2011.html.

Shumow, Lee, and Joe D. Miller. 2001. "Parents' At-Home and At-School Academic Involvement with Young Adolescents." *Journal of Early Adolescence* 21:68–91.

Singh, Kusum, Patricia G. Bickley, Paul S. Trivette, Timothy Z. Keith, Patricia B. Keith, and Eileen Anderson. 1995. "The Effects of Four Components of Parental Involvement on Eighth Grade Student Achievement: Structural Analysis of NELS-88 Data." *School Psychology Review* 24:299–317.

Smetana, Judith G. 1995. "Parenting Styles and Conceptions of Parental Authority during Adolescence." *Child Development* 66:299–316.

Smetana, Judith G., and Cheryl Gaines. 1999. "Adolescent-Parent Conflict in Middle-Class African American Families." *Child Development* 70:1447–1463.

Smith, Jay, Kenneth Stern, and Zhanna Shatrova. 2008. "Factors Inhibiting Hispanic Parents' School Involvement." *Rural Educator* 29:8–13.

Smith, Judith R., Jeanne Brooks-Gunn, and Pamela K. Klebanov. 1997. "Consequences of Living in Poverty for Young Children's Cognitive and Verbal Ability and Early School Achievement." In *Consequences of Growing up Poor*, ed. G. J. Duncan and J. Brooks-Gunn, 132–189. New York: Russell Sage Foundation.

Smith, Marshall S. 2000. "Assessment Trends in a Contemporary Policy Context." In *Analytic Essays in the Assessment of Student Achievement*, ed. D. W. Grissmer and J. M. Ross, 264–272. NCES 2000-050. Washington, DC: National Center for Education Statistics, U.S. Department of Education.

Smith, Ryan A. 2005. "Do the Determinants of Promotion Differ for White Men versus Women and Minorities?: An Exploration of Intersectionalism through Sponsored and Contest Mobility Processes." *American Behavioral Scientist* 48:1157–1181.

Snow, Catherine E., Susan Burns, and Peg Griffin. 1998. *Preventing Reading Difficulties in Young Children*. Washington, DC: National Academies Press.

Souto-Manning, Mariana, and Kevin J. Swick. 2006. "Teachers' Beliefs about Parent and Family Involvement: Rethinking Our Family Involvement Paradigm." *Early Childhood Education Journal* 34:187–193.

Sowell, Thomas. 1981. *Ethnic America: A History*. New York: Basic Books.

Stanton-Salazar, Ricardo D. 2001. *Manufacturing Hope and Despair: The School and Kin Support Networks of U.S.-Mexican Youth*. New York: Teachers College Press.

Steele, Claude M. 1997. "A Threat in the Air: How Stereotypes Shape Intellectual Identity and Performance." *American Psychologist* 52:613–629.

Steele, Shelby. 1990. *The Content of Our Character*. New York: Harper Perennial.

Stein, Melanie R., and Ron J. Thorkildsen. 1999. *Parental Involvement in Education: Insights and Applications from the Research*. Research Practitioner Series. Bloomington, IN: Phi Delta Kappa International.

Steinberg, Laurence. 2001. "We Know Some Things: Parent-Adolescent Relationships in Retrospect and Prospect." *Journal of Research on Adolescence* 11:1–19.

Steinberg, Laurence, Sanford Dornbusch, and Bradford Brown. 1992. "Ethnic Differences in Adolescent Achievement: An Ecological Perspective." *American Psychologist* 47:723–729.

Steinberg, Laurence, Julie D. Elmen, and Nina S. Mounts. 1989. "Authoritative Parenting, Psychosocial Maturity, and Academic Success among Adolescents." *Child Development* 60:1424–1436.

Steinberg, Laurence, Nina S. Mounts, Susie D. Lamborn, and Sanford M. Dornbusch. 1991. "Authoritative Parenting and Adolescent Adjustment across Varied Ecological Niches." *Journal of Research on Adolescence* 1:19–36.

Stevenson, David L., and David P Baker. 1987. "The Family-School Relationship and the Child's School Performance." *Child Development* 58:1348–1357.

Suarez-Orozco, Carola, and Marcelo M. Suarez-Orozco. 2001. *Children of Immigration*. Cambridge, MA: Harvard University Press.

Suarez-Orozco, Carola, Marcelo M. Suarez-Orozco, and Irina Todorova. 2008. *Learning a New Land: Immigrant Students in American society*. Cambridge, MA: Harvard University Press.

Sue, Stanley, and Sumie Okazaki. 1990. "Asian-American Educational Achievements: A Phenomenon in Search of an Explanation." *American Psychologist* 45:913–920.

Sui-Chu, Esther Ho, and J. Douglas Willms. 1996. "Effects of Parental Involvement on Eighth-Grade Achievement." *Sociology of Education* 69:126–141.

Suizzo, Marie-Anne, Courtney Robinson, and Erin Pahlke. 2007. "African American Mothers' Socialization Beliefs and Goals with Young Children." *Journal of Family Issues* 29:287–316.

Taylor, Robert, Linda M. Chatters, M. Belinda Tucker, and Edith Lewis. 1990. "Developments in Research on Black Families: A Decade Review." *Journal of Marriage and the Family* 48:67–77.

Teachman, Jay D., Kathleen Paasch, and Karen Carver. 1997. "Social Capital and the Generation of Human Capital." *Social Forces* 75:1343–1359.

Teale, William H. 1986. "Home Background and Young Children's Literacy Development." In *Emergent Literacy: Writing and Reading*, ed. W. H. Teale and E. Sulzby, 173–206. Norwood, NJ: Ablex.

Teitelbaum, Peter. 2003. "The Influence of High School Graduation Requirement Policies in Mathematics and Science on Student Course-Taking Patterns and Achievement." *Educational Evaluation and Policy Analysis* 25:31–57.

Thernstrom, Abigail, and Stephan Thernstrom. 2003. *No Excuses: Closing the Racial Gap in Learning*. New York: Simon & Schuster.

Tienda, Marta, and Faith Mitchell. 2006. *Hispanics and the Future of America*. Washington, DC: National Academies Press.

Tinkler, Barri. 2002. "A Review of Literature on Hispanic/Latino Parent Involvement in K–12 Education." http://www.coe.uga.edu/clase/EdResources/latinoparentreport/.pdf.

Tomaskovic-Devey, Donald, Melvin Thomas, and Kecia Johnson. 2005. "Race and the Accumulation of Human Capital across the Career: A Theoretical Model and Fixed-Effects Application." *American Journal of Sociology* 111:58–89.

Topping, Keith J. 1992. "Short-and Long-Term Follow-up of Parental Involvement in Reading Projects." *British Educational Research Journal* 18:369–379.

Trumbull, Elise, Carrie Rothstein-Fisch, Patricia M. Greenfield, and Blanca Quiroz. 2001. *Bridging Cultures between Home and School: A Guide for Teachers*. Mahwah, NJ: Erlbaum.

Trumbull, Elise, Carrie Rothstein-Fisch, and Elvia Hernandez. 2003. Parent Involvement in Schooling—According to Whose Values? *School Community Journal* 13:45–72.

Tyler, Kenneth M., A. Wade Boykin, and Tia R. Walton. 2006. "Cultural Considerations in Teachers' Perceptions of Student Classroom Behavior and Achievement." *Teaching and Teacher Education* 22:998–1005.

Tyson, Karolyn. 2002. "Weighing In: Elementary-Age Students and the Debate on Attitudes toward School among Black Students." *Social Forces* 80:1157–1189.

———. 2011. *Integration Interrupted: Tracking, Black Students, and Acting White after* Brown. Oxford: Oxford University Press.

Tyson, Karolyn, William Darity Jr. and Domini Castellino. 2005. "Black Adolescents and the Dilemmas of High Achievement." *American Sociological Review* 70:582–605.

U.S. Census Bureau. 2000. *U.S. Summary: 2000.* Washington, DC: Economics and Statistics Administration, U.S. Department of Commerce.

———. 2006. "Foreign-Born Population—Selected Characteristics by Region of Origin. Table 43." http://www.census.gov/compendia/statab/2010/tables /10s0043.xls.

———. 2008. "Educational Attainment—People 25 Years Old and Over, by Total Money Earnings in 2008, Work Experience in 2008, Age, Race, Hispanic Origin, and Sex." PINC-03. *Current Population Survey, Annual Social and Economic Supplement.*Washington, DC: U.S. Census Bureau.

———. 2009. *Asian/Pacific American Heritage Month: May 2009.* Washington, DC: U.S. Department of Commerce.

U.S. Department of Education. 1992. *A Profile of Parents of Eighth Graders.* Washington, DC: National Center for Education Statistics.

———. 1998. *Parent Involvement in Children's Education: Efforts by Public Elementary Schools.* NCES 98-032. Washington, DC: National Center for Educational Statistics.

———. 2002. *National Education Longitudinal Study of 1988 Base Year to Fourth Follow-Up Student Component Data File User's Manual.* Washington, DC: National Center for Educational Statistics.

———. 2004. *Parental Involvement: Title 1, Part A.* www.ed.gov/programs/title iparta/parentinvguid.doc.

Useem, Elizabeth L. 1992. "Middle Schools and Math Groups: Parents' Involvement in Children's Placement." *Sociology of Education* 65:263–279.

Valdes, Guadalupe. 1996. *Con Respeto: Bridging the Differences between Culturally Diverse Families and Schools: An Ethnographic Portrait.* New York: Teachers College Press.

Warner, David F., and Mark D. Hayward. 2006. "Early-Life Origins of the Race Gap in Men's Mortality." *Journal of Health and Social Behavior* 47:209–226.

Weiss, Heather B., Ellen Mayer, Holly Kreider, Margaret Vaughn, Eric Dearing, Rebecca Hencke, Kristina Pinto. 2003. "Making It Work: Low-Income Mothers' Involvement in their Children's Education." *American Educational Research Journal* 40:879–901.

West Virginia Department of Education. 2010. "W.Va. Board of Education Celebrates October as Parent Involvement in Schools Month." http://wvde .state.wv.us/news/2174/.

White, Paula A., Adam Gamoran, John Smithson, Andrew C. Porter. 1996. "Upgrading the High School Math Curriculum: Math Course-Taking Patterns in Seven High Schools in California and New York." *Educational Evaluation and Policy Analysis* 8:285–307.

Whitehurst, Grover J., and Christopher J. Lonigan. 1998. "Child Development and Emergent Literacy." *Child Development* 69:848–872.

Williams, Heather. 2005. *Self-Taught: African American Education in Slavery and Freedom.* Chapel Hill: University of North Carolina Press.

Wilson, William Julius. 1987. *The Truly Disadvantaged: The Inner City, the Underclass, and Public Policy.* Chicago: University of Chicago Press.

———. 1996. *When Work Disappears: The World of the New Urban Poor.* New York: Knopf.

Xie, Yu, and Kimberly Goyette. 2003. "Social Mobility and the Educational Choices of Asian Americans." *Social Science Research* 32:467–498.

———. 2004. "The American People: A Demographic Portrait of Asian Americans." New York: Russell Sage Foundation.

Yan, Wenfan, and Qiuyun Lin. 2005. "Parental Involvement and Mathematics Achievement: Contrast across Racial and Ethnic Groups." *Journal of Educational Research* 99:116–127.

Zellman, Gail L., and Jill M. Waterman. 1998. "Understanding the Impact of Parent School Involvement on Children's Educational Outcomes." *Journal of Educational Research* 91:370–380.

Zhao, Bo, Jan Ondrich, and John Yinger. 2006. "Why Do Real Estate Brokers Continue to Discriminate? Evidence from the 2000 Housing Discrimination Study." *Journal of Urban Economics* 59:394–419.

Zhou, Min. 1997. "Growing Up American: The Challenge Confronting Immigrant Children and Children of Immigrants." *Annual Review of Sociology* 23:63–95.

Zhou, Min, and Carl L. Bankston III. 1994. "Social Capital and the Adaptation of the Second Generation: The Case of Vietnamese Youth in New Orleans East." *International Migration Review* 28:775–799.

———. 1998. *Growing Up American: How Vietnamese Children Adapt to Life in the United States.* New York: Russell Sage Foundation.

Acknowledgments

We are greatly indebted to the many individuals who played an important role in making this work possible. We want to thank numerous people at the University of Texas and Princeton University for helping us improve this project by reading earlier drafts of chapters. These individuals include Rob Crosnoe, Janeria Dunlap, Linsey Edwards, Tod Hamilton, Mark Hayward, Bob Hummer, Sara McLanahan, Chandra Muller, and Kelly Raley. We want to thank the anonymous reviewers whose input helped shape the direction of this book. We thank Sapna Swaroop, who unknowingly helped to shape our understanding of some issues we grappled with in this book. We thank the students who took part in the focus groups for this study and whose insights pushed us into thinking more deeply about parents' role in children's education. We also thank the Institute for Advanced Study, where we received helpful feedback during the 2009–2010 academic year from an amazing interdisciplinary group of senior scholars. In particular, we thank Danielle Allen, Marcelo and Carola Suarez-Orozco, Paul Attewell, and Seth Moglen. We also want to sincerely thank our partners, Isabelle and Chinyere, whose love, support, and encouragement were unyielding.

   We would not have been able to complete this project without the generosity of various funding agencies. The Maryland Adolescent Development in Context Study—the data set that supplemented some of our analysis—was supported in part by National Institute of Child Health and Human Development Grant R01 HD33437 to Jacquelynne S. Eccles and Arnold J. Sameroff, by the Spencer Foundation Grant MG #200000275 to Tabbye Chavous and Jacquelynne S. Eccles, and by the MacArthur Network on Successful Adolescent Development in High Risk Settings (Chair: R. Jessor). We also received support from STEM in The New Millennium: Preparation, Pathways, and Diversity, a grant funded by the National Science Foundation (DUE-0757018) to Chandra Muller and Catherine Riegle-Crumb.

Portions of Chapter 9 and Appendix B originally appeared in Keith Robinson and Angel L. Harris, "Racial and Social Class Differences in How Parents Respond to Inadequate Achievement: Consequences for Children's Future Achievement," *Social Science Quarterly* 94, no. 5 (December 2013), pp. 1346–1371, © 2013 by the Southwestern Social Science Association.

Index

Achievement: in defining parental involvement, 4–5; problem of raising, 6–7; parental educational attainment and, 7–8, 9f, 32f, 33, 34f, 35, 36f, 37, 38f, 57f; social class and, 7–11, 47–48, 170f, 172; gaps, 7–17, 9f–10f, 13f, 14f–16f, 75, 76f, 77, 78f, 79, 165–171, 173, 195f; race and, 11–12, 13–17; parental involvement as solution for, 17–18; cultural capital and, 46–47; home-based parental involvement and, 48–49, 50f, 51, 52f, 53, 54f, 55, 117f, 118f; parent-child discussions and, 53, 55, 59f, 100–101, 126f; parent-initiated contact with school and, 64f, 66f, 155, 156f, 157f, 158; parent-teacher organization involvement and, 67, 68f, 69, 158, 159f, 160–161, 176f, 177f; event attendance by parents and, 70f, 160f; school-based parental involvement and, 70f, 154–155, 156f, 157f, 158, 159f, 160–171, 173; assertiveness of parents with teachers and, 71f, 72, 161–162, 163f; Asian American attitudes about, 115–116; parenting style and, 190–191, 192f, 193–195, 194f, 195f; autonomy of children and, 191; intrinsic motivation for, 191; punitive parenting and, 191, 192f, 193, 194f

African Americans. See Blacks

Asians: as "model minority," 12, 85, 100; assimilation among, 93; educational attainment among, 93; median income of, 93; resistance model and, 93; experiences of, 93–94; as voluntary minorities, 93–94; diversity of, 99; achievement attitudes among, 115–116; nonverbal communication and, 134; family in culture of, 144; in methodology, 242, 244; increase in immigration of, 276n3. See also Race

Assertiveness, parental: social class and, 37, 38f, 39, 41t; achievement and, 71f, 72, 161–162, 163f; race and, 144–145, 146f, 147

Assimilation, 85, 88; of Asian Americans, 93; of Hispanics, 94–95; resistance model and, 96–97; social receptivity and, 97

Attainment. See Educational attainment

Attendance, at school events, by parents, 69, 70f

Authoritarian parents, 274n5

Autonomous minorities, 275n1

Autonomy, of children, achievement and, 191

Behavior: parent-initiated contacts about, 64f, 66f, 132f, 156f, 158f; school-initiated contacts about, 137, 138f, 139; race and enforcement of standards on, 167

Blacks: behavior patterns in culture of, poverty and, 89–90; antagonistic relationship with education among, 95; experiences of, 95–96; opportunity structure and, 96; resistance model and,

307